_f_**P**

Elijah's Cup

*A Family's Journey into
the Community and Culture
of High-Functioning Autism
and Asperger's Syndrome*

Valerie Paradiž

THE FREE PRESS

NEW YORK • LONDON • TORONTO • SYDNEY • SINGAPORE

THE FREE PRESS
A Division of Simon & Schuster, Inc.
1230 Avenue of the Americas
New York, NY 10020

THE FREE PRESS and colophon are
trademarks of Simon & Schuster, Inc.

For information regarding special discounts for bulk purchases,
please contact Simon & Schuster Special Sales:
1-800-456-6798 or business@simonandschuster.com

Designed by Deirdre Amthor

Manufactured in the United States of America
10 9 8 7 6 5 4 3 2 1

Library of Congress Cataloging-in-Publication Data
Paradiž, Valerie, 1963–
Elijah's cup : a family's journey into the community and culture
of high-functioning autism and Asperger's syndrome / Valerie Paradiž
p.   cm.
Includes bibliographical references and index.
1. Paradiž, Elijah. 2. Autistic children—Family relationships. 3. Asperger's syndrome—Patients—Family relationships. 4. Autistic children. 5. Parents of autistic
children. I. Title.
RJ506.A9 P28 2002
618.92'8982—dc21   2001054718
ISBN 0-7432-0445-X (ALK. PAPER)

6/14/02

The author wishes to thank the Estate of Gertrude Stein for its kind permission to
quote excerpts from "A Birthday Book," first published in *Alphabets and Birthdays,*
and "A Comedy Like That" from *Bee Time Vine.* Special thanks also goes to Marsilio
Publishers for permission to quote Ingeborg Bachmann's poem "Journey Out," translated by Peter Filkins in *Songs in Flight: The Collected Poems of Ingeborg Bachmann.*

Elijah's Cup

A Family's Journey into
the Community and Culture
of High-Functioning Autism
and Asperger's Syndrome

Valerie Paradiž

THE FREE PRESS
NEW YORK • LONDON • TORONTO • SYDNEY • SINGAPORE

THE FREE PRESS
A Division of Simon & Schuster, Inc.
1230 Avenue of the Americas
New York, NY 10020

THE FREE PRESS and colophon are
trademarks of Simon & Schuster, Inc.

For information regarding special discounts for bulk purchases,
please contact Simon & Schuster Special Sales:
1-800-456-6798 or business@simonandschuster.com

Designed by Deirdre Amthor

Manufactured in the United States of America
10 9 8 7 6 5 4 3 2 1

Library of Congress Cataloging-in-Publication Data
Paradiž, Valerie, 1963–
Elijah's cup : a family's journey into the community and culture
of high-functioning autism and Asperger's syndrome / Valerie Paradiž
p. cm.
Includes bibliographical references and index.
1. Paradiž, Elijah. 2. Autistic children—Family relationships. 3. Asperger's syndrome—Patients—Family relationships. 4. Autistic children. 5. Parents of autistic
children. I. Title.
RJ506.A9 P28 2002
618.92'8982—dc21   2001054718
ISBN 0-7432-0445-X (ALK. PAPER)

6/14/02

The author wishes to thank the Estate of Gertrude Stein for its kind permission to
quote excerpts from "A Birthday Book," first published in *Alphabets and Birthdays,*
and "A Comedy Like That" from *Bee Time Vine.* Special thanks also goes to Marsilio
Publishers for permission to quote Ingeborg Bachmann's poem "Journey Out," translated by Peter Filkins in *Songs in Flight: The Collected Poems of Ingeborg Bachmann.*

had used up the large plastic bottles of bright, nontoxic colors that I had plied him with through the winter and the spring. Color was all-important for Elijah. He perseverated on it. That is, he thought mainly in terms of color and did so repeatedly and fixedly all day long. At that time, for example, he had moved into a routine of removing all his clothes and painting his entire body a single color, methodically transforming himself each time into red, purple, blue, or yellow. On that hot morning, Elijah was determined to drum up some paint and finally discovered a full, unopened bottle at the back of a messy closet. Immediately, he proceeded to undress and paint his slender body orange.

"I . . . want . . . to go . . . outside," he said to me in halting speech once he had finished covering himself in paint. Elijah has developmental delays, and all the words he uttered at age seven were hard-won trophies. I did not take them for granted.

"I guess it's okay," I answered. "It's certainly warm enough outside."

I opened the door for Elijah, and soon he was frolicking like an elf, all clad in orange, out on the big, flat bluestone slab—a geological wonder that's just outside our door. Within seconds, the dragonflies descended. It must have been the color of his body that attracted them. They swarmed around Elijah, moving in very close and persistently, ready to alight, then darted off again as he leaped and waved his arms through the air. The dragonflies were so swift it was impossible to count them all, but at least twenty of them attended to Elijah at one time. He was not afraid at all. He moved with them in the choreography, aware of some grand collaboration.

As I watched this vision, I was sent back to a time when I was a teenager living in Germany as an exchange student. I was sitting beside the pond with my host parents, Mama and Papa, in their back yard. The pond had so much life in it and, more important, *above* it. Dragonflies were everywhere, hovering in

Preface

I wrote my first poem to my son, Elijah, when he was two years old. At the time, I didn't know that what I had jotted down one afternoon in an act of desperate self-preservation would eventually become this book. I also didn't know that Elijah was autistic. The poem was about his first seizure, which had abruptly descended on our family, forever altering the trajectories of our lives.

As Elijah's autism came to light, writing poetry and short fiction became my means of cultivating self-respect during a time of profound loss. It helped me get my bearings straight, and soon, what had started out as a survival mechanism became a great adventure. By the time Elijah was seven years old, all the pieces I had written—the many journeys that mined the depths of our autistic life and our entry into a special community of autistic friends—began to feel like a book to me.

On a sunny day in our home in rural New York, something happened that caused me to glimpse the bigger picture of this book. It was during the dog days of August, when the sun was already too hot in the morning and when Elijah was asking me, repeatedly, to please buy more paint at the art supply store. He

Contents

Preface		ix
CHAPTER 1	Elijah's Cup	1
CHAPTER 2	The Gift of Loss	16
CHAPTER 3	Perfect Strangers	30
CHAPTER 4	The Coincidence of Sharron Loree	44
CHAPTER 5	Nietzsche in the Bathtub	59
CHAPTER 6	My Father Was a Yakker	77
CHAPTER 7	Echolalia Fun Fun Fun	98
CHAPTER 8	Balloon Days	110
CHAPTER 9	Cartoons Don't Get Hurt	130
CHAPTER 10	Life Under Glass	153
CHAPTER 11	Playground Comedian	175
CHAPTER 12	Cracking Code	201

Web Sites by and for Autistic People and for Autistic Advocacy — 220
Notes — 221
Acknowledgments — 232
Index — 236

A NOTE ON LANGUAGE

The author has purposefully not used the politically correct term "person with autism" to refer to an autistic person. "Person first" language was developed with the very positive goal of not labeling disabled people in a fashion that is denigrating. However, there is ever-growing sensitivity in the disability community (not strictly among autistics) toward such language. Person first language is perceived by many as a labeling system that rigidly separates disabled individuals from an integral aspect of their identity. A person with autism, for example, "has" something, perhaps something that should be removed or cured. These are implications disability activists wish to avoid. An autistic, on the other hand, is somebody.

For Avis and Greg

the air, and Mama pointed out to me that they were busy laying eggs on the water. That was why they touched down, ever so lightly, again and again, on the glassy surface.

I told Mama that back home in the United States, we children would run away from dragonflies, screaming our fool heads off. Their very name frightened us, and because they were larger than bees, hornets, and yellow jackets, we associated them with threatening danger. This is something that would never occur to a German, young or old, for the Germans perceive these insects as creatures of graceful beauty. The dazzling greens and blues of their slender bodies shimmer in the sun, and their wings are delicate translucence.

I like crossing cultural boundaries. I learned from my German family that this is perhaps one of the most daring and meaningful things a person can do in a life. The day I saw Elijah dance with the dragonflies, I knew I wanted to write a book about autism and cultural boundaries. I wanted to dismantle the fear many people feel toward other minds. Now I'm offering this labor of love to my readers in the hope that it is daring and meaningful to them. I hope that what I have learned from Elijah—to think of autism not as a *mental illness* that absolutely needs a cure, but rather as a *way of life* that possesses a deep history and a rich culture—makes its way across.

CHAPTER 1

Elijah's Cup

Before I knew what a seizure was, my son was taken down. He went down many times from ages two to three. The first was in the kitchen, collapsed on the floor. Later, it happened like a geography dream. Each seizure had its own place and its own season: in the supermarket, aisle two; naked on the rug in my father's home; at the top of Silver Hollow in the middle of the winter. It's not something a person can get used to. Each place and circumstance lodges in the mind indelibly. Each time it's a loss of sudden nature.

I was stirring soup when Elijah fell in the kitchen. A snowstorm had blown in, and we were home for the night. Our little family at the top of Silver Hollow. I was stirring soup around and around in the pot. A marriage stew of seven years, soaking in its own juices. Elijah was walking circles, as he often did. Through the dining room, the living room, the bedroom, back into the kitchen again. His father was writing in the office with the door shut, a forbidden threshold I crossed with caution. A mutual agreement on cool distance. Whenever Ben emerged from his poetry or his newspaper deadlines, we engaged in circular conversations. I suppose that was also part of our agreement.

"Whatever happened to my wedding dress? It's missing from the shelf."

"What's the matter with Elijah? He isn't talking very much."

Elijah walks in circles all around the house. He doesn't turn his head if someone calls his name. We've had his hearing checked, but everything's in order. He's just a late talker. He's just independent. He wants to climb on windowsills and gaze wordlessly through glass. He wants to peel crayons and line them up in rows or play the threshold game and hide behind a door. Open the door, close the door, peek at mommy through the crack. He hasn't called me "mommy" yet. He's just a late talker. He says only the little words, the monosyllables. "Sad, sad, sad, sad." All day long. Or "fun, fun, fun," looking through the glass. He says the words so often they've begun to spin in place. He says them so much that I repeat things too.

"Whatever happened to my wedding dress? I wonder if it still fits."

Elijah tools around the corner and falls at my feet.

"Boom, boom," I say. He's a little clumsy, always falling down. "Elijah goes boom boom," I say again. But he doesn't do a thing. He's lying flat on his face. I take the spoon out of the pot and bend down to help him up. He's flat on his face, and I'm losing him, losing him to the blossoms. To those invisible flowers that take up all the thinking space. Those bouquets of thorns and color, bouquets of ruthless mercy. So many roses and tulips and so little time to think. I call his name, but he does not hear me. I take him into my arms, but he does not see me. Instead, his eyes roll back into his head. His jaw locks and his slender limbs begin to quiver. I call and call, but Elijah does not answer.

It took a long time for the ambulance to reach the top of our steep road. The snow was deep by now, and the Ostranders had

CHAPTER 1

⌒

Elijah's Cup

Before I knew what a seizure was, my son was taken down. He went down many times from ages two to three. The first was in the kitchen, collapsed on the floor. Later, it happened like a geography dream. Each seizure had its own place and its own season: in the supermarket, aisle two; naked on the rug in my father's home; at the top of Silver Hollow in the middle of the winter. It's not something a person can get used to. Each place and circumstance lodges in the mind indelibly. Each time it's a loss of sudden nature.

I was stirring soup when Elijah fell in the kitchen. A snowstorm had blown in, and we were home for the night. Our little family at the top of Silver Hollow. I was stirring soup around and around in the pot. A marriage stew of seven years, soaking in its own juices. Elijah was walking circles, as he often did. Through the dining room, the living room, the bedroom, back into the kitchen again. His father was writing in the office with the door shut, a forbidden threshold I crossed with caution. A mutual agreement on cool distance. Whenever Ben emerged from his poetry or his newspaper deadlines, we engaged in circular conversations. I suppose that was also part of our agreement.

"Whatever happened to my wedding dress? It's missing from the shelf."

"What's the matter with Elijah? He isn't talking very much."

Elijah walks in circles all around the house. He doesn't turn his head if someone calls his name. We've had his hearing checked, but everything's in order. He's just a late talker. He's just independent. He wants to climb on windowsills and gaze wordlessly through glass. He wants to peel crayons and line them up in rows or play the threshold game and hide behind a door. Open the door, close the door, peek at mommy through the crack. He hasn't called me "mommy" yet. He's just a late talker. He says only the little words, the monosyllables. "Sad, sad, sad, sad." All day long. Or "fun, fun, fun," looking through the glass. He says the words so often they've begun to spin in place. He says them so much that I repeat things too.

"Whatever happened to my wedding dress? I wonder if it still fits."

Elijah tools around the corner and falls at my feet.

"Boom, boom," I say. He's a little clumsy, always falling down. "Elijah goes boom boom," I say again. But he doesn't do a thing. He's lying flat on his face. I take the spoon out of the pot and bend down to help him up. He's flat on his face, and I'm losing him, losing him to the blossoms. To those invisible flowers that take up all the thinking space. Those bouquets of thorns and color, bouquets of ruthless mercy. So many roses and tulips and so little time to think. I call his name, but he does not hear me. I take him into my arms, but he does not see me. Instead, his eyes roll back into his head. His jaw locks and his slender limbs begin to quiver. I call and call, but Elijah does not answer.

It took a long time for the ambulance to reach the top of our steep road. The snow was deep by now, and the Ostranders had

The brain pictures showed Elijah's tissues to be normal. There was nothing more to do, so we put him in his car seat and drove back home through Kingston, questioning ourselves at every stoplight. Questioning the past and Elijah's complicated birth. Questioning the developmental assessment he'd had just weeks earlier. *Severe delays in expressive speech. Moderate delays in motor ability.* The seizure was the sealing factor. It made Elijah "delayed" in my mind, though I'd been fighting this notion a very long time. I'd been defending him for months, defending him since birth perhaps. *The midwife came too late.* Defending without submitting. *She came too late and gave me false instruction.* The blindest love is for a child. It's blind and unconditional. If I'm an atheist, my love for Elijah runs close to blind faith, and if I'm a believer, awesome responsibility makes it hard to see the light. In the end, it doesn't really matter. I was defending without submitting.

"Elijah is a different drummer!" my father-in-law once yelled at me. "When are you finally going to see that? I don't trust you anymore! I don't trust your parental judgment! When are you going to see, he's a different drummer?"

My father-in-law boiled over at a family party. He was the first to speak his mind, the first to pick a fight. Elijah was sitting on the floor that day—in usual isolation. And I yelled back—in usual silence. I never argued out loud with my father-in-law, or anyone else for that matter. My arguments were long internal discussions, long internal debates that suspended me in silence. A tape that ran its loop over and over again. Internal arguments need serious attention, especially when they repeat themselves too much. *The midwife came too late.* I learn this lesson time and again. I learn it repeatedly, because denial is a human mystery. Endless secrets and endless revelation lie before me. There's no escaping them. I'm always debating with myself about one thing or another. Always suspended somewhere between defending and submitting. Always poised and fearful of the next revealing, for when it comes, it seizes me, it seems, with too much feeling.

Elijah was "delayed" and sleeping in the back seat, while Ben and I scoured our grieving minds. It was our time of asking questions and of our maturing. Asking questions and maturing can drive two people asunder. The answers become so necessary, so very urgent. So full of obvious departure.

"What were the Apgar scores on the day that Elijah was born?"

"Did the midwife come too late?"

"What's a grand mal, what's a petit mal seizure?"

"Did she come too late? I didn't get to hold him."

"The Apgar scores. Do you remember?"

"They whisked him off. His face was blue. I didn't get to hold him."

Elijah was asleep in his car seat, exhausted from events and sedatives, while we stopped at every stoplight and asked our separate questions. But when we reached the traffic circle, something came upon him. It was a faint sound in the back seat. Soft wheezing. Soft choking. Delicate gulping, like a goldfish just below the water plane. As I turned around to check on him, Elijah's eyes were wide open, but he wasn't the familiar boy of deep musing. There wasn't that gaze of distracted contemplation. His eyes were fixed and locked. No small thing was his object, like the tiny pieces of fibrous lint he often picked off his pajamas. His gaze was fixed on nothing, and his throat made soft music. It convulsed gently for a moment, then his eyes rolled up into their sockets.

"It's happening again! There, in the back seat! Turn around, turn around! Go back to the hospital!"

Just as I said this, the seizure left Elijah's body. His face softened. His eyes closed. He fell back to sleep.

◇

Elijah was admitted to the children's ward where a nurse tried to stick an IV needle in him. The IV needle was a medical precaution, a rude intrusion into his sensitive exhaustion. She probed his tiny arm, but she couldn't find a thing.

"The little ones with little veins are difficult to handle!"

Elijah cried bitterly, and his bewildered face went red. He was a thin toddler, and he had always been a skinny baby. During the first year of life, when most infants were getting fat and chubby with growth chart curves swinging upward full of promise, Elijah's plotted weight never turned. His line went horizontally straight. The doctor was alarmed.

"Your son needs serious feeding."

So for weeks I crawled on the floor, tailing Elijah with baby food jars. He only ate in motion in those thin days. I followed him like a soldier through the trenches. I held the spoon before his face: "Look here! Banana pudding!" But he would crawl right past it. This forced me to improve my feeding tactics. I'd head him off behind the couch, or just as he rounded a corner, I'd spring a spoonful on him like a booby trap. *Slurf, slurf, slurf, slurf.* There he goes down the hallway! *Slurf, slurf, slurf, slurf.* He's swishing in his diapers. Got to get to him! Got to catch up with that lone crawler! His weight was off the curve, and he was traveling at high speed, pausing only to inspect the tiniest things. Pieces of lint, specks of dust, small seeds from the garden. Pausing only now and then to bang his head a little. Just a few repetitions on the open floor, then off again, off the charts and living in abstraction.

When the nurse abandoned the IV needle, Elijah finally got some sleep. I tucked his tired body into the hospital sheets and laid down on a cot beside his bed. Hospital rules allowed only one parent to keep vigil through the night, so Ben left for a hotel down the street. Elijah's sleep was heavy, but his eyelids were delicate. Such a thin layer of skin separates the respite from the hardship! Whenever Elijah opens his eyes, they are onyx brown. They are deep and dark and full of complicated questions. We saw the questions from the start, from the day that he was born. From the day that he arrived, we knew he was a contemplator.

"Such a thoughtful little baby!" all the relatives exclaimed. "Look, he's so intelligent! You can see it in his eyes!"

The first time Elijah smiled, his onyx eyes gazed right into me. It was at a friend's house. Leaves were falling outside, and the air was orange and chilled. Children were running wildly through the house, up and down the stairs, then past their talking parents standing in the kitchen, then out the open door to the back porch autumn. Elijah and I sat alone on the living room love seat, nursing in warm isolation, when he pulled his mouth from my nipple and smiled directly at my face. It was a long smile and so auspicious that I was certain everyone had seen it. But as I lifted my head to receive their warm congratulations, I saw that all my friends had gone outside. I returned my face to Elijah. He smiled again.

"Elijah, another developmental milestone!"

That was early motherhood, so warm and isolated, with all the classic milestones falling classically into place. I'd read of them in baby books and followed them with astute emotion. They were enervating days full of pediatric certainty. But now, in the hospital, each milestone was under serious scrutiny. The banging head. The missing words. The little finger that just won't point. Worlds of weariness were seeping in, worlds of hospital incident. *His face was blue. They wouldn't let me hold him.* Too many puzzles in need of too much attention. I lay on my hospital cot, thinking of our nameless doctor. A neurologist, whom we hadn't met yet, was well aware of our case. That's when I learned that in the hospital, most things happen in the absence of a presence. That's why a doctor is a god. He is an absent presence.

Dozing, brooding, halfway dreaming. Restless in the middle of the night. Tossing, turning on this cot. Check Elijah. Make sure he's breathing. He's so heavy in his bed. Leave the room. Just for a minute. Walk to the children's ward desk and ask the nurse for direction.

"It's down the hall and to your left. Walk directly past the elevators and keep going straight."

Padding, padding down the hall, like a midnight patient. It's so quiet in the children's ward in the middle of the night. Reach the bathroom. Lock the door. Muse about the doctor. Dozing, dreaming. Then, overcome with strangeness. Something is too silent here. The entire ward is quiet. Flush the toilet. Walk back quickly. Walk faster. Then, run! Run! Run back to Elijah! It's too quiet in the children's ward. There's no nurse at the desk! I'm almost at our room and in a panic. I know she is in there. She heard the silence. She heard it very clearly in the middle of the night.

When I reach the threshold, the nurse is bending over Elijah. I gasp aloud, but she raises a firm hand begging me to be quiet. That's when I hear the music again, Elijah's soft goldfish gulping. The nurse lowers her hand and places it gently on his chest. "The midwife came too late," I whisper, approaching Elijah's bed.

"I know that, dear. But there's nothing here to defend. There's nothing to defend and a great deal to learn. Now come closer. This is how you do it. This is how you help a person who's in the middle of a seizure. You see, it's very easy. See how stiff he is?

You shouldn't move him very much. You may roll him on his side. Ignore the other things you've heard, like forcing something in his teeth to keep his tongue from being swallowed." That's what the nurse in the white uniform told me. She was wearing white shoes and white stockings too. "Put those old wives' tales out of your mind entirely," she whispered gently. She spoke almost imperceptibly, like a good teacher. "Never talk too loudly around a person who's in seizure. They are so very sensitive to all that is around them. You see, it's neurological. You may talk Elijah gently, gently, gently through it. Let him know you're here. Touch him, or hold him tenderly, if he's seizing in your arms." As she whispered this, the white nurse caressed my delicate boy and said kind things to him until his taut body sighed and softened.

"Well, he's a bona-fide epileptic." That's what the neurologist-god said when he appeared in the room. "One seizure isn't enough to achieve this kind of status, but two seizures, three seizures, in the space of eight short hours, that's enough for me to grant the title. Your son is epileptic." The neurologist's face began to twitch, and he looked at me through thick glasses. He was in a rush and on the edge of distraction. "Now, these seizures could stop completely and never return again. But medically speaking, your son will always be prone to them. Depending on his age, depending on the season. For now, it's important to do the proper testing. MRI and EEG. We'll start first thing in the morning. I shall sign the order. Good night." He stared at me absently for a moment with his big bug eyes, then abruptly vanished around the corner.

After the third seizure, Ben returned to the hospital where we kept an anxious watch together for the rest of the night. We were learning seizure poise, and I know we both still have it. Once it enters the body, there's no getting rid of it. It's a sixth sense. A tight attention for sudden silences. A high-pitched fear of unexpected departures. Even now, eight years later, when I hear an awesome silence, I must turn my head in Elijah's direction, take his hand in mine, exchange some small words. It's not something a person can get used to. It's a geography dream. Ben and I were poised to travel anytime to any distant country that Elijah took us to. But our fear became so taut it made for unbearable stresses.

Two hours later, Elijah had a fourth seizure. He cried out in his sleep, trembled, went stiff again, then off he drifted, back into deep postictal dreaming. The neurologist-god, who was paged and told of the incident, passed down word to the nurse: "Administer a phenobarbital injection." Phenobarbital is an anticonvulsant, an old faithful drug. It puts a stop to seizures and more besides. It's an ugly pharmaceutical, strangely red and sticky. Eerily effective. It squelches everything, and the reason to squelch seemed immediate. Repeated seizing over short periods of time indicates terrific brain harm. *Status epilepticus,* the pinnacle of seizure possibilities, could occur. It's beyond grand mal, beyond petit mal, and all the latest terminology. It's the kind of seizure that won't desist. Our child could seize and seize and never come out of it. Serious damage occurs to the person, so we agreed to give Elijah the injection. The wicked needle prick made him writhe again. All the prickings and proddings were beginning to wear our family down, pull us down, break us down, and yet so very taut. Our softening would come later. It was still a long way off.

What can I say of Elijah's cup and magnetic resonance imaging? How is it possible to piece two things together? Elijah was a prophet, and according to the Bible, he never really died, but simply walked away. He parted the waters of the Jordan and walked right into the riverbed. That's where he waited for the burning chariot. The chariot came with a fiery horse that took him into the sky. They say he never really died and that he's watching from the shadows. He is a perfect witness, perfectly invisible. Open the door, open the door on Passover night. Elijah will come to the seder and take an invisible drink. He will drink wine from the cup that's laid out for him. What's the nature of invisibility? It's gentle and elusive, a necessary trick. My son is gentle and elusive, and I ask myself this: What does Elijah have to do with magnetic resonance? I am very tired now, past exhaustion, trying desperately to piece these two things together. Did I sleep in this chair I'm sitting in, or did Ben and I talk all through the night? I can't remember anymore. Elijah and the MRI. The MRI and Elijah. What will they find there, in the gray and the white matter? Why is it so important?

The cold morning is shining through the hospital blinds and puts an ugly image on the wall that's all gray and white. It's time to wake Elijah now from his sedative sleep. It's time to surround his head with heavy radio waves. Time to make the nuclei dance in each and every atom. Time to take thousands of brain measurements from thousands of angles. All these perspectives add up to a 3-D composite. It's the same old modern question, and not a question I dislike. But I never expect an answer—an absolute composite. To think that there's an answer makes me squeamish. It's like locking the door on Passover night in hopes of detaining Elijah. Like putting a saucer over his cup. Trap him there! Just to get a glimpse. Like wanting desperately to undermine a necessary human trick. Wanting, wanting, at any cost, to apprehend the benign witness.

We wake Elijah up and dress him for a trip in the car, to go to the MRI lab. We put his socks and shoes on, but before we leave, there are a few things to tend to. It's just protocol. Blood samples, thermometers, urine tests for toddlers.

"Just tape this vial to his penis, and put his diaper over it," says the new nurse on duty.

Crying, more crying. Elijah will never reach the end of it. The moment he stops crying is the moment he is broken. The nurse bustles into the room with more pharmaceutical orders.

"He'll have to drink a sedative to keep him quiet for the test."

This was the beginning of our medication journey. Elijah's cup was poisonous, and yet he had to drink. Phenobarbital, pentobarbital, chloral hydrate, Tegretol, Felbatol, and all their side effects. This was the beginning of a cup of violence. The beginning of pinnings and forcings flat on the bed and the pouring of cruel liquids down Elijah's small esophagus. Liquids that altered everything. His father held his legs down and I his chest and head, while the nurse poured and screeched, "Swallow it! Swallow it!" Elijah spit the red ooze out, screaming. I flattened him down and apologized in the same breath, looking into the onyx, sending a message there.

"Elijah! We are so coarse! Adults are coarse and bumbling!" He screams and spits. The nurse is devastated.

"I hope he's had enough! If he didn't get the full dose, it might not do the trick." Grumpily, she gives us directions to a lab three blocks away.

When we reach the MRI lab, we are told that the equipment is malfunctioning because of last night's snowstorm. Water is leaking through the roof, dripping down onto the precious apparatus. I peer into the testing room at the big daunting cylinder. It's a long coffin in there. Ominous. Ominous. Elijah is in my arms, asleep again and swaddled like a newborn. He grows heavier and heavier as we're being briefed on the procedure. The technician is talking of injecting dye into my son's brain tissues.

"We don't fully know the health risks, but we do get a better image. If you just sign these papers, we'll get a better picture."

I'm distracted by the dripping water. I cannot listen to this nonsense. A small drop is in the testing room. I see it, hanging from the ceiling right above the equipment. It's ever so small, yet it's dangling there. Hanging, dangling, getting full, fuller, fullest. Then it drip-drops down onto the coffin apparatus. The technician talks too nervously and ushers us to a waiting room.

"Be patient," he says. "It's a minor repair."

We wait and wait—we're patient—for two good hours. We are very good, and the magazines are chatty. We are very good, and the furniture is boring. We wait and wait until Elijah starts to moan and the sedative recedes. He stretches and squirms, drifts off again. Then, as if we've just arrived at this awful place, the technician emerges from the back office to tell us that the staff is ready to conduct the test.

"Just sign these dye papers, and we'll get started."

"No dyes," I answer him. "No color. You'll have to content yourselves with the gray and the white."

He shrugs his shoulders and prepares Elijah for the test, but by now my son is only half asleep. He's a big cocoon squirming on the stretcher in white sheets, awaiting transformation.

"This is too much motion for our sensitive equipment!" the technician complains as he tries to situate Elijah precisely and tighten the Velcro band around his head before rolling him into the cylinder. Elijah flails about, only half conscious of where he is. The technician throws his arms up in the air and angrily cancels the test. Oddly, I'm relieved.

"I did not like that cylinder casket," I tell Ben, who nods wordlessly in return. Ben is so fatigued, he can no longer speak. Elijah is moaning and twisting in his arms. "I want to go home, Ben," I say. "Let's go back to the hospital and get the goddamned EEG over with."

To my surprise the EEG was all gentleness, and Elijah slept right through it. A white-haired specialist sifted through Elijah's thick curls and pasted electrodes to his scalp. Fourteen for the right lobe and fourteen for the left. It adds up to twenty-eight symmetrical sites, and there's an extra one for Elijah's small heartbeat. She pastes it to his chest.

"Now, shhhhhhh!" the specialist says, putting her finger to her mouth. When she turns the quiet machine on, the room grows small and intimate. All the lights are out, and the sensitive needles are tracing a message on the long scroll of paper. Peaks and valleys, ebbs and flows. It's all gentleness. When she is finished, the woman removes the electrodes from Elijah's head and washes the paste from his hair.

"We got a good reading," she whispers, shampooing our sleeping boy. Then she sends the results off to neurology for god's interpretation. That will take three days, we are told, and Elijah is released from the hospital. There is nothing more to do, so we gather ourselves up and drive back home to Silver Hollow. Safe and sound with our epileptic toddler.

CHAPTER 2

◌⌒

The Gift of Loss

The gift of loss is many flowers blossoming. So many roses and tulips that there is little time to think. Once the loss has struck the mind with all its thorn and color, there is nothing left to do but begin the telling. A crisis comes. A crisis goes. There is a smell of roses in the room. I know the words I use to do my telling are but transient scents. They are empty-handed gestures. They are medical descriptions. They are explanations that draw just one narrow picture of what has really happened to us.

When the relatives call on the telephone, they express their concern and pity, asking questions about Elijah to which I give the diagnostic answers.

"The EEG was inconclusive. It showed no epileptic activity, no lesions or a focus that might explain the seizures."

Elijah has swiftly become a medical case, and I have begun to speak the fitting language, repeating my conversations with the specialists as I talk to my mother, to my father, to my sisters and brothers on the telephone late into the night. I tell them all about Elijah's tests and Elijah's medications. I tell them all about the biology of epilepsy.

"He's taking 30 milligrams of phenobarbital each day. The phenobarbital stops the unregulated electrical discharge."

But as I speak of Elijah's brain and of its unregulated activity, I drift beneath the surface of side effects and pharmaceutical warnings. I strain beyond the MRI, the CT scan, and the EEG. Beyond the frame in which I'm to contain him. Beyond the frame in which I'm to contain myself too. Untethered in another region, I must be careful what I say. *Be careful what you say in this timeless hour! Be careful of the crises and the impending departures. Be careful of the flowers and how you speak of them. Be careful, for the body must bear each uninvited blossom until the body dies. Be careful, for in the telling, you forge the essence of a life.*

All the while on the telephone, I'm in my undercurrent thinking, alone with the questions that I would like to put to Elijah. *Is a seizure a flower? Is it a thorn sticking in the mind? Does it hurt? Is it color? Is it a long journey? Is it the deepest of isolations, like a solitary poppy, emerging, orange and paper thin, in the quiet garden?*

I would put these questions to him, but Elijah is sleeping in the bedroom in barbiturate sedation. He is sleeping as my voice grows hoarse with each telephone conversation. He is sleeping when I'm cooking dinner. He is sleeping when it's time to eat. He is sleeping whenever my in-laws stop by for a visit. He sleeps and sleeps, and when he does awaken, Elijah is entirely stripped of his monosyllables.

He used to say "ba" for big and "dee" for tree. He toddled around outdoors and laughed at gusts of wind. "Ba . . . dee!" he'd exclaim, looking up at the whooshing branches of a tree. Then he'd giggle gleefully, squat down, and return to his stone investigations. So busy, so very busy, with all the stony objects. Picking them up, one by one, examining their every contour. Then grasping firmly with his two small hands, he'd rock the object back and forth, back and forth, two times, maybe three. Then toss it aside. Systematically.

Elijah would repeat this game, picking up the next stone and running it through his investigative protocol, doing it meticulously, as if he could get to the end of them all. As if Elijah could count every single stone there is in the wide world. As if infinity did not exist. "The limits of my language mean the limits of my world," writes Ludwig Wittgenstein. Wittgenstein, the Austrian philosopher, did not presume infinity when it came to the objects. To presume this, he felt, was a logical failing. For Elijah, each stone he chose was utterly singular. Each stone was silent. Each stone was something he did not have a word for. A compelling investigation conducted according to the strict routine of back and forth, back and forth, two or three times. Did he memorize each contour? Did he note the shade of color? Did he absorb each and every case? "The world is all that is the case," says Wittgenstein. Elijah was thoroughly taken up with the stones, with each and every case, squatting silently like a small frog beside the gurgling stream, squatting with all the objects beneath the high whooshing in the trees.

But now it's winter, and Elijah and I don't go outside anymore. We don't go outside to look for the wizards or to stare into the coals of their reliable campfire. Elijah sleeps instead. He is a medical case. Or he sits sedated on my lap, moving from one speechless emotion to the next. We live our days out together in the living room, confined to the narrow circumference of an old easy chair. Getting up, once in a while, to make circuits of the apartment. As he stumbles from room to room, moaning and crying, I follow him, my hands outstretched, blocking the sharp corners and the painful edges. Elijah is drunk on phenobarbital. Drunk and clumsy and paper-thin sad. His limbs are heavy, his central nervous system is depressed, and a bright red rash has developed on each cheek. The phenobarb

rash, a mix of pharmaceutical side effect and the salt of bitter weeping.

The pinning down on the bed and the sputtering red syrup emitting from Elijah's mouth have become regular traumas in his day. If Elijah swallows too much medication, he recedes into a hypnotic state. If he swallows too little, he runs the risk of *status epilepticus*. He is living within a narrow window of opportunity that the anticonvulsant has afforded him.

"Not too much, not too little! Remember all the warnings!" Ben and I stridently say to one another each time we pin Elijah down and make him cry.

When using Phenobarbital, call your doctor immediately if you develop a fever, a sore throat, sores in your mouth, broken blood vessels under the skin, or easy bruising or bleeding. How would a wordless toddler alert us to his symptoms? *Phenobarbital may cause excitement, irritability, aggression, depression, or confusion—particularly in children or adults over 60.* Elijah always manages to spit the red stuff out, and each time he spits, his father and I snap at one another.

"He didn't get the full dose! Keep him down while I get the medicine bottle!"

"Does he really need more?!"

"How should I know?! It came out red everywhere! Look! It's dripping down his neck!"

"Let's try 5 more milligrams!"

Elijah is howling now. *Symptoms of a Phenobarbital overdose include difficulty breathing, back-and-forth movements of the eyes, appearance of being drunk, fast heartbeat, low body temperature, heavy sedation, coma, and death.* We have become too zealous with ourselves. We are untrained for this. We fume at one another during our graceless dispensations, then Ben angrily disappears behind the office door to *his* undercurrent thinking, behind the sad veil of separation that has come to mean his writing.

Both of us in our undercurrent thinking, we hardly speak to one another anymore, not until it's time to give Elijah the next dose. *Less serious side effects include dizziness, confusion, agitation, nightmares, nervousness, or anxiety.* When Elijah has finished weeping, he goes back to his unhappy tour of all the rooms of the apartment. I follow his every move. I have become his silent shadow. No one speaks in our home anymore, as we navigate the blind corners and the sharp edges. *Phenobarbital is habit forming. You can become addicted to it.* This is the profit of the narrow pharmaceutical. It might erase a boy's happiness and thrust him into synthetic depression. It might destroy his liver, and with time, put cancer in his cells. "And yet . . . and yet . . . ," Ben and I tell ourselves, our backs against the wall, "it has put a stop to the seizures."

"Your uncle Maurice took phenobarbital most of his life," my mother says on the phone.

I never met Maurice. He died in his early twenties. He was mentally retarded, and when my mother was a girl, she helped take care of him. That's when she learned her gentle diligence, sleeping beside her little brother in the same bed at night.

"They say his seizures were due to the whooping cough. He had had a bad case when he was a baby."

"I didn't know Maurice was epileptic."

"Yes. He had seizures all his life. Mom and Dad tried everything. Medications, a special high-fat diet. They even took him to the Mayo Clinic. That was a big deal back then, the Mayo Clinic in the 1940s. The phenobarbital was rough. Maurice took high doses. By the time he reached his twenties, it had caused his gums to grow completely over his teeth."

Phenobarbital was the pioneering barbiturate of the twentieth century. Before it was first synthesized in 1912, the only sedative-hypnotic drugs humans used were opium and alcohol. The barbitals made the twentieth century the century of the tranquilizer, the

century of the sleeping pill and induced, deep unconsciousness. But dangers of death and coma prompted new research and new promises: Valium, Halcion, and the benzodiazepines. These were popularly prescribed in the 1960s. Popularly prescribed for people like my mother, who had too much gentle diligence. Valium for the housewife. Valium for depression. Valium for the Catholic farm girl who left college to get married and raise six children. Soon enough, the drug ran its course in the competitive markets and became disreputable. Then it was replaced by another promise, and another one, and another one. Now, Elijah's father and I are told that there are new "designer drugs," sophisticated anticonvulsants suited specifically to our toddler's epileptic neurology.

"Anything," we tell ourselves with grave hesitation, "anything to escape the coarse barbiturate."

We set up an appointment with a pediatric neurologist in New York City, and within a few days, we're driving from Woodstock down to the big urban hospital. I sit beside Elijah in the back seat of the car, singing songs for a hundred miles. Singing, singing, singing songs like a marathon nursemaid. I dare not stop, or Elijah will shriek in his car seat. His body has become an agitated puppet, and only songs will distract him from his nervous strings. *This old man, he played one,* over and over again. I sing it many times, or there will be trouble. Trouble in the front seat and in the back. I perform my songs with diligence, as I dangle shiny mirror objects before his face. Elijah loses himself there, momentarily, in the twinkling reflections. He stares into the shininess and forgets he wants to cry. But the moment I leave this deep proximity, Elijah falls into despair, and the car is pierced with crying.

"Keep him quiet! I'm trying to drive!" Trouble in the front seat. Ben is angry now.

"Turn the radio off!" I yell back. "It's too loud for Elijah!"

I've begun to snap more than my fair share. I've begun to crack more than I thought I would in a marriage. Since Elijah's birth, I have had to put things on hold. My teaching, my literary translation, my long study of German letters, and my Ph.D. aspirations. I have put them completely aside, so that I may sing *Row row row your boat* ten more times. Then ten more times, *gently down the stream*. I'll just sing the song again, and each time I do, I'll soften the volume one small degree. I'll soften myself for Elijah and take hold of his keen attention. I'll caress his deep listening with my sound increments.

Auditory anchor, auditory anchor, falling down to the bottom of the sea. We are sinking, sinking softly. How far does a voice travel when it's under water? How far can it recede from the surface events? Where in these depths is the telling juncture, the juncture of identity? Is it between the silence and the song? Between Elijah and me? We have gone all the way to the bottom. The anchor has landed, and in between the silence and the song, my son is asking me to become a different woman.

The wheels of the car are rolling smoothly along the paved interstate. Elijah is calm again and thoroughly listening to the sound of my voice. He is serenely attentive. Ben is quiet too, and the radio has been switched off. No more trouble in the back seat. *Gently down the stream.* No more trouble in the front seat either, but I am loathe to continue my anchor song. I am loathe to do it because Ben's satisfaction sickens me. I am sickened by the satisfied presumption that giving comfort is my natural duty.

Elijah's eyes are heavy now. My sound game has nearly ended, but then, without warning, he screams louder than before. His pains come unannounced, and he hits his own head. Elijah has lost the anchor, and Ben is saying harsh words again. We've reached the George Washington Bridge. We're crossing the Hudson River. Elijah is howling, and I have grown too lonely with the presumptions about comfort. Nothing will console my son, and Ben's anger sends me into my harrowing thought, into the thought I do not wish to think. All too soon and frequently I return to Elijah's birth. To the day of his blue face and the administered oxygen. The nurse had placed him in my arms in the delivery room once he was breathing properly, and I began to take the first tentative steps into maternal passage. I was holding an infant boy, divining a new human relationship!

"You're not very good at things like this," Ben said to me, desperate about the oxygen.

I tried to remain "objective" after seventeen hours of labor.

"You're not very good at things like this."

I didn't say a word in reply. Instead, I let blame slip in where the word was supposed to be. It slipped right in and made a stubborn home in my body. That's when this loneliness began, this solitary endeavor. It began at the beginning with the satisfied presumptions. Ben could not help himself then, and he cannot help himself now. He can't resist the sad human contrivance of finding fault.

The blue, blue birth, the little finger that doesn't point, the banging of the head on the wooden floorboards, the stony games and their repetitive protocols, the lack of appetite, the seizures, and the piercing screams. These are Elijah's blossoms, and they are full of thorn and color. These are Elijah's flowers, and Ben and I must bear witness to them. We must bear witness, but we must not bear the blame, for to place blame and bear blame would be to negate Elijah's very existence. And were I to embrace this loneliness, I would embrace blame too. I would put it on myself. I would put it on Elijah. I would put it on Ben, and on everyone around me. I would *use* this sadness to snap and crack and break. I've begun to think the harrowing thought, and I must be careful what I say. *When this is over, when this is finished—*

The new pediatric neurologist asks several questions about Elijah's seizures.

"What happens to his eyes?"

"They go up and toward the left."

"Does he have convulsions? Do his arms and legs jerk around?"

"No. He stiffens. He trembles."

"How long does it last?"

"About a minute. Maybe longer."

"Any other family members with seizures?"

"Val had an uncle who was mentally retarded."

Ben is doing all the talking today, and I'm receding. I'm looking at the pictures of the neurologist's children hanging on the wall above his desk. The medical discussion drones on, and I'm adrift. "No new world without a new language" writes the poet Ingeborg Bachmann. I shadow Elijah around the office. He is nervous and cannot stop for a moment, staking out every corner of the large consultation room, going into the narrow spaces, squatting under tables, pressing himself behind the door. He is looking for containment in this unfamiliar place, while the neurologist's words float on the air like stray pieces of confetti.

"Until we know more, my sense is that Elijah has a form of idiopathic generalized epilepsy."

"Idiopathic?" Ben is dismayed.

"Idiopathic means that no cause has been identified. It's difficult to be more specific about the type of seizures Elijah is having. He has no tonic, no clonic movements, so I'm ruling out grand mal. But there are other possible explanations. We'll have to repeat the EEG."

Elijah has toddled off into a small examination room adjoining the doctor's office. He's always going off into the next room, and I'm always going there with him. Away from all the people and their speaking voices, off to solitary islands of unheard-of shapes and sizes. Like the island hammock we went to at a friend's house last week. We had been invited to a spring picnic and decided to get out of the house for a while, but Elijah remained a measured distance from all the party guests, preferring to be alone.

Swing, swing, swing, swing in the hammock. No people. No people to speak of. If I stop pushing him back and forth, he'll complain. So I stay on this blessed isle with him until he finally falls asleep. Then I make my way back across the long green lawn to the cluster of people who are milling about near the barbecue. As I approach, their smiling faces turn to me, and their voices ask how Elijah is doing. I want to say that I have just left the islands, but all I can manage is a mute nodding of my head. I'm too far gone, too situated in Elijah's solitude, yet the faces seem satisfied with my wordless answer and return to their conversing.

"I suggest you schedule another EEG and sedate with chloral hydrate. And, I must stress, the MRI is absolutely necessary."

Magnetic resonance snaps me out of my picnic reverie and makes my ears prick up. Apparently, the test is going to be important, but it doesn't resonate with me. I remember that morgue drawer in the lab, the rude imaging staff, and the needless sedation that did not serve its bumbling purpose.

"If we find no epileptiform activity on the second EEG, I might suggest putting Elijah on a new anticonvulsant. It's called Tegretol. It has fewer side effects. I know you're wary of the phenobarbital, but we have to wait for the new results. Then we can talk about switching medications. Besides, it concerns me that you live so far away from the hospital." The neurologist scribbles out a pile of new prescriptions and test orders, including one for liquid Valium and syringes. "The Valium is for status seizing. Inject 1 cc if Elijah has an episode longer than three minutes. Do it *right away*, and call EMS."

On the way home in the car while Elijah sleeps, Ben and I turn to necessity, to paying bills and finding a suitable baby-sitter. I have a freelance translation to complete, a dry, academic study of Franz Kafka's labyrinthine fiction. Oh, the irony of it. I have become K. in Kafka's novel *The Castle*, hired to do the job but thwarted in my vain attempts to get to work. In K.'s case, it's the inscrutable maze of human emotional bureaucracy that prevents him from reaching his employer who is in the castle that is perched high up on a hill overlooking a provincial town. If only he could get to the castle, K. would finally get the job done. But queasy interruptions are thrown into his path all along the way. Kafka writes:

> *"Are you waiting for somebody?"*
>
> *"For a sledge, to pick me up," said K. to a village man as K. paused to rest on his way up the steep road to the castle.*
>
> *"No sledges will pass here," answered the man, "there's no traffic here."*
>
> *"But it's the road to the Castle," objected K.*
>
> *"All the same, all the same," said the man with a certain finality, "there's no traffic here." Then they were both silent. But the man was obviously thinking of something, for he kept the window open.*
>
> *"It's a bad road," said K., to help him out.*
>
> *The only answer he got, however, was: "Oh, yes." But after a little the man volunteered: "If you like, I'll take you in my sledge."*
>
> *"Please do," said K., delighted; "what is your charge?"*
>
> *"Nothing," said the man. K. was much surprised. "Well, you're the Land Surveyor," explained the man, "and you belong to the Castle. Where do you want to be taken?"*
>
> *"To the Castle," answered K. quickly.*

"*I won't take you there,*" *said the man without hesitation.*

"*But I belong to the Castle,*" *said K., repeating the other's very words.*

"*Maybe,*" *said the man shortly.*

What I would give to trade my own labyrinth of delusions for K.'s, for the hapless land surveyor's. What I would give to probe an ambivalence other than my own, to return to my occupation as translator in the no-man's-land between German and English. I have become jealous of Ben's work and enraged each time he closes the office door. Whenever we broach the topic of child care, we quarrel.

In the weeks that followed our trip to New York City, Elijah's lab tests were repeated. The MRI failed again because the chloral hydrate made him writhe too much to get an image. The EEG, on the other hand, was the same as the first one, gentle and inconclusive. This meant that we could begin to wean Elijah off the phenobarbital.

It took weeks for the drug's wicked half-life to leave Elijah's body, but as the days passed, he began to talk again. Just one word at first. "Fun," Elijah said. I sat with him in my arms watching videos in the easy chair. "Fun," he said again, as we moved through the pharmaceutical transition, decreasing the phenobarb, increasing the Tegretol a little bit each day. All the while we were watching Charlie Chaplin and his silent comedies. Charlie replaced Elijah's side effects with sound effects, with bonks and bops and clanks.

"Fun . . . fun . . . fun!" Elijah cackled gleefully at the little tramp's wordless pranks, at Charlie's histrionic flirtations with the ladies at a high society party; at Charlie, the lover boy, batting his eyes at a forlorn beauty who is sitting all alone in a restaurant. He's ordered her a meal, wondering nervously how he's going to pay that bully of a waiter for the bill he's running up. Elijah howls at the roller rink stunts, when Charlie trips the bad guys with his devious cane, sending them flat on their faces to the ice, or when he's a gambler, tossing dice, betting everything he's worth on the immigrant ship to America. Charlie throws other things, too, like pies and punches. Elijah is beside himself when Charlie slips away from the police and dodges their angry billy clubs, leaving them puzzled and all alone in the California dust. "Fun . . . fun . . . fun!" It's as if the comical tramp is forever on Elijah's mind, gracing every room he walks into when he does his circuits of the apartment. "Fun . . . fun . . . fun!" Charlie is teaching Elijah the fine art of wordlessness. "Welcome, Elijah," he says, "to the grand silent theater!"

We make a systematic study of Chaplin, rewinding the scenes we like the best to get another look. Elijah is in my arms for hours, sedated but happy . . . but . . . what's this? Uncanny silence. Elijah has stopped laughing, and his body has gone stiff. He's trembling now. He's seizing again, in my arms, and his eyes have gone up to that same high place. I don't get up. I don't call out. I look at the watch on my wrist and begin to clock the seizure. Thirty seconds pass. Elijah is still in it. One minute goes by. What's this? What's this? Thirty seconds later, he's still trembling. Then thirty more seconds. We're just over two minutes now, and if it continues, I'll call out to Ben, "Get the Valium!" But . . . Elijah sighs, and his limbs let go. He falls asleep in my arms without a trace of ceremony.

Ben comes out from behind the office door and approaches the chair we're nestled in. He's come with his seizure poise. I see it written on his body. It's lodged in his hardened brow and on his pained cheeks. It's crying from his outstretched hands that ask a thousand questions.

"What's this?"

"Elijah's just had another seizure."

Stunned, we carefully transfer our boy onto the bed and phone the neurologist in New York, who tells us to increase the Tegretol dose. It works. The seizures stop. Elijah gets a few days' rest, but little do we know that this is the beginning of a long chain of medicinal increments. After a few days' rest, there are a few more words. "Sad . . . sad . . . sad boy," says Elijah, until another seizure bolts through his body. Then he isn't talking again, and the dose is upped. Elijah speaks. Now he is saying "scared." Then, more seizing. More Tegretol. More wordlessness and pinnings on the bed. Seizing. Tegretol. Seizing. Language comes and goes like a wayward friend, and "sad . . . sad . . . sad" fills our lives up in small doses.

Elijah has begun to seize in places that fix themselves indelibly in my mind, on walks in the stroller down Silver Hollow Road, right where the raspberry bushes are, on long nights in our bed, when he's wedged between Ben and me for protection, or in the supermarket, sitting in the shopping cart. Elijah swoons and tilts to the side. Ben picks him up and takes him out. Our eyes are glued to our watches as we abandon our groceries and head for the exit. Just as we're moving out the door, when Elijah has lapsed from seizing to sleeping in his father's arms, a woman entering the store smiles at me with a warm and knowing face. She is imagining some peaceful family scenario. If I could, I would step forward and correct her vision. I would tell her all about the invisible blossoms. "Whereof one cannot speak," says Wittgenstein, "one must be silent about."

CHAPTER 3

∾

Perfect Strangers

"Why is this happening to me?" Ben asks aloud one morning after Elijah has had another seizure. We are sitting in two chairs at opposite ends of the bedroom while our son sleeps on the bed between us. "That's how I feel about all of this." Ben sweeps his hand through the air with a broad gesture. "Why is this happening to *me?*"

"I don't understand you. What do you mean by that?"

Ben looks up at the ceiling and explains to me that *his* idea of fate is personal, a thing that comes crashing down on him from some high authority.

"From God?" I ask.

"Something like that. I just don't know what I did to deserve this."

I'm repulsed by Ben's version of grief. "All I know," I reply, "is that I have to make some changes."

He knows what I'm alluding to. Our words are about to escalate into a well-rehearsed argument about who is getting enough time to work, who should be making child care arrangements, who will drive Elijah to the medical lab for his next blood level check. The weekly blood tests are essential. The Tegretol must be monitored so that it does no sudden damage to Elijah's internal organs. Usually the nurse in the lab can't find a vein in Elijah's small arm, so she resorts to lancing his tiny index finger. Then she squeezes and presses until enough precious red drops have emitted from the surface of his skin to fill a small vial. In the beginning, I elected to do the tests alone with Elijah, no questions asked. I held his flailing arms and legs down for the nurse, then tried to hold him and console him in the car afterward. I did it to avoid Ben's anxious excuses whenever I asked him to go to the lab for a change, or to come along and help.

"I'm tired of this marriage," I say across the room. "I'm tired of our history. I don't know *us* anymore."

Just then, the telephone rings. It's our neighbor from down the road. She has a suggestion. A woman named Sharron Loree might be able to help out with Elijah.

"She has a lot of experience with kids."

"Sharron Loree? What's her phone number?"

"She doesn't have a phone, but you can find her in town. She drives a white van. It's usually parked behind Family. You won't miss it."

"Won't miss it," I think skeptically an hour later, as I'm driving into Woodstock to the town's local shelter. Looking for help for Elijah has become futile. Friends and relatives are hesitant whenever I ask them my desperate favors.

"Can you take Elijah for a couple hours today?"

"I . . . don't think we can do that. How about forty-five minutes instead? It's really too hard. Elijah is difficult. You seem to be the only one who knows how to comfort him."

Forty-five minutes for Friedrich Nietzsche's *Gay Science?* I slump into my quiet fury. There's no time to read for my oral exams at the university, no time for translating Kafka. Ben plays little role in these asking games. He's become too removed for that. He's too high up there with his wrathful god, wondering why all this is happening to him. The more I ask for favors, the more I'm refused, the more I find myself all alone with Elijah. We've begun to leave the apartment for long periods of time. It's a self-imposed exile, from morning to dusk. Elijah is unhappy as we move from one playground to the next, while Ben, at home working, misinterprets our long outings as a gesture of my maternal duty. And now, in yet another false gesture, I'm driving into Woodstock to drum up this ephemeral Sharron Loree, grasping at one more elusive promise of help.

"Don't stay in town too long," Ben had called out, just as I was walking out the door. "I have an appointment. I need the car." Ben's fear has become Ben's work. I've been tiptoeing around our versions grief so long, I don't want to know us anymore.

In Woodstock, I see a van tucked into a quiet corner of the empty public parking lot. No one is around. I turn off the engine of my car and roll down a window. I'll just wait here a few minutes to see if Sharron shows up. I'll watch the mist that's rising off the asphalt. The warm spring air moving into the car urges me to get out and stand among the swirling white wisps. And look there. A woman has appeared as if out of nowhere, as if from the mist. She must have come from behind the van, and a man is walking beside her. They stop for a moment and talk. The woman has a blonde ponytail and an open face. I have never seen her before, but I recognize the man. He has long matted hair and a shaggy beard, and he's wearing a cowboy hat. For years, he's been visible in Woodstock, pushing a shopping cart up and down Tinker Street, collecting cans and bottles from all the public garbage bins. One day, as I passed him on the street, he mumbled "hello."

"Hello," I answered back, shyly looking into his face. Beneath the weathered surface of his skin, I saw that he was stunningly handsome.

The woman with the blonde hair hands the cowboy a paper shopping bag. He takes it from her and walks off in the direction of the shelter. Then she turns to the van and agilely slides the heavy side door open. That's my cue. She must be Sharron. I walk across the parking lot and approach her.

"Are you Sharron Loree?"

"Yes," she answers.

I tell her that our neighbors sent me, two artists who live up on Silver Hollow Road. Sharron says she knows them. She used to baby-sit their children.

"We're looking for a full-time child care person. We have a three-year-old son who has some medical problems, but I have to warn you, it's a stressful situation." Without a trace of hesitation, Sharron agrees to come to our place for an interview.

Two days later her big van is pulling into the driveway.

"I need someone I can rely on," I tell her with little introduction, wincing at my own nervous rigidity as we sit down together at the kitchen table. I'm feeling burned by the last baby-sitter we had, a young woman of eighteen who came for two days, then never showed up again or returned my calls. "We need someone to be here every day. Someone who's mature enough to handle it. I have to get to work. I'm on deadline. This is liquid Valium. These are syringes."

"Where's Elijah?" Sharron asks, cutting through the mustard.

"He had another seizure just before you arrived. He sleeps a lot when he goes through these periods. We're trying to get the Tegretol dose right, but so far it hasn't worked."

I get up from the table and invite her to come peek inside the bedroom door. Quietly, I open it and point to a small cherub nestled in a big puffy comforter on the bed.

"He's a beautiful boy," Sharron declares somewhat loudly.

I whisper back in reply, "We only have a little time to talk. Let's take advantage of it. When Elijah gets up, he'll need all of my attention."

"This is a magical place," she says, stopping to gaze out a

window at the austere mountains that rise up dramatically right behind the house. "It looks like Switzerland up here."

"Yeah. It's remote," I answer, feeling disarmed by her casual ease. "Ben likes it that way, but I think it's too high up. We had a hard winter with all the snowstorms. Why don't we sit down again, and I'll tell you more about the job." I prop my elbows on the table, put my tired face into my hands, and launch into all the tired details of Elijah's hospitalization and the confounding tests. "We still have to get the MRI done, but we have a new appointment at a lab in Albany." Sharron listens as I go through all the narrative motions, but soon I find myself adding new turns to the story. "I would never put Elijah in an institution," I'm surprised to hear myself say. I'm surprised because no one has ever suggested such a thing. "I want you to know," I tell this perfect stranger, Sharron Loree, as if I were speaking to my sole confidante, "I would never do a thing like that."

Something about the quality of Sharron's listening caused me to say this. It's true that we trace our souls by the souls of other people. It's true that what appears to be a series of mere coincidences, of chance encounters and unintentional meetings, ultimately adds up to a life of distinct points of contact. We are not immortal, and our relationships are as limited in number as our own lives are limited in days. I lift my head up from my hands to look at Sharron, who is still listening quietly, and I'm startled by what I see. A remarkable face is there. Sharron's face. It is an elfin face, a moon face. Beaming, wise, and compassionate. Tears are streaming down her cheeks. They are profuse, not a poignant wetting of the eyes, and yet her body does not shake or sway or move in the least. There is dignity in her crying, and she makes no gesture to wipe away the tears. She just sits there looking at me in perfect honesty.

"The seizures make me cry," she says, in the simplest terms.

Who is this elf? This Sharron Loree? How old is she? Does she have a home? Does she have family? Who is this woman with tears for a small boy she has only glimpsed? A perfect stranger. A witness.

"I've met you before," she says, the tears still coming down her cheeks. "I've met you and Elijah before. It was at the flea market. Elijah crawled into my van. Don't you remember?"

"That was you! Of course! What a coincidence!"

Just days ago, during one of our exile trips from home, I had taken Elijah to the flea market to let him wander around and to place myself in the vicinity of other people, even though it was impossible to talk and tarry at the tables full of antiques and gadgets. Elijah roamed freely. He traced and charted, looking for a place where his body could find a situation for itself. Seeing Sharron's van parked there, with the side door wide open, he made a beeline for it and crawled right in. I tried to stop him.

"Don't go in there, love!" I called out, but it was too late.

"That's okay. He can go in my van," a kind voice answered. Sharron climbed inside with him and showed him around.

"You were so nice to us, Sharron. Elijah trusted you, and he liked all your stuff. It was a safe haven, for both of us. Sometimes I think he's in a lot of pain until he finds the next right thing to think about."

"Yeah," Sharron answers. She doesn't seem to need my explanations, and she doesn't respond with the stinging things, with the conversational platitudes I've grown used to, those phrases that push me and Elijah even further away from the few encounters we have with other people. Things like "*all* toddlers are active," or "*all* toddlers like to explore," or "*all* toddlers are impetuous," or "*all* toddlers are exhausting." The stinging things are sometimes hard to recognize in the moment they are spoken, but the aftereffects are not difficult to identify. The aftereffects have caused me to censor my interactions whenever the topic of Elijah's development is broached. But with Sharron, I'm writing my own script, and it's clear that to her, the more original I am, the better.

"I'm sorry I didn't remember you from the flea market."

"That's all right."

"We couldn't stop and talk to you. We never do that. Elijah is very swift, and if I just submit and fly with him wherever he wants to go, I know he's happiest. But I'm afraid one day, while I'm turning my attention elsewhere, he'll walk away. I'll lose him forever."

"Yeah," Sharron says generously. She's not afraid of me. She's not a stranger after all, and there is something more about her . . . but I cannot put my finger on it. There is something *more*. Something *familiar*. Kindred even. "Elijah doesn't look *ill* to me," she says, making no bones about it. The way she talks is clear and simple. "He's beautiful. How could he be *ill*? Who told you that? The seizures are sad. *Those* make me cry." More tears come down her cheeks as she says this, and yet her body remains so calm. "I won't sit on him and give him medications. And I won't do Valium injections. I would never do that to Elijah. So don't ask me to."

"Okay," I say surprised. It looks as if Sharron is staying.

"Don't ask me to do that," she repeats. She is adamant.

"I won't. I won't ask you to do it," I assure her.

"Okay."

The matter is settled. Something about Sharron demands explicitness. Something about her makes me not mince my words.

"Does this mean you're taking the job?"

"Yeah," she answers casually. "I want to see Elijah. I'll wait here until he wakes up. I'll go out to my van and get my work."

When she comes back, she's carrying a briefcase and a large plastic garbage bag full of stuff. She plunks the bag down on the floor.

"These are toys," she announces loudly. "They're for the children. I get them at the free store."

"What's the free store?"

"It's the place at Family where rich people bring things they don't want anymore. You can take whatever you want. It's all free." She sits down at the table again, opens up her briefcase, and sets to work with a pair of scissors. "When Elijah wakes up, I'll show him my toys." She is cutting out what appears to be small colored images.

"What are you doing?"

"I'm an artist." She continues cutting awhile, then, after a few beats, "I have to get these ready for the flea market on Saturday."

"What are they?"

"I take photographs of my paintings. Then I reduce them and color photocopy them. Do you want to see?"

"Yeah. I'd love to."

She pushes a few photographs that are lying on the table in my direction. "I cut them out, laminate them, and glue magnets on the back. It's refrigerator art. People like them at the flea market."

"This one is great!" I tell her, holding up an image of a bride and groom walking a tightrope that's strung perilously above a waterfall.

"Thanks. That one is popular. It's called *Wedding at Niagara Falls*."

"That's hilarious!" I exclaim.

"Thanks." She continues cutting. A long pause goes by, and then, "You wanna see some more?"

"Sure."

Now Sharron takes a large stack of photos from her briefcase and hands it to me. "That's almost all my paintings."

"You painted *all* of these?"

"Yeah, except for the one my boyfriend did. It's in there somewhere. His name was Bill Turk. He died in an avalanche."

"Your boyfriend died in an avalanche?"

"Yeah. In Utah. See that painting, the one you're looking at now? I did that after he died. It's called *Macho Death Message*."

The painting is a grid of images of men involved in death-defying feats. One is shooting heroin. A skull and crossbones is tattooed on his muscular arm, just above a red tourniquet cinched around it. Another man is bungee jumping. Another is aiming a pistol. There's an alcoholic, guzzling liquor from a bottle. There are men riding atop an army tank and various types of vehicles in crashes. And there's a man on skis. A tidal wave of snow is looming behind him.

"How long ago did he die?"

"Two years. I'm still not over it." In the grid of images of male self-destruction is a portrait of Humphrey Bogart, a cigarette dangling from his hardened lips. "I'm still not over it. I moved back to Woodstock after Bill Turk died. I came back here, but my dream is to buy a trailer and live in the California desert. I want to start a day care center and live in the desert and paint. I like baby-sitting. I'm good at it. Painting and baby-sitting."

I flip through more of her images. "This is a strange and beautiful painting." I hold the photo up to show her.

"Thanks," she says, still snipping.

The picture is of a naked man, napping all alone on a couch that is situated in a bleak landscape. The man's back is toward the viewer, and the couch is parked outside an old trailer with silver metal siding. It's a scene of domestic tranquility, but it's uncanny because the whole thing is set on the surface of the moon. The man, the couch, the trailer, just plopped down there on the open plain among the craters. The visible earth is hovering distantly in the black atmosphere, and a dog, its snout turned up, is howling at it. Ah, a cozy place on the moon, far from the madding crowd.

"This is a strange and beautiful painting," I repeat, studying all the quirky details.

"Thanks. It's called *Pursuit of Free Will*."

I laugh out loud at the title.

"Thanks."

"The moon is like the desert, isn't it?" I remark.

"Yeah," she answers. "I want to live in the desert. I want to buy a trailer, and start a day care center."

"And what's this?" I chuckle at the next image I hold up, startled now by my own laughter because I had forgotten what it feels like. "What's this?" The image is a nude woman diving through a ring of fire that is being held out for her by a muscular man in a T-shirt. The woman is perfect in every sense. Perfect breasts. Perfect hips. Perfect diving.

"Oh, that was my boyfriend Bob," Sharron answers with nonchalance, referring to the man holding the flaming ring.

"The man in this picture was your boyfriend?"

"Yes, and the woman is supposed to be me."

"It looks like a circus act!"

"Yes. That's what it was like being with Bob."

Sharron is very dry. She is a little wicked-funny. I'm laughing out loud at her jokes, and all the while she is snipping, snipping, until Ben steps out from his office and walks into our conversation. I introduce him to Sharron. They say courteous hellos to one another.

"Sharron's going to stay," I announce, feeling pleased with myself. "She's going to help us out. And she's an amazing artist!" I point to the images that are scattered all around the table. Ben nods his head half-interestedly. He is distracted and grumpy, standing there long enough for the conversation to go completely dead. Then he goes back to work.

"Gee, he doesn't seem to want to get to know me too well," Sharron says rather audibly as Ben leaves the room. Her face is grinning impishly. I smile back at her in ambivalence. Sharron says what she says in the most direct of terms. She is both reviving and unsettling to me in this serious house of ours.

"Oh, you don't need to worry. He's just autistic. I've had autistic friends before." This was one of Sharron's earliest impressions of Elijah, as she watched him get six seltzer bottles spinning at the same time, while he sat on the kitchen floor. "He's autistic," she said as point-blank as on the day that I had interviewed her for the job. Now, a week later, she, not to mention her frankness, has already taken up a fixed place within our family scenario.

Sharron was the first to say "autism" in our home. My memory of it is mist. But the mist rises slowly after the dawn, and soon the word was turning up in other places. It turned up, for example, on the day Ben and I took Elijah to Albany for another MRI attempt. A new pediatric neurologist, our third opinion, said the word while she conducted the examination.

"How is his speech developing?"

"Slowly. He's saying a few words, but the seizures silence him for days at a time."

"Does he tend to repeat the words?"

"Yes."

"Does he respond when you call his name?"

"No. Usually not, though he sometimes does if I sing. Lately, I've been singing practical things, like 'Eat your lunch' or 'Come over here.' He understands me better that way."

As I answer the neurologist's questions, Elijah, lying docilely on the examination table, is flipping a nearby light switch on and off.

"Let me tell you something," the neurologist says, removing her glasses. "I don't want to frighten you or imply anything without a proper diagnosis, but have you ever thought that your son might have autism?"

"Yes," I answer without a second thought, though why I say it is beyond my comprehension. I know nothing about autism, and yet her words are neither startling nor upsetting. In some inexplicable fashion, it has taken up a presence in my mind. Perhaps it came from Sharron. The mist is rising. Autism. It's familiar. Even kindred.

"The way you describe his speech makes me think that he's echolalic."

"Echolalic?"

"Yes. If you say that he's repeating things, it's possible that he's echolalic. It's a common language manifestation among autistic people. It means what it sounds like. Your son might be echoing words he hears from you or even from the television. But it's not my place to diagnose. You'll have to get a full developmental exam. I can't do that for you." Elijah continues flipping the light switch on and off. He is relaxed with his preoccupation. The neurologist looks at him with a discriminating, professional aura about her. "I think he's getting drowsy now from the sedative. We'll get the MRI done this time. The pentobarbital should do the trick. See there. He's getting sleepy. Just wait here a few more minutes, until the technician calls you."

Elijah's eyelids are heavy. He is nearly nodding out. He is flipping the switch on the wall up and down, up and down. *Echolalia. Echolalia. It means what it sounds like. Echolalia. Onomatopoeia. The lights are going off. Now they're on again. Off and on. Off and on. Echolalia. Elijah is sleepy, sleepy. The lights are completely out.*

Though it's summer and the air outside is hot and muggy, the MRI testing room is a cool refrigerator. Elijah, now sedated, is being rolled into the equipment, but the machine is not a deep tunnel this time. It's a big ring-shaped doughnut.

"Do you want to stay in here for the test?" the technician pleasantly asks us, as he maneuvers Elijah's head just inside the ring. Ben and I nod our heads mutely, astounded that we have come this far. "Okay, then. I'll warn you about the knocking."

"Knocking?"

"Yeah. It can be rather loud. Some people find it unsettling when the superconductive magnet hits the water bath. It causes a series of beats. I just want you to be prepared for it."

We nod again, though our real concerns remain unspoken. I know that, like me, Ben is thinking about Elijah's fear of sudden loud noises. As a nursing baby, he screamed in agony whenever I sneezed without warning, and once, he went into a full panic when the firehouse in town rang its daily noontime siren just as we were passing by on the street. It shattered him for days afterward, as if he couldn't rid himself of the shrill memory.

The technician leaves us in the testing room and closes the door. The chilled air is beginning to move beneath my skin. I sit down on a chair, hold my arms about me to generate some warmth, and look across the room at Ben.

"Are you cold too?" I ask timidly. He is very tense today.

"Yes," he nods soberly. "Cold and tired."

We stayed up late last night with Elijah, making sure he'd be exhausted for the test and possibly sleep right through it.

"It looks like this is finally going to happen," I say with feigned confidence.

"Maybe," Ben answers half optimistically.

Then the first knock strikes with a sharpness we did not anticipate. Our attention darts in unison toward Elijah, but he's still asleep, lying there all alone, his small head of curls encircled by the big technological halo. His eyes are closed and hollowed out by the dark rings beneath them. He is ghostly in this room of white. Next, a series of fast raps resounds in staccato. The din is precipitous and absurd. It makes the room more frigid. Then silence, but only for a short interval. Then more random knocking. Each new percussive movement punctuates my memory, pulling up forgotten episodes of our lives together, like the day we came home from the hospital after Elijah's birth. *Rap, rap, rap* went the loud raindrops against the windows. A violent storm had rushed in off the mountains just as we carried our newborn into our home. We lay down on the bed together, the three of us, and listened to the awesome thunder while Elijah nursed then drifted off to sleep.

Rap, rap, rap. The MRI falls silent. Ben looks across the room at me.

"I think it's all over with," he says.

I nod my head, agreeing.

Elijah sleeps as the technician removes him from a bundle of blankets and lifts him into my arms. Ben and I say nothing to one another on the way back out to the car. Now we're in the car, exiting the parking lot for the street. Elijah, sedated in back, is a familiar scene, when suddenly Ben slams on the brake, slumps his heavy body over the steering wheel, and begins to cry as I have never seen a man cry before. He's entirely cracked open, while his small son in the back seat sleeps through his father's sobbing. Soon, I'm crying too at this harsh irony of a mutual grief that no longer seems to connect us. Ben and I have become perfect strangers, to ourselves and to one another. We are losing it here in the parking lot. We have lost each other.

Three days later we're told the MRI pictured nothing abnormal in Elijah's brain. There are no tumors or misshapen tissues, and his neurology, as always, remains inconclusive. Ben and I have no answers, but I must keep my promise to myself. On the day we receive the MRI results, I tell him I'm moving out. I'm leaving Silver Hollow, for it has made me too remote.

CHAPTER 4

◯∼

The Coincidence of Sharron Loree

By summer's end, Elijah is three years old, and I have found a new home for us. It's a cheerful place surrounded by open meadows and welcoming grasses. Our apartment is in a rambling old farmhouse that belongs to a clown, a man of the silent theater.

"The clown is like Charlie Chaplin," I tell Elijah. "His name is Bob."

Bob is usually gone. The parts of the house he occupies are dark and empty, but he's left some clownish things behind, like the neglected contraption that's rusting out on the grass beneath an old apple tree. It must have been a prop that Bob once pedaled around on stage. Elijah climbs all over the zany vehicle and inspects the spindly spokes, then walks around the big old house and peers into Bob's picture window. Inside, hung in two vertical rows on the high wall, is a collection of antique silk top hats.

"Hat." Elijah wants to go inside and put them on.

"Those are Bob's hats, Elijah. We can't go in there now. Bob's gone. He's on tour."

"Hat . . . hat," Elijah calls out in repetitive longing.

"Yeah, those are Bob's hats. Bob is a clown."

"Clo . . . own," he mimics me. Elijah hasn't had a seizure in more than two weeks. His language is expansive and exhilarating.

"That's right. Bob's a clown. Those are his top hats."

"Toooo . . . p . . . haaa . . . t."

Sharron Loree comes to our new apartment nearly every day.

"Top . . . hat," Elijah tells her when she walks in the door.

"Good talking! Good talking!"

Whenever Elijah tries on a new word for size, Sharron is quick to let him know what she thinks. Now they're sitting together on the floor of the living room, Elijah intently peeling crayons, while I work at my desk in the bedroom. Thanks to Sharron, I'm translating again. "Kafka is perhaps not meaningless but unequivocally ambiguous and hence uninterpretable." Such are the words I must coax from this dry scholarly study, while Sharron, sitting astutely opposite Elijah, speaks from a well of literalness that deeply impresses him. Sometimes her literalness impresses itself on me too.

"You don't have very good toys in your house," she calls out, as I'm wrestling with a passage on hermeneutics and miscommunication. "Elijah needs more glow-in-the-dark. These toys you have here are bourgeois. They're boring."

"Uh-huh," I answer, still working out the tedious language.

A few minutes later, she has something more to say. "You should go down to the clown's house and let Elijah try on all those hats. He needs to go down there." Sharron's presence in the tiny apartment is both comforting and unremitting.

"The clown's out of town, Sharron."

"I know that, but Elijah needs to go down there and try on those hats."

"Haa . . . at," Elijah pipes in.

"Yeah, that's right! Good talking!"

The following night, when Sharron was away from us, a light-bulb in the living room suddenly blew out and made the room go black. Elijah, who had been irritable all evening, let out a long wail in the darkness. I heard him throw his body to the floor and bang his head several times. Groping along the wall, I found a light switch and turned it on, but the illuminated room didn't ease his misery. I spent the next long hour attempting in vain to help him through the sudden trauma. He allowed me to pick him up briefly several times, then tore himself away again, tossing his body down and hitting himself repeatedly on the head before I could stop him. If only Sharron were here! She would know what to do. And, thinking of Sharron, I finally cried out in desperation.

"We're going down to the clown's house to try on those top hats!"

"Haaaaa . . . aaat!" Immediately, Elijah stopped crying, picked himself up from the floor, opened the door of the apartment, and without putting his shoes on, stepped earnestly outside onto the cold deck, heading for the steep wooden staircase.

"Hey, wait for me! I have to get a flashlight!"

"Hat . . . hat . . ." His little voice was receding quickly. I rushed outside to join him.

"Slow down!"

To my surprise, halfway down the stairs, Elijah stopped and turned around to look at me. His small body shone clearly in the bright moonlight.

"Look. It's a full moon, Elijah! You can see everything, even the leaves on the trees!"

"Hat."

The meadows around the house were bathed all in silver.

"I guess we don't need this thing."

I put the flashlight down on the deck and take hold of Elijah's hand. I let him walk barefoot in the cool, early autumn grass all the way to Bob's front door. The sky above us remains wide open. It's a theater of light. I try Bob's door with trepidation. It's unlocked. I stick my head inside. "Anybody home?"

No answer. We pass through the dark kitchen and into the living room, where I switch on the lights.

"Hat . . . ," Elijah says, looking up.

There they are, all twelve of them, waiting for him up on the high wall. A ladder is conveniently perched beside a small loft in the room. I maneuver it near the hats, climb up the narrow wooden rungs, and carefully remove one hat from its peg. Bending down, I pass it on to Elijah. He puts it on. In fact, he tries each hat, repeating the word unabatedly, banishing the cruel incident of the burned-out lightbulb completely from his mind. Then he tries each hat a second time, and a third. "Hat . . . hat . . . hat." He pops one closed and makes it into a flat pancake, causing a cloud of dust to swirl about him in the air. He sneezes several times, saying "hat" in between each sneeze. By the time Elijah is ready to return to the apartment, it has grown very late. We walk back together, both sleepy and sated, escorted by the moonlight, while he moves his beloved word through his lips, all the way around the house, all the way up the stairs, and into his bed, where he easily drifts off to sleep.

Some nights later, I'm making a bed up for Sharron on the couch.

"You don't have to do that," she says self-consciously. "I don't need sheets and all that stuff."

"Why not?" I hand her a blanket.

"You're spoiling me," she answers, slipping between the bed sheets. "It feels like home here."

At the time, I didn't know that Sharron didn't have a home. Since Bill Turk's death, she had been living improvisationally, house-sitting, baby-sitting, sleeping in the van a lot. But summer had come to a close, and she talked about living in a warmer climate. I began to worry that she might go away, that she might make some split decision to drive across the country, which she had done many times before in her bohemian life.

"Hey," she called out from the couch, just as the three of us were settling into our respective beds.

"Yeah?" I replied from the bedroom where Elijah and I slept. His little mattress was on the floor beside my bed where I could keep an eye on his seizures.

"I can be Elijah's grandmother!"

"That sounds just right, Sharron. Good night!"

"Good night!"

In was early September, and Elijah began attending the Children's Annex, a school for disabled children in Kingston. On his first day, a big yellow bus trundled down the long dirt road through the meadows and honked its horn before the house. Together, Elijah and I walked down the stairs of the outside deck, then, seamlessly, without a trace of hesitation, he climbed right into the bus, the same way he had crawled into Sharron's van that day at the flea market. My chest was tight and my stomach heavy. Elijah was but three years old. He would be gone now every day for eight long hours, working a rigorous routine of therapies and early interventions. Inside the bus, an aide who was hired to monitor his seizures was waiting for him. I watched through the window as she buckled my son into a booster seat, absorbing the meaning now of what it meant to "receive services." Yes, Elijah is disabled, I thought, as the bus began to make an enormous revving sound. The engine didn't seem to cause him any visible alarm, though he was distracted by it. I waved at him through the window, knowing he wouldn't see me.

I was used to this by now, but it was not his apparent distance that filled me with sadness on this day, for I knew it was only apparent. It was the thought of allowing so many other people to involve themselves in our lives that was difficult to face. Doctors, special ed teachers, physical therapists, speech therapists, occupational therapists, and social workers.

Elijah was leaving home alone for the big world far sooner than I had anticipated. The aide on the bus tried to coax his line of vision in my direction and make him wave his hand good-bye, but he was too mesmerized by the enormous engine and the high-pitched beeping sound the bus made when it started backing up. The aide shrugged her shoulders at me, then gave a hearty wave herself as the bus carried my son off to his long day in Kingston.

I walk back up the stairs to the apartment and pause on the deck. Far across these meadows, beyond the forests, is Overlook Mountain rising up in the distance. For the American Indians who once lived here, it was a holy site, and for the Hudson River school painters, the most compelling silhouette in the Catskill range. One week ago, when Bob had returned home briefly from his tour, I stood with him here on this deck and watched him subtly trace the mountainous terrain with the hand of a mime.

"Soon the rust will come," he said, implying autumn. "I love when the leaves pass their peak and turn to rust. Rust is melancholy. Rust is loss."

Appropriate words for a clown, I thought, and now today the leaves *are* turning. The first traces of red and orange are visible in the trees. Last night I even felt the rust in the air. I woke up in the wee hours, got out of bed, tiptoed past Elijah sleeping on the mattress, past Sharron sleeping on the couch, and stepped outside the door. There was no moon. The air was crisp and the big indigo sky studded with countless stars. "This is our transformation," I said aloud into the night, and as I said it, a train blew its whistle in the distance, sounding its swift bulk along the rails.

When I went back inside, I opened the window in my bedroom just enough to let the living air in and sat in bed, working with a small lamp on, translating with dictionaries strewn about me. The nights here are becoming increasingly sleepless, and I have resorted to work to pass the time.

Which poet said that when a writer finds voice it's like a shooting star? I can no longer remember. But last night, as I was rendering the academic words, the history of scholarly opinions and counteropinions about Franz Kafka, I paused for a moment—it must have been the rust—reached out for a scrap of paper, and, without thinking all too much, wrote down a poem for Elijah. This has begun to happen with frequency in the middle of the night, but last night there was something more to it. A star shot through the indigo heavens, and it left a pressing question on my lips. "What's the difference between human trust and language?" "Very little" was the whispered answer.

Elijah's school bus is gone now. I can no longer hear it heaving its cumbersome weight in the distance. I go back inside the apartment and find Sharron there on the couch.

"You really need to get some glow-in-the-dark toys or paint or something," she says as I enter. "Elijah will like it."

"Okay. We'll go to town today and get some things," I reply, heading for the bedroom to get to work.

"I'm done," she intercedes, holding up a box of matches for me to see. I stop in my tracks and wonder at her. When I moved into the new apartment, I had found a big bowl of matches left on the kitchen shelf by a previous tenant. It was a jumble of tiddledywinks.

"I guess it's not too safe having these things sitting around," I had said aloud. "I think I saw a matchbox somewhere in these kitchen drawers. Maybe we can dump these loose ones in it."

"I'll do it!" Sharron had offered zealously. "It's the kind of thing I like. I'm good at it." Now she's seated on the couch holding out the box for me to inspect. "Look inside." I slide the matchbox open and find that Sharron has laid each match neatly and individually into well-ordered rows. "Look at them. They're like new, like from the store."

Sharron's quirks seemed to mingle organically with my budding awareness of Elijah's autism. At the school in Kingston, he was now being described in tentative professional language. Elijah, I was told, was "manifesting autistic-like behaviors." He was lining objects up in rows and suffering through transitions. Transitions from indoors to outdoors, from daytime clothes to pajamas, from home to school, from speech therapy, to occupational therapy, to physical therapy, to structured behavioral training.

In the midst of all this, Donna Williams, an autistic woman, had just published a best-selling memoir, *Nobody Nowhere,* and the neurologist Oliver Sacks had profiled Temple Grandin in *The New Yorker.* Temple was a successful design engineer and a professor of animal science. She and Donna were both called "high-functioning autistics," and the media gasped that in spite of their "mental illness," these women could write books, have careers, and be the success stories that they were.

One day, Elijah's school sent home a video recording of Temple Grandin giving a lecture on autism. "Do you want to watch this video with me after I get Elijah to bed?" I asked Sharron late that night. Sharron was game. She would wait for me to ease his restlessness. Elijah was having hard days at school, adjusting to the new environment. He came home anxious and troubled, and at bedtime he tossed and turned, sometimes for hours, on his mattress, trying to bang his head against the wall. I lifted my hand up quickly to the wall to block the impact each time, but I couldn't always anticipate it. Bang, bang, bang went Elijah's head.

"Oh! Don't do that! Don't bang your head!" Sharron called

out gently from the couch in the living room where she was working with her scissors. She said it pedagogically, as if it were something he had to *learn*.

When Elijah finally began to grow calm, he listened to me sing a song he had learned at school. "The wheels on the bus go round and round, round and round, round and round . . ."

"Wound," he joined in with me. "Wound."

"Good singing!" came Sharron's voice from the other room. Her interest consoled him even more.

"The wipers on the bus go swish swish swish, swish swish swish, swish swish swish . . ."

"Sish! Sish!" He cooed some more until his voice was practically a whisper. Then the whisper gave over to silence, and silence to sleep.

"Okay," I said to Sharron, getting up heavily from the mattress and closing the bedroom door behind me. "Do you still want to watch this Temple Grandin thing?"

"Yeah!"

"This video just might be the right kind of grist for our midnight mill," I joked, popping the tape into the VCR. Sharron and I had been staying up very late, talking about art and poetry and failed relationships. I switched on the television and sat down on the couch beside her. Temple Grandin, a hearty woman in a cowboy shirt, appeared on the screen and launched into a dense lecture that was studded with firsthand experience.

"I can't shut out background noise," she explained about her sense of hearing. "I'm like an open mike. I gotta let it all in or shut it all out. I can't modulate." Temple was talking about what she called "sensory scrambling" and "sensory sensitivities," things that most autistics seem to share, though in tremendous variation. One person might have a heightened sense of smell or taste, while another has little or none at all. Sensitivity to sound is extremely common.

Temple's talk was revelatory for me. It mapped the islands that Elijah and I had been inhabiting for so long. She described how as a child, other people's voices sounded like grating and meaningless chatter, unless they spoke very slowly and clearly to her.

"Sharron!" I exclaimed. "Elijah has those sensitivities! That's why he's always going off to be alone! It's too much input to handle all at once!"

Though I had been told that Elijah was autistic, Temple's articulate insights into her own lived experience made a way of life congeal in my mind. Elijah's perceptions of the world were suddenly palpable to me. Temple talked, for example, about how difficult it is to transition from one sensory mode to another, like switching from visual to auditory awareness. The world for an autistic child is a highly fragmented place, and any traditional cohesion it might have is constructed through a long and arduous process of piecing together disparate sensory elements.

"All my thinking," Temple explains, "goes from specific to general." This is also the case for emotions and social behaviors. Temple, who describes herself as a "visual thinker," was able, over the course of many years, to integrate various functions that most of us take for granted. She did it by accessing a vast catalogue of images she had built up in her mind: "This thing that people call thought, facts and emotions all merged together. . . . I don't have that. My memory works like slides. I speed search the CD-ROM. I look at the slide. If I hold it up on the screen in my mind, it turns into a video. Then it gets sound, and then it gets emotion. But they don't come up all together."

If Elijah is a visual thinker, and I'm beginning to suspect that he is, then he is standing at the very beginning of a long project of archiving. Our repetitive games and songs and deep preoccupations suddenly have their reasons. Beginning with "the specifics" that Temple had talked about, Elijah is building up a lexicon of pictures, sounds, and other disparate elements. The small threads on his pajamas, the seeds from the garden, the stones, the top hats.

I was dumbfounded and grateful all in the same breath. Temple Grandin was speaking *directly* about autistic life. Clearly, she was sowing the seeds of Elijah's future. When her long lecture came to an end, Sharron and I watched the whole thing through a second time. We stayed up the entire night, riveted to the revelation, until—we didn't even notice it—the sun was about to rise. My mind was on fire. I got up from the couch, walked over to the television, and switched it off.

"I'm not working today, Sharron. I'm taking the day off. Elijah is autistic. I *see* it now, but I have to let it all sink in." I plopped back down on the couch beside her. "How uplifting Temple Grandin is!"

"Yeah," Sharron answered with her familiar brevity.

"I think I need to get a little sleep now, before Elijah wakes up. Maybe I can squeeze in an hour. I can't believe we stayed up all night watching that!"

The sun was now shining in through the windows with a soft, promising light. That's when Sharron broke the silence in the room, and what she said was so auspicious, I believed her with every fiber of my being.

"Val, I think I'm autistic."

Sharron then proceeded to tell me all about "Simple Sherry." That's what the kids in school had called her when she was a girl. Joking and teasing, they said things like "Nobody home" or "She's out to lunch." Some kids would mock her gestures and hang their mouths open at her, making dumb expressions. When this happened, she protected herself by being "spaced out," or by staring out the window of the classroom most of the day. Like the sensory scrambling Temple had described on the video, Sharron had moments of aural-visual jumbling.

"When I heard the children's pencils scratching on paper in the classroom, the *sound* of the scratching would produce two large cartoon characters in full color right in front of me. I thought I was the only one who had to contend with these characters. I dreaded it."

The sensory confusions and the teasing isolated Sharron in her childhood. She spent most of her time in the schoolyard, alone, repeating over and over again the solitary games she made up. "I used to find a certain kind of bush. I pulled a leaf off the bush and snapped it in half. I snapped it a lot of times until it had a striped pattern on it. Then I would throw it away, get another one, do it again."

Unasked questions were being answered. Now Sharron knew why she didn't like to comb her hair. Why she didn't want to brush her teeth or change her clothes whenever there was a shift in the weather. Why she couldn't wear underwear. Why her nerves were always on edge. Why she kept turning the radio and the television off when everyone else wanted them on. Why she neatly lined those matches up in the matchbox just the other day. Order was satisfying in a world of sensory instability and ephemeral social expectations. It's why Elijah was spending more and more of his time after school lining objects up in rows, his toys, his markers, any obvious group of things.

Sharron had been living on an unnamed margin all her life. She couldn't keep a conventional job. "I always got fired because I didn't fit in." She was "weird." She was "strange." Employers told her that she was too self-absorbed, too demanding in ways that weren't clear to her. She talked too loudly because, like Temple, she didn't have a sense for modulating sound. "'Lower your voice,' they would tell me."

Not long after our auspicious night with Temple Grandin on the video, Sharron was diagnosed with Asperger's syndrome, a high-functioning form of autism that was getting a lot of attention in professional circles. On the heels of her diagnosis, in 1994, the same syndrome was officially included in the American Psychiatric Association's *Diagnostic and Statistical Manual of Mental Disorders (DSM-IV)*. Sharron was of the first wave of diagnoses of Asperger's syndrome that soared in the 1990s and completely reconfigured the known incidence of autism in the population. Researchers are still reeling from this paradigmatic shift. In 1975, the estimate was that 5 in every 10,000 people were autistic. By the year 2000, it was reported to be as high as 1 in 100.

The *DSM-IV* uses the phrase "autistic spectrum" to describe a group of people with a wide range of functional abilities. Elijah was on the spectrum too. He watched the soap bubbles I sent drifting out from the round O of the bubble stick. He stared and stared into their oily opalescence. On rainy days in our small apartment, when all the windows fogged up with condensation, he moved from one pane of glass to the next, methodically wiping away all the moisture. I trusted Temple Grandin that these repetitions and sensory fascinations would accumulate into a rich life, and Sharron was living proof. Elijah might not answer me when I called his name or acknowledge me in word as "mommy." He had other things to tend to, the specifics. When he couldn't reach a high spot on the window, I pushed a chair out for him, or I steadied him with my arms, as he balanced on the back edge of the sofa, erasing the opaque wetness.

"You're doing a fine job, Elijah. It's all clear."

"Cle . . . arrr."

The coast is clear. Everything is transparent. The autumn days are growing shorter. The sky is royal. The sun is wrapping itself around the farmhouse, shining in at angles I had never imagined before. Ben stops by from time to time and takes Elijah out for a few hours. When they leave the apartment, I lie down, depleted,

on the couch and read Donna Williams's memoir, another watershed event in the history of autism. Donna writes about the time when she was Elijah's age and how she discovered that air itself was full of visual possibility: "If you looked into nothingness, there were spots. People would walk by, obstructing my magical view of nothingness. I'd move past them. They'd gabble. My attention would be firmly set on my desire to lose myself in the spots, and I'd ignore the gabble, looking straight through this obstruction with a calm expression, soothed by being lost in the spots."

Donna Williams was slapped by her mother whenever her mind drifted toward the soothing things or when she seemed to be ignoring other people. High-functioning adults like Sharron and Donna had been living invisibly for years. They did not fit the classic autistic picture that for decades had dominated public imagination. At most, they were dismissed as "eccentric," as "mad," as "narcissistic." Autism, when Sharron was a girl, meant extreme removal, extreme disability, but Asperger people were hovering unseen on the fringes of so-called normality. They "passed" to a degree, yet their exclusion was most profound. Sharron wasn't living in an obvious institution. She wasn't living obviously at home with obvious support from professionals and family. Her disability was "unassuming."

Elijah, unlike Sharron, was pegged early. His delays in language and in gross and fine motor movement were obvious, and so were the seizures. But what remained unclear was where Elijah might find himself at Sharron's age, as an adult living on the autistic spectrum.

"Wound, wound, wound," he'd say, gently rubbing his hand along the tire of our car.

"Yeah, 'round,' Elijah." His tiny hand stroked and patted until it went all black with tar. "Let's go inside now and wash up for dinner."

"Wound." He wants to stay longer. In the moment, a small breeze picks up, and Elijah laughs at the sound of it. The sound of it, the curve of it, the fine detail. Elijah's perceptions are more than fundamental, more than joyous, more than painful. He takes me to his sensory islands, just as my friend Sharron takes me on intellectual journeys of light shining in at unimagined angles. It's true that we trace our souls by the souls of other people. It is no coincidence.

CHAPTER 5

༠~

Nietzsche in the Bathtub

Zarathustra, Friedrich Nietzsche's philosopher-hero, has his special islands too. "New paths do I tread," Zarathustra proclaims as he emerges from his cave of brooding solitude and sets out for what he calls the "blessed isles." Leaving the cave means abandoning old ways: "New speech comes to me . . . weary I grow, like all creators, of the old tongues. My spirit no longer wants to walk on worn soles. . . . Like a cry and a shout of joy, I want to sweep over wide seas, till I find the blessed isles where my friends are dwelling. And my enemies among them! How I now love all to whom I may speak! My enemies too are part of my bliss."

The definitions of autism and Asperger's syndrome in the *DSM-IV* are like the worn-out soles that Zarathustra speaks of. In the *DSM-IV*, there are words that I cannot bring myself to say about Elijah. Words like "lack," "deficiency," "impairment," and "failure." Condescension litters the *DSM-IV* and betrays a burdensome psychiatric history. Elijah, by definition, has "marked impairment" in his "use of nonverbal behaviors." It's true, he doesn't point, he makes little eye contact, and he rocks the stones and other objects back and forth repeatedly. He also "fail[s] to develop peer relationships." He leaves the room whenever other

children come over to play, and he doesn't approach a fellow toddler to snatch a toy away as most "healthy" three-year-olds
might. He "lack[s] spontaneous seeking to share enjoyment." He
engages in "restricted patterns of interest." This, the *DSM-IV*
emphasizes, is "abnormal."

My enemies too are part of my bliss. The professional literature on autism, which I rely on for information about Elijah's
way of life, is impossible to embrace wholeheartedly. Elijah fits
the diagnostic picture, and yet he is being framed by a language
that cannot shake its negativities and technicalities, a language
so cautiously self-involved with clinical precision that it overlooks the problem of its own ephemeral standards and presump-
tuous conventions. "It's normalist," Sharron would say.

The scientific dialects of condescension long preceded not
only Elijah's birth but the "discovery" of autism itself. "Every
cretin is an idiot, but every idiot is not a cretin; idiocy is the
more comprehensive term, cretinism is a special kind of it."
The German psychiatrist Wilhelm Griesinger wrote this in
1850. It was a landmark proposition, heralding the dawn of
differentiation among the various types of "mental deficiency."
Over the next 150 years, bodies and minds would become med-
icalized as new syndromes were zealously catalogued. Often a
discovery bore the name of its colonizing hero. In 1980, for
example, "Kanner's syndrome" became the official title for
autism in the *DSM.*

Leo Kanner had devoted his life to child psychiatry. He was an
early voice in the field, publishing in 1935 the first book on psychiatric childhood disorders ever to appear in North America. It
soon became a cornerstone text for medical students and
remained so for many decades. More than anything else, however, Kanner has been credited for having "discovered" autism
when he published, in 1943, his first case studies of eleven boys.
Kanner's research marks an important moment in autistic his-

tory. It was the beginning of a decades-long process that would distinguish autism from schizophrenia as it appeared in children, validating autism as a distinct way of life.

In the early 1980s, when Kanner's syndrome first appeared in the *DSM*, the profession of psychiatry was beginning to legitimize itself again after having lived in the shadow of Freudian psychoanalysis for nearly five decades. The *DSM* served as a tool in a political power struggle between two camps: the psychoanalysts and the biologically oriented psychiatrists. Priding itself on diagnostic data that would lead to clinical standards in diagnosis, the *DSM* promised a new objectivity in the mental health field, which had been obscured by Freudian ideals.

But pure objectivity is impossible. Although the drafters of the *DSM* struggled to cling to the hard facts, "they were buffeted by ideological lobbies," says medical historian Edward Shorter, "and forced to make a series of concessions." Concessions for good reason. Feminist and gay activists of the 1980s revealed that if the *DSM* was the scientific document it claimed to be, it was just as much a political tool. They criticized the inclusion of homosexuality as a "sexual deviation" and said the "self defeating syndrome" was sexist in its claims that it occurred more often in women than in men.

In the midst of this sea change, Lorna Wing, an autism researcher of the post-Kanner generation, was revitalizing the long-buried research of Hans Asperger. Wing showed how Asperger, unbeknown to most of the English-speaking world, had identified autism, or at least a high-functioning subtype of it, in the publication of his postgraduate thesis in Austria in 1944. Coincidentally, Asperger called the condition he identified "autistic personality disorder." Both Asperger and Kanner had used the same word to name what appeared to them to be a new syndrome, and it turned out that their research shared some similarities. The boys they studied showed "a lack of or inadequate social relatedness" and "had difficulties in the areas of affective reaction, nature and range of interests, and social use of language."

Once Asperger's research was reintroduced in the 1980s by Lorna Wing as a syndrome both similar to and different from Kanner's autism, it was subsequently included in the 1994 publication of the *DSM-IV*, at the very moment of Elijah's and Sharron's diagnoses. Wing coined the phrase "autistic spectrum" and stressed the idea of an autism continuum that ranged from high-functioning to less abled people. By the 1990s, professionals had come to see that Kanner had been documenting case studies of younger children who were less functional and often mentally retarded (though the phrase "mental retardation" is viewed today among some disability activists as seriously lacking in precision), while Asperger was describing older children who were verbal and not labeled retarded.

I didn't know the details of such things at the time of Elijah's diagnosis, but the burdensome psychiatric history was all too palpable. If autism was first "discovered" by Kanner and by Asperger, then it's important to frame their research within its larger cultural contexts, such as the power struggle between the psychodynamic view of autism that was on its way out and the neurobiological perspective that was rising to celebrated heights.

Both Kanner and Asperger happened to be Austrian. Kanner, a Jew, emigrated to the United States in the 1920s, while Asperger remained in Vienna. During the early years of their careers, widespread belief in the sterilization of the disabled, as a way of elevating the human race and protecting the gene pool from contamination, was present not only in fascist Germany and Austria, but in the United States as well. Medical leaders of these nations wanted to correct social problems by scientifically halting the growth in the population of those who were perceived as "unfit." In fascist Germany, the eugenics program was taken to nightmarish extremes. Not only were the disabled sterilized against their will, but they served, as early as 1940, as a kind of pilot program for what would become the Nazi death camps for Jews, gypsies, intellectuals, gays, and lesbians in the years that followed. Holocaust historian Henry Friedlander writes:

> *The euthanasia killings—that is, the "systematic and secret execution" of the handicapped—were Nazi Germany's first organized mass murder, in which the killers developed their killing technique. They created the method for selecting the victims. They invented techniques to gas people and burn their bodies. They employed subterfuge to hide the killings, and they did not hesitate to pillage the corpses. . . . The killers who learned their trade in the euthanasia killing centers of Brandenburg, Grafeneck, Hartheim, Sonnenstein, Bernburg, and Hadamar also staffed the killing centers at Belzec, Sobibor, and Treblinka.*

The eugenics campaigns of Germany and the United States were similar in some respects. Both countries wanted to shape forcefully a society of economically useful individuals, while decreasing the fiscal burden of institutionalization, incarceration, and charity. In the United States, public opinion against eugenics was more vocal than in Germany. Leo Kanner was incensed by such campaigns. Targeting Schiklgruber, a prominent neurologist of the day who was a strong supporter of euthanasia for the feebleminded, Kanner writes,

> *Let us try to recall one single instance in the history of mankind when a feebleminded individual or group of individuals was responsible for the retardation or persecution of humaneness in science. Those who caused Galileo to be jailed were not feebleminded. Those who instituted the Inquisition were not mental defectives. The great man-*

made catastrophes resulting in wholesale slaughter and destruction were not started by idiots, imbeciles, morons or borderlines. The one man, Schiklgruber, whose IQ is probably not below normal, had in a few years brought infinitely more disaster and suffering to this world than have all of the innumerable mental defectives of all countries and all generations combined.

Kanner's words are extreme in a time of extremity, and the implications of fascism ring through them. Kanner was known to take up other causes. During World War II, he assisted fellow Jewish physicians from Europe when they arrived as refugees in the United States, and he was blacklisted during the McCarthy era.

Leo Kanner came to America in 1924, long before the rise of Nazism. Originally, he had aspired to be a poet, but after finishing medical school in Berlin and experiencing the German depression of the 1920s, he abandoned his literary dreams and emigrated. By 1928, he had worked his way to Johns Hopkins University, where he conducted research until his death in 1981. Kanner's arrival in the New World also predated the ideological wave of Freudian psychoanalysis, when the mystique of the Old World European therapist had taken hold in America, clouding the objectives of treatment for autistic people for decades. "History," writes Shorter,

moves in odd ways. What ultimately converted [the] chic therapeutic boomlet [of Freudian psychoanalysis] into a mass ideology shaping almost every aspect of American thought and culture was the Holocaust. In the 1930s, fascism drove many analysts who were Jewish from Central Europe to the United States, where they lent the strippling little American movement the glamour and heft of the wide world. . . . [But in] the New World . . . the refugees

*brought with them a stifling orthodoxy, a reflexive adher-
ence to the views of Freud and his daughter Anna that
American analysis was never able to outgrow and that ultimately caused . . . its death from disbelief.*

Many therapists in Sharron's younger days possessed hardened
vestiges of this wartime legacy. Their analyses of their patients
were patronizing, and their opinions, rarely supported by evidence, were accepted as received truths. In terms of autism, it was
believed that the autistic child had experienced some kind of emotional assault, generally from a mother who was so cold and aloof
that she caused her own child's disability. The project of psychodynamic therapy was to draw the child out of his or her shell.

One notorious example of the Old World refugee therapist
was Bruno Bettelheim, a contemporary of Kanner and a fellow
Austrian émigré who was among the first groups of Jews to be
arrested during the Nazi annexation of Austria and incarcerated
in the early work camps. Eventually, Bettelheim was released
from Germany. He fled to the United States, where he established
a career in child psychiatry. In his work, Bettelheim took a strong
antiparental, and particularly antimaternal, approach to autism
and sensationalized his vision of the "refrigerator mother."
Drawing analogies with life in the concentration camps, he compared the mothers of autistic children to Nazi SS guards. At the
time, few people knew that Bettelheim had faked his credentials
and was using fictional data to support his research. In 1944,
with a forged resumé that suggested a stellar academic career in
psychoanalysis in Austria, Bettelheim had made his way into a
post as the director of the Orthogenic School for Disturbed Children at the University of Chicago. By the 1960s and 1970s, he
was famous. Publicly, he was charming and compelling, a racon-
teur who appeared on TV talk shows and wrote best-selling
books, such as *The Empty Fortress* and *The Uses of Enchant-*

ment, that enthralled readers with his popular psychoanalytic notions. Behind the closed doors of the Orthogenic School, however, he raged at his young, overworked female employees (sometimes psychoanalyzing them and driving them to tears after hours in the back office) and chastised parents of disabled children for damaging their own offspring.

Although he never took as hard a line as Bettelheim did toward parents, Kanner was susceptible to the Freudian hold on the culture. In fact, it was Kanner who originally coined the phrase "refrigerator mother" and claimed, with little critical repercussion, that "from the beginning" his patients had been subjected to "parental coldness, obsessiveness, and a mechanical type of attention to material needs." His autistic children "were left neatly in refrigerators which did not defrost. Their withdrawal [seemed] to be an act of turning away from such a situation to seek comfort in solitude."

But Kanner expressed many conflicting messages in his writings about parents and about the etiology of autism. At various points in his career, he said that there seemed to be a genetic link, but he also felt that the way the child was raised was important. In *In Defense of Mothers: How to Bring Up Children in Spite of the More Zealous Psychologists,* he writes that there is "no raid shelter from the verbal bombs that rain on contemporary parents. At every turn they run up against weird words and phrases which are apt to confuse and scare them no end: Oedipus complex, inferiority complex, maternal rejection, sibling rivalry, conditioned reflex, schizoid personality, repression, regression, blah-blah, blah-blah and more blah-blah." Metaphors of war ring through Kanner's language, as do his own frustrations with Freudian jargon. This is part of the burdensome history of autism. Kanner, apologetic and patronizing all in the same breath, is confessing his mistrust of the ideology that had overwhelmed his profession, as he further urges mothers to "regain that common sense which

had been yours before you allowed yourselves to be intimidated by would-be omniscient totalitarians."

Meanwhile, Hans Asperger was in Vienna developing his own studies of autism, until his career was interrupted by the war against the Allies, in which he served as a medical officer. World War II is probably one of the main reasons that Kanner and Asperger knew nothing of one another's research. The two men were living in enemy countries. Kanner did not know that in 1944, Asperger had published four case studies of boys who showed difficulties in social integration, who did not like being distracted from their own thoughts, who had showed limited facial and gestural expression, including the classic stiff gaze, which one "can never be sure" whether it reaches "into the far distance or is turned 'inwards.'" Asperger said their language was "soft and far away," "shrill," or "over-modulated." Often speech didn't seem to be directed toward the person spoken to, but as if it went into empty space. Asperger called his patients "little professors" because they had clever-sounding language. They invented words and spoke more like grown-ups than children. Often they had highly specific interests and fixations involving a large degree of memorized fact.

Like Kanner and Bettelheim, Asperger was also interested in the parents of these children, for many of them seemed to manifest related, incipient traits. He was certain that autism was genetically transmitted, and he sympathized with parents, whom he felt deeply understood their children. Unlike Kanner and Bettelheim, Asperger's career went largely unaffected by the cultural influences of Freud. In fact, researcher Uta Frith writes that Asperger "turned the psychodynamic proposition on its head" and viewed autism as "a deep affective disturbance at the biological level," a perspective that was unpopular at the time but is most prevalent today in the professional fields.

As a person, Hans Asperger wasn't motivated to communicate his findings beyond his close circle of fellow researchers, which is another reason that his important study of 1944 remained unknown for so many years. His daughter, Maria Asperger Felder, describes her father as having been a "distanced man" who seemed to possess some of the traits of the very syndrome he had so carefully documented in his case studies. As a child, Hans had special talents involving language and memory. During his first year in school, "he was constantly citing the Austrian national poet Grillparzer," and throughout his life, "he was known to use a limited number of quotations, which often included his own statements. He had a hard time finding close friends. . . . [He was] unreachable and intensely interested in the German language, constantly preoccupied with [his] quotations, well meaning, but with a tendency for outbursts if anyone made fun of him, isolated from [his] family without any real interest in socializing." Asperger himself once said that one had to be a little autistic oneself in order to understand autism.

Before the war broke out, Asperger worked in the University Pediatric Clinic of Vienna side by side with his assistant, Sister Viktorine Zak. Asperger called Zak a genius. Her therapeutic approach to children was legendary. Tragically, she was killed when the children's ward of the clinic was destroyed in an Allied bombing of the city in 1944.

In 1940, four years before the publication of Asperger's study, the systematic killing of disabled children in Viennese clinics was already well underway. Although Asperger did not castigate the sterilization and euthanization of the disabled with the kind of outspoken rage that Kanner did, between the lines of his study can be read a plea for the social validity of autism in a culture murderously bent on eliminating the unfit. Asperger's paper was apparently delayed in its publication because he was not a Nazi party activist.

If a war and Asperger's own autistic-like tendencies kept his work from being known on a broader international level, America's affair with psychoanalysis was a third inhibiting factor. After the war, in the 1950s and early 1960s, psychoanalysis peaked in its sway over American psychiatry. In this sort of climate, Asperger's biologically based approach to autism was unpopular at best. By the 1970s, however, clinicians were becoming disaffected by the "blah-blah, blah-blah" of Freudian theory that Kanner had criticized. Professionals wanted to diagnose their patients based on symptoms rather than on theories about underlying causes. This is when the *DSM* began to carry important political heft, becoming the battleground of professionals as they thrashed out their differences regarding mental health.

When Lorna Wing revived Asperger's work, it was accepted into a psychiatric community that was turning its attentions to the promise of psychopharmacology and neurological and genetic research. Although at the time of Elijah's diagnosis, and still today, the autism community was celebrating having overcome the legacy of psychodynamic therapy and the specter of Bettelheim, the "power in [present-day] psychiatry to prescribe medications," writes Edward Shorter, "coupled with the latest researches into the functions of the brain and genetics, is itself pressed by a new ideology that is backed by corporate pharmaceutical companies." Psychiatry's own diagnostic sense is becoming distorted. "Illness categories have ballooned in proportion to the market niches the drug companies lay claim to."

Diagnoses of Asperger's syndrome soared in the 1990s, and researchers are madly scrambling to gather data about this way of life. There are many open-ended questions. Is the rise in diagnoses due to environmental problems, such as pollution, or due to the measles, mumps, and rubella (MMR) vaccination? Or has diagnosis simply become so sophisticated (in the same way that it has for attention deficit disorder, dyslexia, and obsessive-compulsive disorder) that it has revealed a large number of high-

functioning people in the population who would not have been
considered autistic even twenty years ago? This was the case for
Sharron. One thing is certain: all the nervous scrambling and
admitted need for more research has not affected prescription
patterns in the least. Some autism researchers warn that people
being diagnosed with Asperger's syndrome today are often
receiving "medication following a regime that has little basis on
empirical data."

"Do you really believe," Nietzsche asks in *The Gay Science,*
"that the sciences would ever have originated and grown if the
way had not been prepared by magicians, alchemists,
astrologers, and witches whose promises and pretensions first
had to create a thirst, a hunger, a taste for hidden and forbidden
powers? Indeed, infinitely more had to be promised than could
ever be fulfilled in the realm of knowledge."

Elijah's identity is encumbered by the paradox that in the
moment autism was first identified, it was also loaded up with
cultural values produced mainly by professionals. How will I
hear my son's voice if it's entangled in such a legacy of wartime
fear, cultural misogyny, and ideological posturing? The answer
seems to me to be found as much in Temple Grandin, in Donna
Williams, and in my friend Sharron as it is in any of the medical
and psychiatric literature. I don't want the alienating aspects of
medicine and psychiatry to cloak our lives in dark ignorance.
Before the emerging voices of direct experience, language about
autism resided mainly within the ideology of othering—of holding up one type of mind to another type with heavy-handed
implications as to which of the two is lesser, unhealthy, or in
need of cure. The dialects of science have changed over the years,
but the basic hierarchical divisions have not. "Brain diseased,"
"feebleminded," "mentally ill," "insane." Would Elijah, had he

the vocabulary, choose to speak of himself this way?

"Craaa . . . cker."

Elijah is moving a new word from his mouth today as I dangle a food reward in front of his face. I'm trying on the rigors of his special educational program, attempting to establish some therapeutic continuity from school to home to school again. The withheld cracker, which Elijah wants more than anything else to eat, is his cue that first he must speak.

"Craaa . . . cker."

The therapy "works," but I remain ambivalent, coaxing words from a small boy as if from a parrot held captive in a cage. Polly wants a cracker! Behold, Elijah speaks! We are all bumbling along with our trials and our errors and our successes, be they medical, be they educational, be they familial. What I want to hear is Elijah's voice of experience, unencumbered by the second parties, the "objective" observers, and even the voice of the parent. But it remains unclear where he is on the spectrum and whether he will one day verbalize his life so that I might have more understanding.

"Where are your greatest dangers?" asks Friedrich Nietzsche. "In pity," the philosopher answers himself:

> *What do you love in others?*—My hopes.
>
> *Whom do you call bad?*—Those who always want to put to shame.
>
> *What do you consider most humane?*—To spare someone shame.
>
> *What is the seal of liberation?*—No longer being ashamed in front of oneself.

Reading Nietzsche's philosophy for my Ph.D. exams has

opened up a can of worms in the light of my son's diagnosis. Each morning, after I put Elijah on the bus to school, I return to the apartment and draw a bath for myself. The exam deadline is looming, and I have found that I can read this strident German philosopher—with his outrageous, perennial anti-Semitism and self-congratulating misogyny—only while sitting in hot water. I get into the bathtub and open up a book, readying myself for another onslaught of contradiction, for Nietzsche is a philosopher who both inspires and disgusts, leaving one to ponder whether he is to be accepted or vehemently rejected. His writings on shame and pity challenge me. Am *I* ashamed of Elijah? Do I pity him? Do I pity myself perhaps, and if I do, does this have anything to do with the negativity and condescension that riddle psychiatric jargon? I am ambivalent. I am both with and against the worn-out language that teeters perilously on the edge of shaming my son, as it leads the way to cultural attitudes that frame public thinking about who he is.

I agree with the specialists that Elijah must work to speak, to learn to use the toilet, to eat with a fork and a spoon, to get a job, to make friends, to have, if he chooses, a companion in life. With the help of therapies, he must adapt in some fashion to a sensory and social climate he and the generations of autistics before him have had little role in shaping for themselves. But I am also looking for signs of a two-way street. I want to cross borders with Elijah and help him find the authentic expression for his experience. Would it not be unprecedented to cast off the worn-out soles that Zarathustra speaks of when he journeys to his blessed isles?

The Woodstock Elementary School has become one of our new islands. On weekends, Elijah and I drive there and park near the playground, which he is only mildly interested in, preferring instead to run around and around the school building, as he inspects all the doors and peers inside each window.

"It's locked," I tell him at an obscure fire exit at the back of the building that has a small high window on it that he can't reach. I lift him up to look inside. "It's locked. We can't go in there."

"In," he says. I set him down on the ground again, where he pauses, knowing exactly what I'm about to say.

"Okay, next one," I announce, and then he takes off running around the corner to a glass door and puts his hands and face against it. Inside is a long corridor lined with symmetrical doors leading to the classrooms. "It's locked. We can't go in there."

"In."

"Okay, next one."

We map the school several times, never skipping a single door or opening. We even explore a dirty stairwell where a smashed window has been covered over with plastic. No one knows it's down there except Elijah, me, and maybe a janitor. Oh, the detail of it all! The fine grain of it! I know the boiler room window of the elementary school is broken and that it hasn't been replaced in weeks. And there's something more I've learned from Elijah: the small high window of the emergency exit at the back of the school is made of reinforced glass, and there's a layer of chicken wire nested inside it.

After he is satisfied with the door routine, we walk away from the school to a certain vantage point on the playground that opens up to a view of a large vent that's slowly turning on the roof. The vent has long metal flanges that spiral up as it rotates, creating an illusion of swirling lines evaporating into thin air.

"Wound," Elijah says.

Is he a cretin or an idiot?

"Yeah, Elijah, the vent is *round*."

Elijah likes things that rotate. At home we set several small toy tops spinning along the floor and watch how their colors change as they gradually lose speed. We put our faces close up to an electric fan.

"Watch your fingers!" I flip on the switch. "Now, do this: Aaaaaaahhhhhhhhh!" I sing into the moving blades. Elijah is enthralled by the song. It reverberates in the air around him.

"Aaaaaaaaahhhhhhhh!" his small voice sings.

"Now, let's do it together. When I say three. One, two, three: Aaaaahhhhhhh!" I model this game until he gets the drift of it. One, two, three, we're singing together, embraced by our own symphony.

What *is* therapy? What is identity and diagnosis and oppression? "Elijah doesn't look *ill* to me," Sharron said long before we knew he was autistic. Does Sharron feel this way about herself too? She has become irritable and sleepless since she was given the label of Asperger's syndrome. She has been backtracking, putting on new lenses to review and correct a lifetime of misunderstandings and false junctures with relatives, friends, lovers, and employers. Sharron doesn't yet know how to wear her autism, nor do I know how to wear Elijah's, let alone guide him in wearing it himself. I have become irritable too. Ben has pared down his time with Elijah to but a few hours a week, and I am beginning to feel exhaustion to the bone. Sharron and I have spats. She comes around to the apartment less often, so I have little help with Elijah. I'm buying food on credit cards. The Kafka translation is getting sloppy. My insomnia is extreme. I have become a single mother of a disabled child, and there is little time now to ponder questions about autistic history. The afternoons and evenings alone with Elijah deplete us, as we hobble from one sensory crisis to the next. On one such afternoon, the phone rang.

"Hello?"

"I have to tell you something." It was Ben's voice, and an unfortunate tone was humming through it. "Your stepmother just called here, Val. She couldn't reach you." He paused. Something was humming. "Your father has cancer of the bone marrow. I'm really sorry."

The next morning, when Sharron came over for a visit, we got into a bad fight. It ended with my opening the door of the apartment, pointing outside with a brittle finger, and telling her to get out. A few days later, I lost the Kafka job.

No chance of reaching the castle now. Sharron has left town in her van. She's off on a quest, seeking her autism, and I'm alone in the bathtub, unemployed and reading Nietzsche. Steam rises off the water and clouds up the sliding glass door that encloses me in the tub. I page aimlessly through *The Gay Science:* "Our personal and profoundest suffering is incomprehensible and inaccessible to almost everyone; here we remain hidden from our neighbor, even if we eat from one pot." I close the book for a moment and wipe away the condensation that has covered the glass door. I wipe it away as Elijah would, were he here right now. But he is in school, and I open the book again: "But whenever people *notice* that we suffer, they interpret our suffering superficially. It is the very essence of the emotion of pity that it strips away from the suffering of others whatever is distinctively personal."

My father suffers. He is approaching death. The blood cell counts are looking bad, and he has no desire to talk to me on the phone when I call him. Elijah suffers. I wipe the away the condensation, but the hot bath obscures the glass again. I suffer. Ben suffers. We will divorce. "They wish to help," Nietzsche continues, "and have no thought of the personal necessity of distress, although terrors, deprivations, impoverishments, midnights, adventures, risks, and blunders are as necessary for me and for you as are their opposites." This is the time of midnights. How not to be small within these worlds of loss that swirl about me in the bathwater? How not to pity Elijah, my father, Ben, myself? The condensation won't go away. There's no transparency. I will allow us our suffering, but no pity.

CHAPTER 6

ᝍ

My Father Was a Yakker

"It all boils down to the odds, to probabilities." These were my father's famous words when I was a girl. I heard them often, growing up as I did on blackjack, knowing as I did to hit on soft eighteen when the dealer has a nine showing. "Chances are the dealer will bust. It's all in the numbers, Val. It's Boolean algebra."

It took my father two years to work out his blackjack system. That was in the late 1960s when no one had personal computers. He sat at the dining room table surrounded by stacks of paper and calculated into the long nights. My father was not a professional gambler. He was a dentist. And yet, for a time at least, pit bosses in Las Vegas knew him by sight and discreetly prompted their dealers to reshuffle the deck whenever he was sitting too nicely at the blackjack table. He was counting cards, assessing deck values, and following all the golden rules of his special system.

"*Always* split a pair of eights or aces. *Never* split a pair of fives."

Not only had he perfected his method but he yakked to anyone and everyone who might listen to it. He was zealous about the game, and his one-sided dialogues moved with rapidity from "one important point worth remembering" to the next. Some people actually sought him out. They knew of his expertise. They were gamblers from around the country who wanted to discern the fundamentals of his notorious system. When they called him on the phone for a consultation, he launched into long-winded technical digressions, gesticulating wildly as he paced the kitchen. His other listeners were more unsuspecting. They were individuals who suddenly found themselves on the receiving end of his uninvited elaborations.

"Go down for hard doubles on eleven, on ten if you have the dealer beat," he explains to a deliveryman who is busy unloading boxes out behind the dental office. The deliveryman looks slightly baffled and harried, but my father doesn't seem to notice this. He just gabs and tails the guy by a few paces, punctuating the crucial points with his lively hands.

"Disadvantageous odds can be changed to an *almost even game,* if you know just *three things.* When to *split,* when to *hit,* when to *go down for doubles.*"

"Dad?" I'm a teenager now, on the brink of a quiet rebellion. "Dad?" There's no answer. He's sitting at the kitchen table writing an article for a dental journal. "Dad?" I raise my volume. I'm standing but a few feet away from him, and for a moment, in my new rebellion, I catch a glimpse of what an oddball he truly is. Always the pioneer in his field, always making a national name for himself, he scribbles away there fixed on his words, yet entirely oblivious to my presence. "Dad!" a fourth time. Still, no answer. So I resort to the trusty strategy, the one that never fails, even though I cringe at doing it.

"Dr. T," I say with sarcastic formality.

"Huh? What?" He looks up. "Did you say something?"

Our family jokes about his absent-mindedness, about how,

driving in the car, yakking and gesticulating too much, he forgets the way home and needs to be reminded of when to turn.

"Make a left up here! Hey, slow down! That's our house you just passed!"

When he's too far gone, all we have to say is "Dr. T." That's the special name his employees at the dental office use to cue him to attention. He looks up enthusiastically, ready to parley with the willing interlocutor on one of his pet topics: nitrous oxide, dental insurance, teeth bleaching, and dice games. And don't forget the most beloved philosophy of blackjack.

"Remember, ace-rich and five-poor decks have a player advantage."

His gambling knowledge came down to me and my siblings as distilled and unassailable principles. We learned them in our family card games on long Sundays after church. For the love of odds, for the love of probability, I was one in six children seated at my father's blackjack table, just looking for attention. His happiness was in the mathematical tabs he kept on the hands he dealt out to his admiring progeny. He'd flick the cards out, face up, with a confident wrist, loquaciously coaching us while his fast mind assessed the particularities of each child's hand in relation to his own. He talked and talked about casino rules, about how much better it is to play downtown Vegas in the older establishments than in the big hotels along the flashy strip.

"Hey, split those eights!" he sounds out, pointing at my sister Marie's cards. Marie is the youngest. "And you," he says to me. I'm next in line of the deal. "You should take a hit on that hard twelve. See here, I have a seven showing."

"Okay, then, hit me." He deals me a ten, and I bust.

"Twenty-two. That's the breaks, kiddo. Chances were you wouldn't bust. I was counting. And what about you?" He passes quickly over me, turning to my brother Conrad. Conrad is the aficionado among us. "You're staying on those two face cards, aren't you?" he asks in exaggerated jest. Conrad returns with a smirking smile. He's a chip off the old block and knows my father's system inside out.

Yak, yak, yak, yak. Deck values and numbers and percentages. Yak, yak, yak, yak. I rarely got a word in edgewise. Living with my father was a long-running commentary that wouldn't turn off. With all the repetitive banter floating in the atmosphere, I had no choice but to absorb the most golden rules.

"*Always* hit on soft seventeen, Val. *Always.*"

Now he's sending hits out to the rest of my siblings, winding up the deal at his own hand with a brief speech on how to play the grind. The grind is beyond me. I'm in my rebellion. I'm soft and seventeen, drifting away from his overbearing theories, having thoughts about leaving home. Then, dramatically, he flips his down-card over, snapping all six of us to attention. Swiftly and competitively, we scan his cards, calculating where we stand in relation to our dealer.

"Fifteen!" he calls out. "*Hard* fifteen! Dealer must hit." He flips a card off the deck with authority, basking in our anticipation. It's a six. He totals out at twenty-one. "Dealer takes all!" he announces, bemused and grinning broadly as he rakes in all our chips. "Chances were I'd bust. I was counting, you know."

And what *do* I know? What do I see? Beneath his pedantic, animated jesting, my father is "far gone." He is calculating. He's thinking most agilely about the in-between places, about the questions inside the questions like: Why didn't the deck, in this context of multiple particularities, turn its cards out the way the odds say it should? He's inside his question inside the question. He's shuffling and reshuffling the deck, and when he returns from this meditation, he reminds us once more, as he has reminded us ad infinitum, that if we kids just continue playing along, adhering strictly to the system, eventually, we'll be a tough match to the dealer's natural advantage.

The chips we use are red, white, and blue. The small grooves around their edges make them stack up neatly. They are reliable chips, but in a pinch, we gamble with wooden matches, or we collect our weekly allowances and play for real stakes.

"Place your bets!" he calls out, beginning a new deal. "And remember, I just shuffled. The deck is no longer in your favor."

I'm one in six, fifth in line from oldest to youngest. How might this affect the odds of communicating with my father? Just weeks before he had learned of his multiple myeloma, I called him in a moment of despair and asked if I could borrow some money. The separation from Ben was taking a toll on me, I explained. Elijah was still having seizures and missing school a lot, which made it hard for me to work consistently. The car I had was falling apart, and I needed to find a cheap replacement fast.

"Welcome to the *real world,* Val," was his answer. He too had been divorced. He too had struggled, nearly broke, not with just one child but six. He would not lend the money on principle. It was *my* time of hard knocks. I, the intellectual, the removed and temperamental one, still stuck in my soft rebellion, should buck up and face the truth of where a Ph.D. in German literature might be getting me. I should lend myself the money on a credit card. "Make a plan. Pay yourself off in installments."

Welcome to the real world. Welcome to the real risks and the real stakes. My father and I had become estranged by the time I had reached soft seventeen. I moved far away from Colorado, taking my quiet aspirations with me, to Germany, to Japan, to Alaska, and India, and China. Then I settled in New York, no longer willing to parley without some sign of mutuality, without some gesture on his part that we might communicate beyond his standard monologues and his beloved narrownesses. And yet, in the wake of Elijah's epilepsy, our odds had been improving. My father had begun to take an interest in us and was calling more often. For my part, I was feeling less stubborn about his faulty communicative habits. I phoned him from time to time too, but our tentative web of awkward relations was suddenly interrupted by the cancer.

My father is watching death now. He is far gone, and I cannot burden him with reports on Elijah's development. I cannot tell him about brilliant Sharron and how the crucial friendship suddenly went so sour, leaving us all alone in the tiny apartment. Isolation is rising beyond my grasp. It has become incontrovertible. There's no more room for external crises in my Colorado family. All my siblings are feeling fraught, because at the age of fifty-nine, the master of probability is dying on us. He cannot beat the system.

"He's lost all his eyelashes," says an older sister, Ann, angrily on the phone when I call to ask about the chemotherapy. Ann has just quit her job to help nurse my father through his illness. She is feeling fraught, but I cannot leave Elijah to go to Colorado, just as I cannot bring myself to tell her that two days ago, when Elijah and I walked out of the apartment to meet the school bus, he had a seizure in the threshold of the doorway. Elijah had been nervous all morning, and he howled as I put his winter boots on and zipped his coat up.

"It's cold outside! You must wear these things!" He is struggling with the change in weather. The added layers of clothing magnify his sensory trauma. Outside, the school bus is honking and honking. I struggle with his mittens, abandon them, then open the door for us to rush out to the impatient bus driver. But as I reach for Elijah's hand, he balks and falls to the floor. I kneel down beside him, put his head in my lap, and let the seizure take its course.

Oh, for the love of a witness! Oh, for family! Sharron is gone. Ben is gone. My siblings are far away. I lift Elijah up and carry him to the sofa. The bus is honking and honking. If only my father could see us now. If only he could see Elijah sprawled out on the sofa as I frantically run outside to wave the bus driver off.

"He's not going to school today!" I wail and fly back inside the house. If only *this* were calculable, like a neat stack of poker chips cashed in at fifty cents a pop. If only I could ask my father *my* question inside a question.

"Dad, what is the probability of an epileptic episode occurring in the threshold of a doorway? What are the chances of that? And Dad, lyrically speaking, should I take it as a symbol and make a poem of it? Where might that get me?"

I wrap Elijah up in an old quilt that he has grown fiercely attached to. One more day of missed school. One more day of missed freelance work. One more day of lonely seizure poise. Elijah has taken refuge in that old quilt that I have carried around for years. I took it from my Colorado home when I began my rebellion. Elijah has been pulling at its loose threads for weeks, and now I see that a large hole has opened up. A seam has come undone, and beneath the faded patchwork, I catch a glimpse of the original blanket. My god, that's *my* blanket in there! It used to cover my childhood bed until it mysteriously disappeared one day.

What is the probability of receiving such symbols on a day in the life of my father's passing? What are the chances that Elijah will ever remember him? Once, they threw stones together on the shore of the Arkansas River. What are the odds that Elijah will recall how hard he laughed each time my father's stone made a hollow sound as it skipped across the water? *Plop, plop, plop, plop.* Is their love calculable? Can the repetition of a stone thrown again and again wrap itself up into a question inside a question, into a spiraling equation that equals eternity?

I know I must whisper softly.
I must take your hand.

I must lead you to sleep,
lead you to eat,
lead you to water
and snow pigeons and geese.
Orange, red, blue, green.
The leaves are rustling.
They fall down and rest on a place
in the road you'll never forget.
They fall too soon.

You're wrapped in an old quilt
and I whisper to you softly.
I lead you to sleep.
The rock skips one, two, three
then sinks.
You go too soon
and the quilt is old and tattered.
Seams undone.
Look inside.
Look inside the holes.
That is where the geese fly backward
and the snow pigeon bleeds.

"Hi."

"Sharron?"

"Yeah, it's Sharron. Hey, did you know that autism is genetic?"

"Sharron! Where are you?"

"I'm in Michigan. But I was in Syracuse for a while, and I'm going to California in a few days. Did you know autism is genetic?"

"Well . . . I guess I've read something or other about it."

"I met Jim Sinclair in Syracuse. He's an autistic activist. I'm meeting lots of autistic people. Have you ever heard the word 'neurotypical'? Isn't that funny? That's the word autistics made up for straight people."

"Yeah, that's funny. 'Neurotypical.' I like it."

"Me too. How's Elijah? Is he still having seizures?"

"I don't know. I mean, we've put him on a new medication called Felbatol, and he hasn't had a seizure in over three weeks."

"That's good. Tell him: 'Sharron says hi.'"

Sharron has begun to call from the road, and she usually does so with a mission. She usually has some kernel of knowledge to impart like: "Autism is genetic." We speak for but a few minutes, just long enough for her to emphasize the essential points, then we hang up quickly, because when Elijah hears my voice talking for too long in the apartment, he becomes miserable. Sharron's calls cause me to wonder about my family picture, about my father and his loquacious intensities, and about his mother (my grandmother) who obsessively memorizes all the prices of products in the supermarkets, then comes home to report incessantly on them, driving everyone nuts.

Unlike classic Kanner autism, which is usually associated with delayed or limited expressive language (and sometimes complete or periodic muteness), Asperger's syndrome can be a very chatty and preoccupied way of life. Many Asperger people have pet topics that involve recitation of voluminous facts, and they don't engage in conversation with conventional pragmatics. It's why my father often seems to broach topics completely out of context and limited to his focused interests. In recent autism research, inquiry is being made into "executive function," or "the many skills required to prepare for and execute complex behavior, including planning, inhibition, mental flexibility, and mental representation of tasks and goals." My father's "lack of common sense" and apparent "absent-mindedness" have been a running joke in the family, but now I see such phrases peppering descriptions of autistic behavior in all the books on the subject.

It's also said that to varying degrees, autistic people don't possess theory of mind, or the "ability to think about and act on information about [one's] own and others' mental states," like beliefs, intentions, and desire. Some autism researchers have given this phenomenon the unfortunate title "mindblindness." It's a difference in the structure of thought, and it's probably why communication with my father sometimes feels like two ships passing in the night. Often a distinction is made between first- and second-order theory of mind. "First-order . . . involves prediction of someone else's mental state, whereas second-order . . . involves recursive processing of one person's mental state about another person's mental state (e.g., 'Mary thinks that John thinks that . . .')." Researchers have begun to feel that theory of mind explains the social disability that is central autism spectrum diagnosis.

In her book *Mindreading,* Sanjida O'Connell derogatorily refers to the "strange and sad world of those who suffer from Asperger's syndrome" because they do not possess a theory of mind. They do not have "the ability to understand that other people also have mental states such as thought, desires and beliefs about the world. Theory of Mind is the hallmark of humanity: knowing the workings of another person's mind allows us to be compassionate, cruel, concerned and conniving. We rarely respond to people solely on the basis of their words and deeds, instead we use our understanding of what we believe others think to predict their behaviour." Although O'Connell's (and other researchers') perceptions open up important views about the mind and the social implications of communication differences, some of their ideas are presented at the expense of the autistic person's identity. Elijah, according to O'Connell, is excluded from humanity because of his alternative neurology. He is being set apart in "a strange and sad world."

For some researchers, the "stiff" gaze and the lack of eye con-

tact—which autistic people are generally described as having—
play a key role in the development of theory of mind. Indeed, I
call out my family members' names: "Dad?" "Elijah?" Neither
looks up in answer. Neither joins my gaze. In my father's case, it
saddens me. For most of my life, I felt ignored and overlooked by
him. But now, in the wake of Elijah's diagnosis, I am consoled by
our family's genetic intersections. My father, my grandmother,
and even I all seem to possess autistic *shadow traits*. Geneticists
call this BAP, or broader autism phenotype. Their studies show
that BAP features occur at a higher incidence among parents and
siblings of autistic children than they do in families with no
autistic members.

Researchers Susan Folstein and Susan Santangelo write:

> *[i]n concept, BAP is similar to both autism and [Asperger's
> syndrome], but the traits and the behaviors are not usually
> severe and sometimes have adaptive value; it usually does
> not come to clinical attention. Individuals with BAP gener-
> ally lack the markedly restricted interests or striking diffi-
> culties of getting along in the workplace that plague indi-
> viduals with [Asperger's syndrome].*

Perhaps Hans Asperger himself was in the BAP range.

In the film *Rain Man*, Dustin Hoffman plays an autistic man
named Ray who has savant mathematical ability. When a waitress in a diner inadvertently drops a box of toothpicks, sending
them to scatter all over the floor, Ray takes one look at them
and knows precisely how many there are. The number, Ray later
tells his brother, appears as an image in his mind. In another
scene in *Rain Man*, Ray counts cards at a blackjack table in Las
Vegas and ends up winning so much money that he and his
greedy brother, the neurotypical instigator of their gambling
spree, are asked to leave the casino. This scene in the movie res-

onates and entwines itself with family stories of my father, who was not a mathematical genius, but his facile numerical musings and preoccupation with gambling odds are shadowy cousins of savantism.

If my father, and his mother before him, were carrying Elijah's autism genetically, then it must have passed through me. How shall I reconcile these familial collisions? I stand between my father and my son, enraged at Dr. T for "ignoring" me as his daughter, yet protective of Elijah whom I defiantly perceive as neither "mindblind" nor as living a "strange and sad life."

"Who is the person with a hidden form of autism?" ask researchers John Ratey and Catherine Johnson.

> He is the odd duck. His difference from "normal" people is readily apparent to all of us; we recognize him as being somehow off. It is only his kinship to the Rain Man that we have missed. We should add the word "he" is in all likelihood correct; while autism at the low end of the spectrum affects two boys for every girl, at the high end there are five autistic boys for each autistic girl. . . . It is quite possible that as we move into the very mild, undiagnosed cases, the sex gap grows wider still. Mild autism may be overwhelmingly a disorder of men. On the other hand, it is also conceivable that at the highest end of the spectrum we will eventually discover more females, not fewer.

I have begun to see my shadow syndrome in my preference for solitary activities and in my need for sameness in particular aspects of my life. As a child and as an adult, I have had intense periods of preoccupation with tornadoes, depending on the degree of stress I'm feeling. The image of the tornado, wreaking sudden havoc and causing extraordinary and paradoxical forms of damage, takes hold of my mind in what is perhaps a kind of perseveration, the rigid thought patterns or extreme focus that many autistics experience.

Growing up as a kid in Colorado, I felt bored, sensitive, and isolated as I observed the social culture around me, feeling uncompelled to jump in and participate in what seemed superficially meaningless. I wasn't entirely aloof, but I preferred being with only one friend at a time. Too many people made me edgy. The social stimulation made my stomach ache. I went through periods of extreme "shyness," as others labeled my seemingly removed or quiet behavior, rehearsing social situations in my mind over and over again, both before and after they had occurred, sometimes speaking them aloud to myself. I still do this today. It's a kind of mental exercise that makes me feel safe. I just like the *sound* of words *spoken aloud,* in poetry, in theatrical dialogue, and in foreign languages.

By the time I reached junior high and then high school, I relied on the rigorous routine of academics to help me negotiate and organize my life around something stable and reliable. I got only A's on report cards and tests, and when I did receive my single B in geometry in high school, I wept bitterly. My mother always tried to tell me not to "take things so seriously" at school. I was "oversensitive" and "moody." All of these traits are common experiences that many Asperger and BAP people describe.

I dreaded the moments between classes in high school, when I had to dash from one room to the next, dodging all the other bodies in the hallway, afraid of bumping into them, entirely unable to stop and socialize. Nervously, all I could think was the phrase "air pockets . . . air pockets" over and over again in my mind. Repeating these words to myself kept me focused, so that I could find the open spaces in the busy hallway and slip in and out of them all the way to the next class. Perhaps it was a question of executive function.

I was well liked in school and known to be a "brain" among

my peers and accepting of just about anyone. This reputation carried over into college, with the exception that I had few friends there. I did very little socially in college. I was the nerd who always studied. This was the time of my first conscious depression. When the other students on my dorm floor caught wind that I was sensitive to touch, mistaking it for being ticklish, they would lie in wait for me in the stairwell. When I came down the stairs from the study lounge, they'd pounce on me and tickle me until I couldn't move. It was all in fun, even to me, but I was amazed at how I always fell into paralyzing passivity, unable to defend myself. What wasn't funny were the aftereffects, which would sometimes ring through my body for several days afterward. Sitting in seminars, I would fear that someone taking notes beside me might graze my arm with a stray hand or an elbow. The slightest motion triggered me, and I'd jump electrically in my seat.

In college, I met Ben. He was a graduate student in English literature and far more stimulating to talk to than my undergraduate peers, most of whom were interested in sex, drinking, and making a lot of money when they finished school. I've known Ben since I was nineteen. My friendship with him freed me briefly from my isolation and depression, but our marriage four years later was no panacea. I began deferring to Ben's intense confidence and burly social ease and eventually receded into the gray life once more.

Had their commentary not been so value ridden, the myth of the refrigerator mother and of the aloof parent that Kanner and Bettelheim had highlighted in some of their research probably had some validity in genetic terms. It is plausible that they were writing about high-functioning autistic parents or about parents like me within the broader phenotype. Hans Asperger was outspokenly *uncritical* on the topic of parents and emphasized their extraordinary relations with their autistic children. Today, the powerful role that parents with shadow traits can play in an autistic child's life is beginning to be more fully acknowledged. Asperger specialist Tony Attwood writes that "should a parent or relative have had . . . [autistic] characteristics when younger then they have a unique advantage that is invaluable in helping the child. They know what [the child is] going through. They have empathy and can offer advice based on their own experiences."

In the winter of Elijah's first year at school, there was a series of unremitting snowstorms. The Children's Annex closed its doors each time a new front passed through the region. This was typical of upstate New York. The snowplows often didn't make it to our rural road for long stretches of time. The temperature fixed itself in the low teens. There was nowhere to go, and even if there were, the car was often buried in deep snow. Elijah's seizures had subsided completely the moment he was placed on Felbatol, but the wintry disruptions to his weekly school routine continued to afflict him with heartrending torments.

Socked in the apartment, he grasped desperately at anything he might use to anchor himself, like the familiar images in his picture books. He sat before a low shelf on the floor and rifled systematically through each and every page of each and every children's book we owned, scanning all the images that he had glimpsed countless times before. His repetitions were mounting to the extreme. Their insistent pervasiveness was stunning to behold. Each of Elijah's actions became well-rehearsed events. Each word spoken was echolalic. The long days trapped inside the house and inside the repetitions forced themselves deep into my psyche. I began having dreams at night that I can describe only as dreams of autistic structures of the mind. I woke up in sweats, having just executed long calculations. They were extended logic problems, replete with scientific symbols that I freely understood and manipulated with ease, translations of a kind, from neurotypical to autistic thinking. When I awakened from these philosophical excursions, I felt deep physical relief. It was as if I had cracked a code, as if I'd been returned to a former way of life that I had once belonged to but had long forgotten.

Ben and I have maintained an imbalance far too long now. We've allowed the weeks of my sole caring for Elijah to add up to months. I am running thin and thinner. I am losing weight and sleep. I have begun to ask Ben for help in a tone of voice that I cannot seem to shake, a desperate tone that scarcely cloaks my indignant rage. One day, after a tense exchange on the phone, Ben finally agreed to have Elijah spend a night at his house so that I could get some rest. We arranged for a date and a time, and obsessively, I began to count the hours. I didn't count them casually, trapped in this small place with Elijah, ravaged by the winter storms of discontinuity.

He's flipping through the picture books one more time, and the same music is playing on the stereo over and over again. Elijah cannot bear it if I change the cassette or attempt to read the picture books aloud to him. He becomes more fragile, so I give up and leave him to his repetitions. But if I stray too far away, to wash the dishes or answer the phone, he soon moves into a panic. It's as if he requires my steady but silent presence to assure him that he exists. I'm counting the hours now until we go to Ben's house. I am maintaining. I'm keeping the space around my son intact, helping him hold his sensory life together by a thin thread.

When it's time to get Elijah dressed for the ride to his father's house, I headline each article of clothing before putting it on him. It's a proactive trick I learned from the capable staff at Elijah's school, from all the Sister Viktorines who work so diligently and empathically with him. It makes the transition less traumatic, lessening the blow of inevitable change, preparing Elijah for what will happen next.

"Look. I'm going to put your jacket on." I hold the little coat up in his line of vision. "I'm going to put your jacket on," I enunciate clearly and consistently. "Now I'm going to zip it up."

"Up," says Elijah.

"That's right. I'm zipping it up." He is not unhappy in the moment, and I'm maintaining. "Now the boots." I fit the first boot on with his cooperation. "Okay, next boot," I say slowly.

"Boot . . . boot." Elijah is satisfied with the careful dialogue.

"Yeah. Boot. And now, out the door."

"Door."

"Yeah, the door . . . and then to the car."

"Car."

"Yeah, the car, then Daddy's house."

We open the door and walk out into the icy night together. I'm anticipating Elijah's sadness. Every time we leave the house in this disruptive winter, he cries out and tries to run back inside. But tonight, as we make our way through the deep snow, he's remarkably silent. Step by tedious step, everything we do is funneled into a careful meditation.

"Don't lose that thought, Elijah. We're going to the car."

"Car."

The powdery snow sifts into the tops of our boots. It's too deep for Elijah to manage, and he whimpers. I bend down to speak to him in my careful language.

"I'm going to carry you."

"Carrrrry you," he nearly sings.

I heave him up in his bulky clothes and wade through the heavy snow. The air in my lungs is painful. Elijah cries out at the dark, but we are maintaining. I put him into his car seat, buckle him up, dig out the wheels of the car, and scrape away the stubborn ice. All the way to Ben's house, Elijah remains serene, and I have gone from counting hours to counting minutes, driving intentionally through the snowy streets of Woodstock.

When we reach Ben's house, I see that all the lights are out, and his car is not in the driveway. Then I hear another soft whimper and startle when I realize that it's not Elijah's, but my own. Something is not right here. Ben's house is completely dark.

"Something is going to happen," I say involuntarily aloud. I park, open the door, get out of the car, and leave Elijah there with the engine running and the heat turned on. I try Ben's door. It's unlocked. I go inside the house, walk directly to his office, pick up the phone, and dial the number of Ben's best friend, George, whom I have known for years.

"Hello?" a voice answers.

"George?"

"Yeah?"

"It's Val. Something is going to happen."

"Where are you?"

"I'm at Ben's house. He's supposed to be here, George. He's not here. Something is going to happen to me."

"Where's Elijah?"

"He's outside in the car. I can't do it anymore, George."

"I know, sweetie. I'm on my way."

I hang up the phone. I'm dizzy, and then I'm on the floor. My arms and legs thrash about me. My voice is loud. It screams, and now I'm looking at my quiet hand, resting on the floor just inches from my face. I see that it is covered with wrinkles, and my bones protrude clearly beneath the gray skin. This vision puts my body in motion again. My limbs work the air violently, and I call out to no one. Then, suddenly, I'm on my hands and knees crawling out the front door. I make my way through the snow to Elijah, open the car, and unhook him from his seat. Without a word, he gets out, walks right past me, and heads toward the house. I crawl behind him and collapse just in the entry, then numbly watch as he sets out into the large dark rooms of Ben's house that are now beyond my reach. I lie there in the front hall and wait for George. I lie there with indifference, no longer able to care if Elijah is in danger.

George helped arrange for a baby-sitter and took me to the hospital.

"When was the last time you ate?" a therapist asked as I lay on a stretcher in the same emergency room that Elijah lay in on the night of his first seizure.

"I . . . don't remember."

"When was the last time you slept?"

"I . . . don't know that either."

I was given the diagnosis of depression and sent home with a prescription of sleeping pills. I did not see Elijah for a solid week. He remained with Ben, who later told me that I had been confused about our appointment. I had miscalculated and arrived with Elijah one day too early. Ben was out of town. But something had forced itself to the surface in the dark driveway that night. It came out thrashing and screaming, then abruptly it receded again into a numbness that surrounded me in a thick fog. I did not miss Elijah in the least during my week in bed, but gradually, as I regained my strength, I awakened to the damage of my isolation. That's when I concluded I would no longer sacrifice my body or my mind to rectify the sad imbalance between me and Ben. This was the beginning of our shared parenthood. Our autistic son would live in *both* our homes. I made plans to go to Colorado to see my father.

Dr. T's head had grown thin and hairless. I sat beside him on the bed where he lay most of the day sleeping, oblivious to my presence, until one evening, on an energetic whim, he suddenly announced that he wanted to go out for dinner. He had the strength to do it. So my stepmother, my father, my older sister Jane, and I all huddled around a small table in a quiet steak-house for an hour. My father listened to us talk, smiling vaguely and unable to engage with his usual loquacity. When the subject turned to Elijah, I tentatively revealed what I had come to Colorado to say, turning directly to my mute father.

"Dad, I've been reading about autism, and there is evidence that indicates it's genetically determined, at least partially."

My father nodded his skinny head. I had his genuine interest, as I had never had it before.

"I think, Dad, that there are people in *our* family who have some autistic traits. I see them in Grandma, in the way she obsesses on certain things, in the way she's always on edge. And I see them in you too." There was a long silence at the table. My words felt like lead in my mouth. I tried to explain. "You know how we call your name and you don't answer because you're so preoccupied? Elijah does that too. It's very common. It's *classic*, in fact."

"You should talk, Val," my sister Jane suddenly piped in. She was obviously miffed. "When you were young, we used to call and call *your* name, and you *never* answered us."

"Yes." My father agreed with her in a weak whisper.

Jane's words were salted with an angry impatience that reminded me of my own disappointed attitudes about my communicative disjunctions with my father. Her words shocked me into a memory I had never had until that evening, right there in the restaurant. It was an early memory of sitting extremely close to the television set, so that all I could see were the tiny dots on the screen. It was those colorful dots, not the big picture, that compelled me so. "Val . . . Val . . . Val . . ." Had someone called my name? I could hear it in the periphery, but I didn't turn my head. "Val . . . Val . . ." I was too entranced with the specifics to be able to listen.

That night, after we had returned from the restaurant, my father came into my bedroom and held out his hand.

"Here. Take this," he said, passing something to me discreetly, as if he were palming an ace. "Pay off some of your debts."

Into my hand he placed a thick roll of bills. He always carried cash that way, as if a poker game could manifest at any moment out of the thin air. My throat tightened with tears.

"Thanks, Dad," I whispered, looking up to meet his gaze, but the yakker had already vanished.

CHAPTER 7

Echolalia Fun Fun Fun

"Hi, I'm Emma Missouri." A robust woman with short red hair and kind blue eyes greeted me in the doorway of a house I was interested in renting. I was there for an interview. "Come inside!" I walked into a cozy living room with a warm fire burning in the woodstove.

"It's nice here," I said, feeling shy.

"Welcome to Brookside Cottage," Emma returned cheerily. "That's what I call this place because in the spring you can hear the brook outside. It flows right past the house. Come into the kitchen. I'll make you some tea." The kitchen smelled like cinnamon and basil. Something was baking in the oven. Emma offered me a chair at the table and jumped right into the details. She was looking for a new roommate because the previous tenant had just moved out. "The house isn't well insulated, but heating with the woodstove keeps the electricity bill down—"

"Before you go any further," I interrupted her, "I have to be honest and tell you that I have a very complicated life."

"Complicated?" Emma asked mildly sarcastically, as if nothing could be too difficult.

"I have a little boy. He's three and a half years old."

"That's wonderful! What's his name?"

"Elijah."

"Wow! A heavy-duty prophet's name!"

"Yeah, and he's certainly living up to it." Emma, standing in the middle of the kitchen with a teacup in each hand, threw her head back and let out a loud laugh. She was wearing a purple apron with the words "Kitchen Butch" printed across the chest. I smiled at her gaiety. Brookside Cottage was an easy place to be. "Elijah lives with his dad most of the time. I'm taking a little break."

"This is good," Emma said approvingly. "This is *very good*."

"Eventually, he'll live with me again, part of the time. I just want to make sure you're okay with that."

"Children are people too," was her reply as she busied herself with the tea.

"I'm glad you feel that way, Emma. Most of the advertisements in the newspaper say: 'No children. No pets.'"

She chuckled at the equation and rummaged around the kitchen cabinets. "Where *is* the honey?"

"There's something else you should know."

"What's that?"

"Elijah is autistic, and he has a seizure disorder. He 'tantrums' a lot. At least, that's the word they use in the autism books. I find it inappropriate."

"Of course you do," she said solemnly, sitting down to join me at the table. "It's demeaning."

"Elijah is very sensitive. I can try to keep him in my room when he's here, but that might be difficult."

"Why would you want to do that?"

"So as not to disturb you."

"This is *your* house, too you know. There are three bedrooms upstairs. You and Elijah can have two of them, but you don't need to lock yourselves in, for goodness sake!"

"There's . . . something more."

"There's more?!" Emma is teasing now.

"I've just split up with my husband, and a couple months ago, I found out that my father is dying of cancer. I'm depressed, Emma. I can't live alone anymore. I can't live alone with Elijah. It's become too much. That's why I answered your ad in the newspaper. I'm in therapy, trying to get my strength back so that I can be Elijah's mother again."

"Uh . . . Excuse me, but aren't you Elijah's mother *now*, as we speak?" Emma asks, pointing out the obvious.

I nod my head. "I just need a break. I can't function if I'm 'on' all the time."

"Of course you can't." Emma spells it out: "You need a break, *and* you're Elijah's mother."

"I think I can stay on top of the bills and my share of the rent, but it's going to be precarious. I'm on the edge."

"You're on the *cutting* edge. I can see you bleeding." Emma gravely pushed a steamy mug of tea across the table in my direction. "Milk? Honey?"

"No thanks," I whispered, my throat swollen with emotion. "I just think you should know these things before you make a decision about our moving in. Elijah and I are a handful." Before I could say another word, Emma leaned into the table and caught my gaze.

"MOVE IN," she said emphatically.

"Are you sure?"

"JUST MOVE IN." Her voice was confident.

"Okay. We'll move in."

"Good."

"Nice apron, by the way," I said, pointing at the words on her chest.

Emma cackled. "This is going to be very good!"

Soon Emma and I were building fires in the woodstove early each morning before work. We sat in rocking chairs and mused and laughed and confided in one another. Emma told me all about the lesbian theater of the 1970s and her previous life as an actor and director. She spoke about art and music and the stage *all the time*. She was passionate and alive. I talked about German literature and my readings on autism.

"You know, Emma, I was chronically depressed in my marriage, but now I see that I was depressed long before I ever met Ben, even before Elijah was born."

"Tell me about it," she replied knowingly.

"I've read that depression is common among autistics, *and* it's common among their family members too. I think I fit the picture."

"You've got a lot on your plate, Val. You might consider antidepressants for a while."

"Yeah. That's what the therapist is suggesting."

After our morning chats staring into the fire, Emma commuted to a job she couldn't tolerate at a new age healing center across the Hudson River. She was gone all day long, while I worked upstairs in my bedroom, finishing up freelance projects. I also made my first stabs at the dissertation, for I had been notified, much to my surprise, that I had passed the oral exams at the university by the skin of my teeth.

As the weeks went by, I was able to see Elijah more consistently on an alternating schedule with Ben. Brookside Cottage was a lovely place when the deep snows of winter began to melt and the Catskill bluestone appeared in view again. The small stream beside the house babbled just as Emma had promised it would. It babbled and bubbled, and so did Elijah. Nearly every word that landed at end of my sentences was pitched right back to me by my parrot companion.

"It's time for a bath."

"Baaaaaath."

"I'm going to turn on the water."

"Waaaaaateeeer."

The Buddhist knows that deep within the mantra are forgetting and transformation. There's more to repetition than meets the ear. If you make a deep study of words, if you go into the well of echoes and the fugue of contrapuntal voices, language, says Kenneth Rexroth, begins to "glow." It becomes an "aesthetic object." What might the objects have to do with repeated autistic speech? Temple Grandin says that autistic children often experience object impermanence. It has to do with sensory processing. When Temple was a little girl, riding in the car to her speech therapy class, she always took along a little purse with a comb tucked inside it. All the way to the lesson, she opened that purse up again and again to make sure the comb was still there. Might the repetition of a word be a similar kind of anchor in a world of human vocal variation? Gertrude Stein, describing the development of her poetry, writes that she was "enormously interested in hearing how everybody said the same thing over and over again with infinite variations but over and over again until finally if you listened with great intensity you could hear it rise and fall and tell all that there was inside them."

In the bathtub, Elijah's speech becomes more fluid. Water is a second skin for him. It calms his body and makes his eyes shine, and his facial features become distinct and expressive. "Boat . . . boat . . . boat," he babbles, splashing around with a beloved object in his hands. His bath has become a synesthetic pool of things and words: plastic puppet heads that he removed from their puppet bodies, all the letters of the alphabet that once stuck magnetically to the refrigerator door, and a miniature ceramic tea set with matching plates, cups, saucers, a creamer, a teapot, and tiny spoons.

"Elijah, that's a spoon." I name each object as he picks it up.

"Spoooooon," he says rocking it in his hands in reverence. He holds the spoon under water, studies it, takes it back out again, and lines it up carefully beside the other objects on parade along the edge of the tub. "Spoooooon . . ." He names the thing so intently it begins to shine. It glows like a poem, like "The Birthday Book," by Gertrude Stein:

Who was born January first.
Who was born in January first.
Who was born and believe me who was born and believe me,
*   who was born who was born and believe me.*
At that rate.
Let us sell the bell.

Who was born and believe me for this reason, this reason the reason is that the second of January as the second or January, February or the second or January, he was born and believe me the second of January. The second of January as the second of January.

"Echolalia is a good sign," says Temple Grandin. "It means that receptive language is getting through." When an autistic person repeats what is heard in the environment, it's like "verifying a telephone number." Autistics have complex speech processing. Temple wasn't echolalic as a child, but she had to hear the words spoken slowly to understand them. Otherwise, it was all grating gibberish. Asperger children don't exhibit echolalia at all in the early years of childhood. They tend to be loquacious and eventually come to speak—sometimes pedantically, sometimes beyond their years—with erudite acumen about a specific field of interest. Some researchers comment on the clinical fuzziness between Asperger's syndrome and high-functioning autism and have set their sights on defining them as separate subtypes. The theory goes that those who are echolalic, or who have obvious delays in speech, are high-functioning autistics as opposed to their Asperger counterparts, who don't exhibit these language differences in early childhood.

But the line remains fuzzy. For all autistics, anywhere along the spectrum, a sensory processing problem can cause a child to run away if the stimulus is too overwhelming to integrate. That's why Elijah leaves the room whenever gabbing friends stop by. On the other hand, if the processing problem is mild, it can generate intense attractions, like Temple Grandin's long-standing visual fondness for automatic doors. She gets a thrill just watching them open and close. Some autistics fondly call these sensory pleasures "stimming." In a sense, Gertrude Stein was verifying linguistic telephone numbers in her writing. Language patterns thoroughly compelled her. From this fixation, she developed a singular poetics that set her apart from her modernist contemporaries.

Elijah's language has thrust me into the well of echoes and the conundrum of meaning, leaving me to ponder how neurotypicals presume communication works. I know that echolalia is more than rote repetition of what is heard in the immediate environment. It is a particular expression of consciousness. I use the therapies I'm shown at Elijah's school, coaxing him to push the envelope of his language repertoire, holding out a cracker for him to eat if only he says the word. But I do not want to equate ability thoughtlessly with neurotypicality.

> *March the eighteenth may we blame no one and in this way reconcile ourselves to every obligation.*
> *March the nineteenth formerly not at all and now nearly as contentedly nearly as candidly nearly as swimmingly nearly as neglected, not as neglected as at all and so forth.*

March the twentieth melodrama.
On March the twenty-first it is our duty to call a halt.
On March the twenty-second likewise.
And on March the twenty-third witnesses.
March the twenty-fourth able to be able to be able very able
   he is very able he is a very able man.

Elijah is getting strong and stronger. He has new deep interests. As the winter snows begin to disappear, we listen to Robert Schumann's Quartet for Piano, Violin, Viola and Cello in E-flat Major, opus 47. Glenn Gould is on piano. Emma pulled this romantic fugue out of her music collection one day, and Elijah, hearing it for the first time, became entranced.

"Schuuu . . . mann . . . Schuuu . . . mann," he now sings, mimicking my German pronunciation of the composer's name with precision. When I pop the cassette into the stereo, Elijah becomes purposefully animated. He paces joyfully around the room, absorbing every figuration, sometimes taking me by the hand to join him in the sweep of musical emotion. Emma opens the door of the bedroom and peeks inside at us, catching me at a failed attempt to do a pirouette for Elijah. I topple to the floor. He squeals with laughter. I get up again and exaggerate my clumsiness.

"This quartet is *wild,* Emma!" I call out to her through the tempestuous strings. "Schumann is all over the place!"

"*You two* are all over the place!"

"This is the *fifth time* we've played it tonight!"

"Uh . . . I noticed," she replies with her jesting sarcasm.

Elijah tugs at my hand again, signaling me to stop talking and do more ballet stunts. I bumble about the room to his happy shrieks. It's *scherzo: molto vivace,* and he is wailing with glee. But just as the movement come to a close, I must dash to Elijah's side and prepare him for the ensuing silence. It lasts only a few seconds, but when its suddenness takes the room, he plunges into deep despair, weeping at the loss of "Schuuu . . . mann! Schuuu . . . mann!"

"Shhh . . . shhh . . . little one," I whisper, holding him through the silence.

"Schuuuuu . . . mann," he cries woefully, tears coming down his cheeks.

"Yes . . . Schumann."

Andante cantabile. The melancholy cello finally resounds, and Elijah's tense body begins to soften in my arms. He remains limp there, lying in my lap on the floor, moving himself into the wistful music that he has thoroughly committed to heart. Now he's humming the gentle piano that has mixed itself in with the longing strings. Tears come down my cheeks too. "Schumann," I whisper to Elijah, "was a romantic."

"All over the place," Emma says again, still standing there. Then she quietly closes the door and leaves us to be alone together.

I don't know how many times Elijah and I listened to that quartet and to Schumann's other romantic fugues. I lost count, just as I have lost count of the endless times we listened to Bach's Goldberg Variations with our friend Glenn Gould on piano. Years later, Gould would become an autistic icon for some Asperger families and would be said to have had Asperger's syndrome. But what did we know of autistic culture then? I was on a steep learning curve with Elijah, living out his fixations. It was Schumann who first taught me how to follow my son's lead, how to take risks, how to journey into untold intensities.

The months passed at Brookside Cottage like the lines of Stein's "Birthday Book." April, May, June, July. Elijah was getting stronger and stronger. By summer, he was frolicking in all the swimming holes that Woodstock had to offer, and at Ben's house, he dove to the bottom of the deep end of the pool to retrieve the objects I threw in for him. Then he swam back up to the top, bursting through the surface with a face of bright contentment.

"Fun . . . fun . . . fun!" he called out. Stronger and stronger.

Elijah hasn't had a seizure in seven months, and on rare occasions, he's begun to say as many as three words lined up in row. On the day he turned four years old, he even sang "Happy Birthday" to himself from beginning to end. He sang it echolalically, four times in a row, as if he were making up for all the past birthdays when a cake, a present, birthday candles, and invited guests were just a pile of disparate elements in a roomful of gibberish. But this year, the parts cohered into a celebration he recognized as genuinely his own. "Fun! Fun! Fun!" he called out, staring into the flickering candles of the cake, surrounded by loving family members. That was in the warm month of July.

July because July because because July because.
July the first because July the first. July the first because.
July the second jealously.
July the third in a place in the place in the place of it.
July the fourth as everybody as a sample as a sample as
*   everybody.*
July the fifth come too come to place come to places come as
*   comfortably.*

The repetitions piled up that summer and moved into fall and winter, but they weren't always strictly "fun." Three deaths happened in my family, echoing the serial nature of our lives. The first to go was my grandfather, my father's father. He died of old age in August. I took a plane out to Colorado to attend the memorial service. It is an uncanny act to watch a parent lose a parent. I sat in a place in the church where I had full view of my father and the anguish that registered on his thin, gray face. Soon, I thought, I will be losing that man sitting over there, across from me in this church, and an echo of his very visage of grief will appear on my own face.

August, September, October. In October, the crickets made loud music in the woods around Brookside Cottage. We had a timeless string of Indian summer days with blue skies and warm, dry air. Emma and I left all the windows of the house open to let the crickets' sounds in. I called Dr. T on the phone every evening in October, and each time our conversation repeated itself. There was little left to say. Hospice had been called in. Our entire family was suspended in waiting . . . waiting . . . for Dr. T to cross over. On the telephone, his voice was nearly inaudible and vied with the cricket symphonies outside my home.

"Hi, Dad."

"Who is this?"

"It's Val. How are you feeling today?" I ask, scrambling quickly from window to window in the living room, rolling them tightly shut, so that I can hear his small voice.

"Uh . . . It's . . . okay today," he nearly whispers.

"I just want to say hello," I tell him, using the very same words I used yesterday.

"How's Elijah?" he coughs.

"Very good. No more seizures, Dad!" I attempt to sound confident, as if the epilepsy were a thing of the past, but Elijah will be prone to seizures for the rest of his life.

"I'm glad he's good."

"Me too." Then there's a long pause, followed by some wheezing. I hear some muffled words that I can't make out and realize that I've left one window of the room wide open. The crickets are chiming in. "I can't hear you, Dad! What did you say?" Frantically, I roll the last window shut, and all the background noise is suddenly erased. My father musters the energy to repeat himself. His voice rings more clearly through the receiver than it has in days.

"I said . . . you're the best, Val."

Dr. T is crossing over.

"Thanks for saying that. It means a lot. Elijah went through a hard time. It's *still* hard."

"I know." Now Dr. T is weeping. "I have to hang up the phone."

"Okay. I'll call you again tomorrow."

November first. First and ferries. Ferries, to go across ferries.
November the second. Cross he looks.
November the third across the end across the end and where
  to cross the, and where is it.
November the fourth where is it.
November the fifth what is the what is it

My father crossed over on November tenth. He died of cancer of the bone marrow. Again, I flew to Colorado for yet another funeral. Again, I stood in the cemetery and in the receiving line, numbly exchanging sympathies with all the faces of all the guests who had attended my grandfather's funeral. Again, I experienced the hard lesson of impermanence.

Six weeks on the heels of my father's ferry came his mother's. It was unexpected. Again, again, again, the echolalic deaths. My grandmother was found dead one morning in her bed. Some family members postulated the reasons. Perhaps she hadn't taken her medication that night. Perhaps it was slightly intentional. My grandmother died of a broken heart in the month of January.

Who was born January first.
Who was born in January first.
Who was born and believe me who was born and believe me,
  who was born who was born and believe me.

CHAPTER 8

Balloon Days

Because of death or in spite of death—I don't know which—
Elijah and I learned about expansion. These were our balloon
days, when both of us had grief for lost relations. Temporarily,
Elijah had lost me, and I had lost my three dead ones. On balloon days, you learn to expand. You fill up the empty space and,
in spite of sadness, discover lofty new dimensions of the self. But
not without pain. As if caught in a horrifying slow-motion
dream, my attempts to see Elijah were thwarted again and again
by the depleting funerals in Colorado and my inevitable dips
into depression. Elijah, requiring vigilant routine just to make it
through a day, was pressed to his limits by my erratic absences.

The first lesson in expansion is to rid oneself of judgment.
Ben's house became Elijah's permanent home base during the
funeral months. It had many rooms, and Ben had hired a live-in
nanny. I wanted to judge that big house. I wanted to judge that
nanny. Their very presence magnified my feelings of guilt and
incompetence. I wanted to judge Ben most fiercely of all, as he
coolly worked in his spacious office, convinced that I had abandoned all responsibility to our son. Death had turned my life
into a mire of emotion, until I could no longer distinguish who

or what I was mourning. Often I had to cancel Elijah's visits to Brookside Cottage, and as Ben assumed the new demands of caring for our son, he became all the more estranged toward me.

Emma was exasperated. "You're a single mother with no family in this town! YOU HAVE A DISABLED SON!" She was moving into another well-intentioned rant, designed to remind me of the obvious. Having just postponed Elijah's next visit in a heated exchange with Ben on the phone, I had mumbled something about being a "terrible mother." That got Emma going. "You have no financial support! *By your wits* you're covering both your expenses and Elijah's at Brookside Cottage, with no help from anyone! It's more than most women can do. You should be proud of it!"

"I miss Elijah, Emma, but I can't do it."

"I know that, honey."

"I need some rest. I'm going to my room to take a nap."

"Good. Try to put it on a back burner. Elijah will be back here again. You'll see."

Elijah was now four and half years old and struggling to learn to use the toilet at school. His teachers decided it was the right time for him to make the transition out of diapers. "Mommy!" he called out one day, sitting on the toilet at school where they had worked out a reliable potty schedule for him. This was the first time Elijah called me "Mommy," and detailed reports of his progress came home in the daybook. The daybook was a diary of notes exchanged between home and all of Elijah's therapists at school. It was crushing for me to read it, because in between the lines I saw that our separations had pushed Elijah to his limit. He had no choice but to expand. "Mommy." The word came out, and I was nowhere to be found.

Elijah developed a special fixation during our months of mourning, and it stayed with him for years afterward. He became compelled by balloons, the same way he had been so mesmerized by the clown's top hats. This balloon fixation became our perilous rite of passage toward renewed stability. It began as a simple ploy on my part: a trip to Woodstock's general store to buy a helium balloon *if* Elijah was willing to go to the supermarket first. The approach took hold. He had enough passive language to grasp the situation—that is, if I explained and elaborated and talked us all the way through it. He needed constant verbal fortification to keep a firm grip on the procession of environments we moved through, going from home, to car, to supermarket, to car again, then finally, to the balloon store. Each transition inspired dread, but with the balloon as destination firmly lodged in his mind, Elijah was able to leave the myopia of home and venture out into what lay beyond our front door.

"Do you want to go to town and get a *balloon?*" I ask, strategically ending my sentence with the most compelling semantic content.

"Balloon!" he replies, scooting toward the door. I'm ready for him, with his coat and boots in hand. He allows me to put them on. "Balloon."

"Yeah. But first we're going to the *supermarket,* then we'll go to *Houst's.*"

Houst's is the name of the general store that sells the helium balloons, but we have to keep things straight. In the car, all the way to the supermarket, I must remind Elijah of our itinerary. Then, once in the supermarket, I repeat it several more times, while pushing him up and down the aisles in the shopping cart and madly grabbing enough food off the shelves to last a few days. Ben is out of town, and Elijah is staying with me at Brookside Cottage for nearly two weeks. It's the longest time we've spent together since all the funerals. Elijah's patience is running thin now, and we've been in the supermarket only five minutes.

"Balloon!" he says forcefully. I respond by calmly reviewing the planned sequence of events.

"First we shop *here,* then we go to *Houst's* for the *balloon.*"

We finish the shopping with little incident, then finally drive on to the general store where Elijah has a sophisticated mental picture of what awaits him there. Before I have even opened the door to Houst's halfway, he has quickly shot inside and darted over to a quiet corner where the balloons are displayed in small bins. He scans the countless colors and patterns. Elijah is choosing bright orange today. He holds the balloon in his small hand and stares into it.

"Orange," he softly chants.

The daybook from school reports that Elijah is now labeling three colors appropriately. One of them is orange. This moment in the general store must have deep meaning for him. "Orange," he repeats many more times until I interrupt his reverie with a cue to take the balloon over to the lady at the cash register, who by now has become used to our frequent appearances. For the past week we've been on a binge, coming into Houst's at least once a day, sometimes twice, if our other repetitious schemes at home become too stressfully rigid and we need to replace them with new ones. Elijah stands before the woman at the cash register and does nothing. I lightly touch his arm to prompt him through the next step, which is to pass the balloon across the counter to the lady. She reaches out and takes it from him.

"Thank you! You've made a nice choice today." Elijah waits silently. A few moments pass. He's becoming mildly frustrated by her talking and by what seems to be an uncalled-for delay. "Okay, then," she says, "let's go fill it up." Unaware of his invisible anxiety, which I'm registering as a red flag, she casually walks out from behind the counter and makes her way over to the helium tank. Elijah falls in behind her. He's right on her heels, following this next step of the ritual as if according to some rule book. At the tank, I sidle up behind him, gently pull his body close against my legs, and cover his ears with my hands.

"I'm doing this for the loud whistling sound," I remind him, not wanting to repeat last week's disaster.

The woman fits the opening of the balloon over the spout of the tank and begins to fill it up. Though the high-pitched whistle penetrates my hands and causes him to stiffen, Elijah watches, transfixed, as the balloon looms large and as its color changes mystically from an opaque orange to an almost translucent peach. It bulges so extremely in size that suddenly I'm struck with panic. The balloon could pop and devastate our nearly successful mission! But the lady finally removes it and casually ties it off.

"What color ribbon do you want?" she asks Elijah, who has no answer. He's stimming. He's so taken up with the change in the state of the balloon that he is rendered wordless.

"Any color will do," I answer nervously on his behalf, now feeling a strong impatience rising up his spine as it presses hard against my legs.

"He's shy, isn't he?" the woman remarks, beginning to feel a little awkward about us. She's probably wondering why we keep coming in here every day. Elijah is about to burst now. He's had enough social interaction for the moment. He wants to high-tail it out of here, but he contains himself. I feel the effort in his body. He's committed to that orange balloon.

"You're doing a good job," I whisper as he zeroes in on the woman's busy hands that are cutting a long piece of orange ribbon from a nearby spool.

"This is a nice color. See?" She holds the ribbon up. "It matches the balloon!" When she finishes tying the ribbon to the balloon, she bends down and passes the end of it to Elijah. "Now, don't lose it!" she sweetly admonishes him.

"Lose . . . it," he answers back. I'm thrilled to the core by this. It's the first time, after a week of practice, that Elijah has spoken directly to the checkout lady.

"No, silly," she corrects him, "I said *don't* lose it." Elijah doesn't respond to this. "You might want to tie it around his wrist," she adds, cautioning me with this advice. "You don't want to lose that pretty balloon, now, do you?"

I shake my head guiltily "no." Of course not. A lost balloon is grounds for tears. A lost balloon, rising up into the atmosphere never to be retrieved again, means certain tragedy for any child. But little does the lady know that I'm feigning, for Elijah has far different plans in mind.

"Outsiiiiiiiide!" he screams shrilly, startling the woman to the quick and sending her bustling back over to the cash register.

"Okay," I attempt to say with a firmness that I hope will grab his attention, but Elijah is now so stressed he might not make it through the full routine. I bend down close to him without making direct eye contact. It would be too much for him right now. "First we have to *pay* for the *balloon*." I say the words clearly, looking into the thin air beside him. He's about to throw himself on the floor and bang his head. The situation is snowballing. "C'mon, let's do it!" In a last-ditch effort, I take his hand up in mine with awkward confidence, and we proceed to the cash register, just barely in possession of ourselves. Then Elijah, with his new balloon in tow, bolts for the exit.

"Here!" I call out frantically to the checkout lady and toss a dollar onto the counter.

"Thank you!" she chimes back. "Bye-bye!" she adds cutely, wanting to assuage Elijah's puzzling discomfort.

"Say 'bye-bye,'" I cue him, darting to his side in the open doorway, realizing painfully in the same breath that I sound as if I'm speaking to a baby who's just learned to wave at strangers.

"Bye . . . bye," Elijah replies, slowly and arduously integrating his rash movement out the door with his speech. He's entirely out of earshot of the woman, for the door has swung closed behind us. Eventually, he'll say "bye-bye," and "hello," and all the other greetings appropriate to neurotypical discourse. He'll say them at the right time, in the right place, with the right vocal intonation. He'll say them while making the right kind of eye contact and with the right amount of distance between his body and someone else's. But these things are methodically *learned* hand over hand for an autistic. They must be practiced as a reliable system.

We've landed outside in the center of town on the busy main drag called Tinker Street.

"Let go!" Elijah yells. He wants to release the balloon and watch it fly up into the heavens. After all, it's why we came here in the first place. It's what he's been working up to ever since we left the house.

"Wait!" I interject. "We'll let it go, but let's walk over to the *field*."

"Let go!" he insists again.

"Yeah, at the *FIELD*. C'mon." I take his hand and lead him down Tinker Street. The big orange balloon is tugging on its ribbon above us, as we slip around a corner and walk one more block.

"Let go!" Elijah happily sings when the field comes into view.

"Yeah, *IN THE FIELD*," I remind him again, still so rattled from his shriek in Houst's that I could scream too. There are moments such as these when life with Elijah becomes so narrow, so rigidly charted and overdetermined in every action and word, that I could burst out in fits of anger and resentment. But—I don't know what comes over me—I suddenly see the poignant humor of it all, and I laugh out loud at this crazy, lonely comedy routine we've put together, the one I have no chance of escaping. Elijah's balloon fixation has implicated me. I have no choice but to submit and persevere with him.

He tugs on my hand, picking up the pace toward the field. My eagerness for today's launch is suddenly growing more palpable. It's rising warmly from my stomach, like butterflies, moving up into the region of my heart. We step out onto the field. It's the same open space where the flea market happens in the summer, where Sharron used to park her van, but today the field is empty. It's winter. We crunch through the hard crusty snow, and before I even have the chance to cue him on it, Elijah releases the balloon.

"Oh! You scoundrel! You let it go!" I tease him.

The orange globe shoots straight up into the gray sky. It goes up and up, drifts momentarily sideways on a breeze, then moves more directly upward again. Elijah carefully monitors every motion.

"High! High! High!"

"Yeah, it's going high up."

"Small!" he adds.

"Small?"

"Small! Small!" he elaborates, still looking up. I'm surprised to hear Elijah use this new word in our balloon context. At the Children's Annex his teachers would call it "spontaneous speech," which he has been expressing with more frequency. Spontaneous speech is language that is neither cued nor prompted nor otherwise pedagogically extracted from him. It's utterly authentic to the situation. We stand there together in the field as we usually do, tracking the balloon until it completely disappears from sight.

"Small!"

"I get it! The *balloon* is getting *small*."

"Small," he says again, pleased that I grasp this perception of things.

"Yeah! The farther away the balloon goes, the smaller it *looks*."

"Small," he affirms satisfied by my description, which he himself cannot summon forth as speech. Elijah is happy and expansive. It has been a good balloon day.

᠎

Over the course of several months, as Elijah's stays at Brookside Cottage become more frequent and regular, we go into Houst's and add new layers of experience to his social repertoire. Soon he is saying the word "helium" all day long, pressing me to engage with him in repetitious talk about "helium balloons" that "float in the sky" and "air balloons" that "stay on the ground." After countless trips to the general store, the tedious social formulas of "hello" and "bye-bye" and "What color do you want?" become less nerve-racking for him. Elijah even chats the checkout lady up, saying five choice syllables the moment he walks in the door: "Heeee. . . . liiii . . . um baaa. . . . looooon." Then he makes a bee-line for the bins.

"What color are you going to choose today?" the woman calls out as he passes by the counter with no answer. He's now making his selection all by himself and brings it back to the cash register without my prompting.

One day, as the woman and I waited for him to return to the counter, I revealed to her that my son was autistic. I thought our camaraderie with her had made it safe.

"There's nothing *wrong* with him! He's perfectly *healthy!*" she challenged me, incredulous that I would suggest such a thing.

I fumbled for an answer. "Well . . . of course there's nothing *wrong*. He's autistic. That's why we come in here all the time." I had hoped to enlighten her about our ritual, but she just shook her head in disbelief.

That's the day I learned about invisibility and how far Elijah could depart from neurotypicality and seem to go unnoticed. Friends even criticized me for falling victim to "those awful labels that only stigmatize the child," but I found their remarks overly simplistic. Sure, I had my bone to pick with condescending language, but not with the word "autism" itself. Such quickness to deny or minimize Elijah's way of life were insulting in the early years, before I learned that I would have to let go of public ignorance the same way Elijah lets go of his balloons.

A year had passed since I moved into Brookside Cottage. Though Ben and I were divorced, something had changed for the better in our family dynamic. I saw it in the daybook one spring morning as I sat on the back porch of the house reading all of Ben's notes to the school. I began with the day that Elijah had first moved in with Ben, after my depressive episode and trip to the hospital. In the course of this year of loss, gruff Ben had become a mother of sorts! It was right there in the daybook in his notes to the teachers, in a language that was surprisingly taken up with the sophisticated minutiae of child rearing. "Elijah," he writes during the toilet training period, "has been tired this week and [is] off his food in the evenings at dinner. . . . He feels badly that he's still not pooping in the potty. 'I can't,' he sometimes says to me. 'You can,' I say. 'Don't worry.' He smiles and gets happy. 'Sorry!' he says. 'Don't worry, you're doing fine,' I answer. He grins and relaxes."

Much had improved between me and Ben, and by summer we were caring for Elijah mutually on a steady routine that he could count on. My grandparents had left me some money, and when the inheritance came through, my jealousy and judgments of Ben's home and Ben's nanny began to lift. Money made it possible for me to work part time and use the rest of my day to focus on Elijah's intense needs. I returned to the dissertation, a study of the German Jewish poet Else Lasker-Schüler, whose life as a writer and single mother of an unusual child had profound resonance for me. Lasker-Schüler was fast becoming my literary mentor. I also began translating German again and eventually returned to a teaching position at a private liberal arts college where I had taught in the past. Elijah and I moved out of Brookside Cottage and back into our old apartment in the clown's farmhouse. We still saw Emma Missouri all the time. Emma was family, but when I bumped into Bob one day in town and was told the apartment was free, I missed the open meadows and the big starry skies at night. I wanted to go back there with Elijah and reclaim a life that had been interrupted by calamity and depression.

That was the expansive summer of Elijah's fifth birthday, when Ben and I sat beside the swimming pool at his house, discussing whether to move forward on a plan to wean Elijah off his anticonvulsant. The neurologist in New York city had given us his blessing. Elijah had been seizure free for more than two years.

"Mum, Dad . . . watch this!" Joanne, the nanny, called out to Ben and me as she cued Elijah to jump from the board of the swimming pool. He jumped without inhibition, diving far far down to the bottom.

"What a little guppy!" Ben called out proudly from where we were sitting. Then he turned back to me, his eyes wet with tears. "You know, Val, during those months when Elijah was living with me most of the time, it changed my life. It humanized me."

"Me too. Things are getting better, aren't they, Ben?"

"Yes," he said. "You're a good person, Val."

"You are too. Can I tell you something?"

"Sure."

"Please take care of yourself, Ben. You're overworked. Elijah and I both need you."

"Yeah."

One of my new freelance jobs involved translating German documents for the science writer Dennis Overbye. Dennis was working on a book about Albert Einstein, and I was to render some of the physicist's unpublished personal correspondence into English. I met Dennis once a week and sat beside him in his office, translating Einstein's letters aloud into English as I read the German original to myself. Dennis pecked away at the keyboard, transcribing my words.

A few months into the job, I began to hear reports from autism circles that Einstein was probably a high-functioning autistic with Asperger's syndrome. As I deciphered Einstein's handwriting in his letters to his family and to his closest friends, I began to read intimations of autism between the lines. As a small child, Einstein was thought to be a dullard, at least that's the word his grandmother used to describe him, and his parents were certain that he was subnormal. He was prone to emotional outbursts. He was solitary and taciturn, and he fled from the raucous sounds and sights of parades. He had a speech delay, showed signs of echolalia, and possessed a deep affinity for objects. "He was well past two," writes Dennis Overbye, "before he made any attempt at language. His most memorable utterance was at two and half when his sister, Maja, was born. Apparently expecting some kind of a toy, he demanded to know why she didn't have any wheels. Until the age of seven he had the curious habit of repeating softly to himself every sentence he said."

Einstein also seems to have had delays processing language, for there was a lag time, or hesitation, before he answered questions that were asked of him. Ilana Katz, an Einstein scholar and parent of an autistic child, says young Albert was "withdrawn" and "avoided contact with other children his age, preferring to play by himself." When he reached school age, he was taunted with *Biedermeier* by his teasing classmates, the German equivalent for "wonk" or "nerd." Academically, Einstein's strengths and weaknesses in subjects were notable for their polarized extremity, a common autistic trait, sometimes called "scatter."

On the one hand, Overbye writes, "he got good grades in math," but "his precocity displayed itself only fitfully to those charged with his formal education." His Greek professor "at Munich's Luitpold Gymnasium, where he was enrolled at the age of nine, is said to have informed in front of the whole class that he would never amount to anything at all."

Einstein's life was one of serial preoccupations and intense focus on a limited number of interests at one time. They began as a child with his zealous study of the Jewish faith (much to the surprise of his secular parents), which he abruptly dropped at age twelve in exchange for mathematics. During his summer vacation that same year, says Overbye, Einstein "worked his way through the entire gymnasium mathematics curriculum, including calculus, sitting by himself for days on end proving theorems and solving problems in textbooks that [his father] brought home for him."

In spite of his obvious strengths in math, he did not graduate from the gymnasium, having been expelled for his disruptive classroom behavior. To his good fortune, however, a formal education at a higher institution was not denied him when he managed, with some difficulty and postponement, to be accepted into the Swiss Federal Polytechnical School in Zurich. Unlike most other universities at the time, the Polytechnical School did not require a gymnasium degree in order to be admitted. Once enrolled, Einstein spent most of his time there perseverating on physics. Other subjects proved to be a challenge and a chore, because he couldn't bring himself to study subjects that didn't involve his intense interests. He found the professors' lectures to be an intrusion to his own process, and he often skipped class, preferring to study alone and intensely. His peers reported that "he didn't listen to anyone" and "didn't follow directions in the lab." He was known to pay no heed to social constrictions, stepping "out of the everyday world whenever he wished." The invisibility of Einstein's autism attracted the same sort of neurotypical commentary that is often said of autistic youths and adults today. They are "in a world of their own." They are "eccentric" and "aloof," seeming, on the surface, to find no need for emotional relationships with others.

Einstein had obvious neurological differences. He might have been epileptic, and he definitely stimmed and perseverated. "There were the strange occasions," writes Overbye,

> *on which he would go into some sort of trance or seizure, as if he had just disappeared into his own world. Later he would claim to have no recollection of what had happened. . . . Throughout his entire life the people around him [remarked] on his ability to suddenly withdraw from even the most raucous surroundings to concentrate on some thought of his own. . . . To the outside world and even to himself Einstein looked a little unworldly.*

Compelling fixations remove one from normative social milieus. Elijah's balloon routine is a good example. He has no compunctions about letting go and feels no sense of loss for the object. In fact, to hold on to the balloon is a disruption to his perseverative fascination with the spatial experience of how distance changes the apparent size of an object. In the very early days of our routine, Elijah used to release his balloons right on Tinker Street, but invariably some passerby would make a disparaging remark or even scold me. This is why we go to the field for our daily launches. Some neurotypical expectations are too intrusive. It's probably why Einstein didn't go to his university lectures. Before he reached genius status in the public mind and was hailed as an important physicist, many of Einstein's teachers and employers thought he was a loser or a social dropout; in fact, he was fixated on finding his way through the maze of complex questions that eventually led him to the theory of relativity.

With tremendous effort, Einstein managed to graduate from the Polytechnical School, though his grades were mediocre. Following graduation, most of his classmates were hired for teaching positions at the school, but Einstein was not. He attempted to do some private tutoring at first, got fired for his casual teaching methods, then managed to wangle a job at the Swiss Patent Office in Zurich, where his unconventional dress and social habits were tolerated. He wore slippers and informal clothing to work. In fact, he always preferred wearing worn-in garments that were soft and melded to the shape of his body, probably because of tactile sensitivities.

The Swiss Patent Office, where Einstein often stayed after hours to work on his own projects, became the famous location of the development of his theory of relativity. Einstein said of himself that his scientific ideas first came to him as images, after which he had the hard task of putting them into words and understandable equations. "For example," writes Steven Pinker,

> *from imagining himself riding on a beam of light and looking back at a seemingly frozen clock tower, he developed the theory of special relativity—that time, length and mass vary with the relative motion of an event and an observer. From imagining himself inside a plummeting elevator and seemingly weightless, he developed the theory of general relativity—that gravity and acceleration are the same.*

Temple Grandin compares her experience of visual thinking with the thought experiments that Einstein used in his development of physical ideas. Elijah's spatial sensitivity appears to be keen, yet he possesses few words to express the heightened experience of it. In the swimming pool at his father's house, I watch him through my goggles as he swims about and scans the volu-minous underwater universe he's traveling through. His eyes are always wide open. Elijah even smiles underwater! When he comes up for a breath of air, I paddle over to him and take his buoyant little body into my arms.

"Elijah, why do you open your eyes in the water?"

He hesitates, thinking hard on the words he will summon forth. "It's . . . a . . . room," he answers brightly.

Had he been born in our contemporary era of learning dis-abilities and special education, young Einstein would most likely have been identified for an early intervention program similar to the one at Elijah's school. Einstein's delayed speech and echolalic tendencies would have called for intensive speech therapy. His outbursts would have made him a candidate for behavioral and social skills training, not to mention his seeming aloofness and insensitivity to others' feelings, which proved to be devastating for his relationships with his family. But this was not the para-digm of the 1890s when Einstein was a boy. What has remained, however, is the legacy of autistic invisibility.

For two years, the artifacts of Einstein's life swirled around me in my work for Dennis Overbye, begging one question: If Albert Einstein was autistic, did Elijah possess a social history that he might call his own? I wasn't equating my son with Ein-stein, or thinking, or hoping that one day Elijah might be deemed a genius. I just wanted to ponder this: If autism is a neu-rological culture unto itself, who might its historical role models be? Certainly, Elijah had *living* models. There was Sharron, for instance. There were Temple Grandin and Donna Williams. As a woman and a writer, I knew how crucial my own models were. I had Else Lasker-Schüler. I had Virginia Woolf. I had Mary Woll-stonecraft. This made me ask, did Elijah have Einstein?

"I . . . want . . . a . . . baaa . . . looon," Elijah says, as we pass by Houst's one day on our way home from the playground.

"You want a balloon?" I'm surprised that he even noticed Houst's, and even more surprised that he's put together such a big sentence so quickly. "Sure. We have time."

I pull the car into the parking lot behind Houst's, still astounded at the effortlessness of the dialogue we just had. We haven't been to Houst's in months. We no longer need the balloon routine to get out of the house, although balloons themselves have taken up a large presence in our lives. Since those first trips to town, we have moved on to water balloons and their many possibilities. We throw them at one another outside in the meadow yelling, "Free shot! Free shot!" We freeze them overnight, then toss them off the deck onto the hard rocks below and listen to them shatter. We dump a pile of water balloons into the bathtub so Elijah can pop them underwater and watch them slowly shrink in his hand. We blow them up with air, draw funny faces on them, then deflate them and study the fine cartoon lines that are left. We paint them. We plaster them. We line them up in muffin tins. We put small bells inside them, blow them up, and shake them around like musical instruments.

We enter Houst's through the back door—which no longer confuses Elijah or makes him cry as it once did whenever our routine was altered—and walk down the long, faded linoleum aisle to the far end of the store where the balloon bins are.

"Oh! They've restocked! Look at all the choices!" I exclaim. "What color do you want?"

"Elijah . . . wants . . . flowww . . . errrrs." Though he's begun to use the pronoun "I" more often, Elijah occasionally falls back into third-personing himself. I see the balloon he's describing.

"Those aren't flowers; they're fireworks. Do you know what fireworks are?"

"Yes," he answers somewhat stiffly and formally. "Firrre . . . worrks."

"Fireworks *look* like flowers exploding in the sky. So you're kinda right."

"Elijah . . . wants . . . firrre . . . worrks."

"Yeah. Let's take the balloon to the counter."

Just as I turn to go to the checkout, Elijah stops me, pushing my hand toward the balloon bins.

"What . . . col . . . orrr . . . do . . . you . . . want?" he asks, attempting to use his "up-down speech." At school, his language therapist is working with him on asking questions that are inflected rather than monotone.

"You want *me* to choose a color?"

"Yes." He sounds like a small robot.

"Okay. Hmmm . . . Let's see . . . I'll take this black one."

Elijah stands there stiffly. I know his hesitation means he's working out a response to the words I just said, so I wait a few beats for him to pull them out. "That's . . . not . . . black."

"It's not?"

"It's . . . pur . . . ple."

"It's purple? Really?"

"Yes."

"Huh, it looks black to me."

"It's pur . . . ple."

"Would you like some helium in those balloons?" a girl working the cash register asks us. She must have replaced the checkout lady we used to know.

"Yeah. Thanks." The three of us walk over to the helium tank where I cover up Elijah's ears. The girl begins by filling up his balloon first. We watch the small fireworks expand into big bouquets. "Beautiful! They *do* look like flowers, Elijah."

"They're . . . firrre . . . worrrks." Elijah watches the girl tie a red ribbon to his balloon. I can feel his mind chewing on the fact that she didn't ask him which color ribbon he wanted, but he doesn't have the response time to speak out loud about it.

She hands the balloon to him, then fits mine onto the spout of the tank.

"Wow!" she says. "I don't think I've ever seen a black balloon before."

"It's . . . pur . . . ple," Elijah corrects her.

"Purple?"

"Yes."

"Hmmm . . . maybe," she says halfheartedly and begins to fill it up. As the balloon grows, it transforms itself miraculously from black to deep purple.

"Elijah, you were right! It's purple!"

The girl nods enthusiastically in agreement. Elijah is visibly pleased with this inside knowledge. We pay the girl at the cash register.

"Thank you!" she says cheerfully.

"You're welcome," Elijah answers, and we walk out onto sunny Tinker Street, making our way to the field as a matter of course. It's summer, and our balloons are bobbing in the breeze above us.

"Hey, Elijah. You're going to be six years old very soon. Can you believe it?!"

"Yes."

We walk out to the center of the field, where, unannounced, Elijah's fireworks rise up into the sky.

"Let . . . go," he mechanically instructs me, tugging on my elbow.

"You want me to let go of mine too?"

"Yes."

"Okay, here goes." But I find myself hesitating. "*You* do it." I hold my balloon out to him.

"No," he says.

"No?"

"No."

"Okay, here goes!" I release the purple balloon and up it flies, joining Elijah's fireworks. "I've never done that before!" My heart is pounding. "Now I know what it's like!" Elijah is silent, holding my hand and watching our two balloons grow small together on their upward trajectories. "Thanks for showing me how to let go."

"You're . . . wel . . . come."

CHAPTER 9

c2—

Cartoons Don't Get Hurt

Sharron bought an old boat, docked it in a coastal town outside Los Angeles, and set up house there. *Desirée* was the boat's name. She had two defunct engines but she was seaworthy.

"It's cozy here," Sharron chimed happily on the phone. "It's like a floating Woodstock hippie cabin."

Desirée wasn't the trailer-in-the-desert scenario Sharron had dreamed of when we first met, but it gave her homey solitude and independence. Monthly rent for a boat slip was far cheaper than for an apartment, especially on the small dock where she lived among fishing boats and a few live-aboards like herself. At last, Sharron could semiretire in a warm climate. She did some baby-sitting, and she continued to paint.

"Where did you hang up Elijah's portrait?"

"It's in his bedroom."

Some months ago, I commissioned Sharron to do a portrait of Elijah. "I want him to look like Little Lord Fauntleroy," she had said at the time. "I want him to look like an autistic prince." In the portrait, Elijah's gaze is full on, looking right into the viewer, as he sits on an ornate, sculpted wooden chair that's perched outdoors on a grassy knoll. The blue sky and its white clouds are floating by behind him.

"Are you in the clown's house?"

"Yeah."

"I like thinking of the two of you in that big old house. It's beautiful there."

"Yeah, we love this place. It's so much happier now, especially since Elijah came off the anticonvulsant. You'd be amazed at his talking!"

"Hey, you should really go to Autreat. Elijah is six. He can handle it."

"Autreat? What's that?"

"It's a retreat for autistic people. Jim Sinclair and ANI are organizing it."

I had heard of Jim Sinclair many times before. Sharron talked about him often, using words like "angel" and "saint" to describe him, and I knew she was serious. Jim is a cofounder of Autism Network International (ANI), a grassroots advocacy organization run by autistics for autistics, one of the first of its kind in the world. Although the core organizers of ANI are all "high-functioning," the group extends its vision of independence and autistic self-awareness to the entire spectrum. Its members, an international network of autistics, communicate by way of an Internet list. Some of them, like Jim, a graduate student in rehabilitation counseling at the School of Education at the University of New York in Syracuse, are highly trained educators and disability advocates.

"Take Elijah there. It'll be good for him," Sharron urged me.

When the brochure and registration forms for Autreat arrived in the mail, I only had to see that year's theme, "Celebrating Autistic Culture," to know that Elijah and I would attend. Within a few weeks, we were making the six-hour trip north to the Finger Lakes with the back seat of the car filled with Elijah's most stimulating objects. We brought along our cadre of classical composers on cassette and the soundtrack from Disney's *Pinocchio*, Elijah's latest musical compulsion. Earlier that summer, when my mother had come to New York for a visit, Elijah lay on the couch beside her one muggy afternoon while reciting the entire dialogue of the *Pinocchio* movie from beginning to end. He did it once and only once, speaking all the roles aloud in a savant flash of memory.

The trip to Autreat was a perilous journey. I had long abandoned most travel that wasn't directly in the vicinity of Woodstock, including trips to Colorado to see my family. But the Finger Lakes were possible, and if I was to trust my hunch with Sharron, it would be worth the sacrifice. The very words "autistic culture" had been humming in the back of my mind like a question mark ever since I had begun my research on Albert Einstein. Now was our chance to experience it firsthand, without the professional filters that often seem to overwhelm most information about Elijah's way of life.

During our first hour on the road, Elijah rifled through hundreds of stickers I had brought along to keep him busy in the car. He feverishly peeled them and pasted them onto a large piece of cardboard like a small machine with his strict and narrow concentration. In the rear-view mirror, I saw the waxy paper backings of the stickers piling up in the back seat like fluffy patches of snow surrounding him. When he had peeled the very last sticker from its paper, he let out a screech. Quickly, I popped the *Pinocchio* soundtrack into the tape player to redirect him, but to my dismay, I had forgotten to rewind it.

"REEE. . . . WIND!" he bellowed when he suddenly heard Pinocchio's boyish voice singing mid-song: *I've got no strings to hold me down, to make me fret or make me frown.* I fumbled with the stereo buttons, which only magnified his anguish. Elijah continued screaming until I was finally able to start the tape the way he liked it, beginning with Jiminy Cricket's opening solo accompanied by the melodious harp.

Once Jiminy finished his sweet song, the puppet maker Geppetto's workshop instrumental, with all its cuckoo clocks and music box effects, resounded in our small car. Geppetto is Pinocchio's oddball father, a tinkerer, an inventor, and an absent-minded loner. The ticktock sound, the ringing bells, and the complex orchestration of chimes and hiccups and corks popping from champagne bottles made us both contemplative and silent. Was it just all the autism literature I had been reading, or was Elijah's visual thinking emerging into fullness? I couldn't get inside his head, but I was convinced that every time we listened to that soundtrack, he was simultaneously playing the animated movie in his mind's eye.

A good hour passed. We listened to *Pinocchio* a second time, and the sun rose higher in the morning sky, heating up the car, which had no air-conditioning. We listened a third time, and then a fourth. After the fourth, I had reached my limit, but before Elijah could screech again, I headed him off at the pass, handing him a crayon from a fresh box of 64 Crayolas I had purchased just for this occasion. Looking at him in the rear-view mirror again, I watched his expression go from despair to animation the moment he saw just what I was holding out to him.

"Cray . . . on," he said. His little hand snatched it up. "What . . . color . . . is . . . it?"

"That's Burnt Sienna."

"Burrnt . . . Si . . . enna."

"Yeah. Are you going to peel it?"

"Yes." Elijah is giving more yes and no answers to questions now rather than repeating what I have asked him.

I look in the mirror again. His concentration is mounting. He peels and picks the paper from the crayon until it's completely clean, then casually tosses it aside on the back seat where the hot sun is pounding down through the window. I have more serious matters to think about than melting crayons, like pacing myself with the remaining sixty-three. I hand him the next color. We go from Silver to Salmon and on to Carnation Pink. Then Periwinkle, Brick Red, Indigo, and Aquamarine Blue. Each time I hand him a crayon, Elijah waits for the word, then repeats it aloud after me before commencing with his peeling. Yellow Orange. Spring Green. Violet Red. Chestnut. When we're halfway through the box, I turn around and take a quick glance at the back seat. Elijah is supremely focused, to the exclusion of everything else. Broken crayons litter the seat, getting oily in the sun. And those lovely bits of colored paper he has peeled have mixed themselves in with the white mounds of snow around him. A few stray stickers are stuck to the window.

"Are you okay back there?" There's a long pause. No answer. "Are you okay?" I ask again, suddenly feeling a pang of loss. I'm reminded of Dr. T and *his* supreme focus.

"Elijah?"

"Yes?"

"Are you okay?"

"Yes."

"Good. Are you ready for another crayon?"

"Yes."

I pull the next color out of the box. "Wow! You're gonna like the sound of this one! Purple Mountain's Majesty." I pass it back to him, and he takes it.

"Pur . . . ple . . . Moun . . . tain's . . . ," he hesitates.

"Majesty."

"Ma . . . jesty."

Elijah never uses crayons to draw pictures, but he is deeply invested in the colors. For him, they are a visual language game. At home in Woodstock, we buy sets of markers at the art supply store—a new destination he never passes up whenever it's offered him—then we go back to the apartment and practice out loud. "Light Blue." "Medium Blue." "Dark Blue." The marker sets have all the basic primary and secondary colors in different shades. I say, "Medium Green." Elijah mimics me, removes the cap from the marker, and draws one line of fluid color on white paper, watching it absorb into the paper's fine fibers. Then he turns to the next blank page of the sketchbook he's drawing in to do another color. From time to time, I ask him to please save paper by drawing more than just one line on a single sheet, but he gets irate with such suggestions. He even refuses to make his colored marks on the less expensive recycled newsprint. I tried it out on him once, but it didn't work. Perhaps newsprint is too gray for him. Perhaps the line he gets is less satisfying visually. Once Elijah has methodically peeled all 64 crayons, he is edgy. Autistic children tend to require constant focused activity, or else the carefully constructed cohesion they're experiencing begins to disintegrate stressfully. We listen to a classical fugue for the umpteenth time, but this does not appease Elijah. All the windows of the car are wide open now. We're sweating in the midday heat, but we're closing in on our destination. Elijah moves into a panic.

"Just a little longer," I try to console him, to no avail. He is screaming now, and with Schumann spilling out the open windows, we finally roll into the parking lot of an old 4-H camp.

"We're here! We're here now! Let's get out!"

Elijah scrambles the moment I open the door for him and moves himself quickly outside into the open air. We see other tired, agitated people just arriving too. They are autistics from all along the spectrum, coming in from distant points around the country and the rest of the world. Some have come with family and care providers. Others have traveled independently. After settling our things into our assigned cabin, I put a blanket down on the green grass just outside the main lodge of the camp, where Elijah and I lie down and begin to decompress. He's close beside me, listening to the songs I sing from *Pinocchio* just loud enough to hold his wandering attention.

We are on our island, marked out clearly by the perimeter of the blanket. From here Elijah and I have our first encounters with other autistics who have come to the retreat. Two of Sharron's LA buddies stop by, introduce themselves, and say they've heard a lot about us. One is a world traveler involved in peace actions. The other is an urban planner at the Los Angeles International Airport. Sharron is beginning to have a reputation as an autistic networker, and thanks to her, I know all these people by name. We meet Dan Asher too, a visual artist from New York City who traveled to Antarctica to photograph ice. Then a small genderless person with a delicate physique and long dark hair appears, flanked by two alert service dogs.

"Are you Valerie and Elijah?"

"Yes, we are."

"Sharron Loree told me about you. The orientation is about to begin in the main lodge."

Jim Sinclair was immediately familiar to me, though I had never met him. Part of this had to do with Sharron's loving and enthusiastic descriptions of his work, and part of it had to do with the peace I felt just listening to his voice. Jim's mind is penetrating. He speaks like crystal. Years from now, at a future Autreat, while astutely listening to Jim lecture on the topic of ethical and respectful treatment of disabled people in the realm of behavioral management, Elijah would turn to me and whisper, "Jim Sinclair makes everything clear for me." Crystal clear. Ironically, Jim's voice, a beacon in the blossoming disability movement among autistics, didn't begin to speak words until Jim was twelve years old, a very late age for an autistic who talks. Now in his thirties, Jim has become the quintessential activist. Always harried, always overextended, his sharp, analytical mind and intimate commitment to autistic people emanate confidence and comfort to those around him.

As he introduced the particulars of Autreat at the orientation, Jim seemed to me a candle burning brightly at both ends. Clearly, he was the soul Sharron had described, an intellectual descendant of Helen Keller and Louis Braille. And like these early activists, who transformed the paradigms of communication for the deaf and the blind, Jim's pioneering ideas on autism were being received with ambivalence, and sometimes outright rejection, by major organizations like the Autism Society of America (ASA) and More Advanced Autistic People (MAAP). These organizations are supported and run mainly by parents of autistic people and by professionals in the field. Until very recently, the mainstream assumption, even within these organization, was that autistics were incapable of truly knowing their own needs, let alone voicing their own decisions about those needs. Jim was one of the handful of autistics at the time who were introducing basic concepts of self-advocacy. He modeled his ideas on the successes of the deaf community and other groups within the disability movement. Because he was one of the very early voices of this new wave, Jim was perceived as a threat to the status quo. Some members of ASA even went so far as to claim that Jim wasn't autistic because he was so capable of thinking for himself. In truth, he was expressing challenging and necessary opinions. This response is all too familiar in any movement. In the early days of women's activism, for example, when advocates were struggling for women's education, they were often met with the dismissive argument that being women, they were simply uneducable, so why bother.

There's much to do in a lifetime, and Jim was burning brightly that day at Autreat. He had lived longer, with multiple disabilities, than the medical establishment had expected. Jim is autistic, has a motor disability, and is biologically neuter, that is, he possesses no sexual organs, and is therefore neither a man nor a woman. Although he uses the male name "Jim," he prefers to be viewed as he is: as sexless.

Some twenty or thirty participants of Autreat stood in that lackluster lodge for the orientation (others remained outside or in their quiet cabins), putting up with the grating acoustics that caused the sound to bounce wildly off the cement floors. How very different this environment was compared to the big autism conferences that I had attended in comfortable hotels in various American cities, in places where mainly neurotypicals gathered to talk about their children, about their students, and about their patients. Here the tables had been turned. These autistic people didn't have comparable means or comparable influence in medicine, research, and education, but everything about Autreat was planned by its members, from the T-shirt design, to the workshop topics, to the social rules. Jim described, for instance, the color-coded badges that had been distributed to all the participants.

"These badges can be worn around the neck. A red one indicates that the person wearing it does not wish to speak to anyone, *at all*. Yellow means that the person wants to be approached and spoken to, *but only by friends*." The following year, green was added, meaning *anyone* can approach.

Respect for solitude was key. Each autistic participant had a cabin to retreat to, alone or with support people and family members, and no one would be forced to participate in activities. It was perfectly legitimate in this environment to isolate oneself

as a means of preventing or recovering from sensory shutdown. Photographs and videos could be taken only with permission and only outdoors, where the flash did not assault those with visual sensitivities. Perfume and cigarettes were disallowed for the same sensory reasons.

As Jim spoke, it was immediately clear to me that Elijah and I were involved in a grand experiment. We were probing, with a group of autistic pioneers, what it means to claim one's environment without a domineering culture breathing down one's neck. For my part, I decided right then and there to devote myself to Elijah's needs and to his perseverative interests within the realms of safety. I would walk where he wished to walk. I would play whatever games he wanted to play for as long as he liked. I would lie around with him in our cabin for hours, listening to *Pinocchio*. There were no other responsibilities. I had no writing deadlines, no texts to translate, and I was happy to have the burden of the ever-pressing dissertation off my mind.

That night, Elijah and I slept in our cabin in sleeping bags on squeaky metal bunk beds. Just before we nodded off, I switched the flashlight on in the dark room and shined it up into the high ceiling from my top bunk. The adventure was beginning.

"Look at all the lines and angles up there, Elijah!" I call across the room over to his top bunk where he lay. I moved the flashlight slowly in an arc through the air. "The shadows in the rafters are pretty, aren't they?"

"Yes."

"Elijah, do you like this place?"

"Yes."

The next morning at breakfast in the main lodge, some participants were sporting buttons on their collars that said, "I survived behavior modification." Others wore T-shirts—which a child member of ANI had designed—proclaiming, "Cure all neurotypicals, but don't cure me." There was a swimming pool at the camp, which heartened Elijah and the other autistics who had a similar penchant for water. "High-functioning" and "low-functioning" became inconsequential here. There was no hierarchy of who was "more abled" and who was not. Some people talked. Some didn't. Some sat at keyboards in wheelchairs. Some had stereotypies, like hand flapping or tics with the head. Some were mentally retarded.

Like a stone tossed into a quiet pond, Autreat was a series of rings spreading out from the main lodge. At each ring that emanated outward from the center, I'd find an autistic person, walking alone in the woods, reading a book, playing a musical instrument, talking to himself, being helped with a keyboard by a support person, having intellectual discussions with friends, or watching the sun set over the rolling green farmlands. Each person I encountered had a particular constellation of sensitivities and deep interests. Each was a star in the sky, and Elijah was a part of that universe I was watching from the shadowy wings.

Jim Sinclair says that until very recently, most attempts to help autistics have been based on the notion that one should be normalized behaviorally. "Expecting that we learn to 'act normal' socially," he says, "is sort of like expecting blind people to learn to drive cars instead of teaching them skills to use public transportation." At Autreat, I learned that autistics feel they can be helped with more important things than constantly making eye contact or mimicking what is thought to be appropriate social behavior. I learned that more than anything else, they need help in identifying and communicating their needs, monitoring their levels of sensory stimulation, and knowing how and when to remove themselves from overwhelming situations before they reach a "meltdown state." Instead of teaching how to deal with sensory and social overload, Jim says that educational programs tend to focus on extinguishing behavior, like hand flapping, that might actually be "an attempt to communicate or to cope."

Often, these trained behaviors "are valued for no other reason than because they're considered 'normal.'"

The camp had an aura of acceptance about it. It was a rarified place. Elijah and I played all day long without concealing our repetitions or interrupting them before he wanted to stop. We didn't have to go off to an isolated field to commit our unconventional acts as we did back home in Woodstock with our balloon routine. We stood outside the main lodge, playing shadow games for hours, watching our dark silhouettes rise up from our feet and project themselves against a wall made golden by the sinking sun. The more the sun slipped toward the horizon behind us, the more our shadows became distinct. We played animation games, running toward the building to see our figures grow small and crisp around the edges. Then we ran away again, becoming amorphous giants, making our shadows chase one another, and they shook their angry fists, ranting funny cartoon phrases.

"Dag . . . nabit!" Elijah yells happily. His shadow is very small compared to mine, for he is standing far ahead of me, close to the building.

"Are you Yosemite Sam?"

"Yes."

"Oh yeah?! Take that you lily-livered varmit!" My towering silhouette bonks Yosemite on the head with its shadowy fist. Elijah laughs wildly and runs away from the building, his figure looming larger and larger. Then he takes a position right beside me, his eyes pointedly directed to our collaboration on the wall. "Look at those two big galumphs over there!" I exclaim.

Elijah cackles at nonsense words whenever I say them. He likes the sound of "galumph" and "frumius bandersnatch." He likes when I call him by his nickname, "Skrumpshk."

"Let's walk through each other again, okay, Skrumpshk?"

"Yes."

I take one step backward, then slowly move my body directly behind Elijah's. Our shadows merge on the wall.

"What a BIG galumph!"

Elijah chortles.

It wasn't all breezy being at Autreat. In fact, it threw me completely off balance. In my cusp status as a "cousin"—a word the other parents with shadow traits used to describe themselves—the rarefied environment I was suddenly immersed in was both deeply familiar and deeply strange. Sometimes I felt left out and ignored. Other times, I was concerned I would make some kind of neurotypical social faux pas. Then there was the autistic humor, all the inside jokes and special language that I didn't always get. There was isolation, repetition everywhere, and enervating stress with Elijah, yet I was tangibly crossing over into his life further than I ever had before. I liked the challenge of my discomfort.

When our long weekend came to an end, so had the summer. Elijah and I made the long trip back to Woodstock, where he was to begin first grade in a special educational class at Woodstock Elementary School. His classmates there were more verbal than his peers at his previous school had been, and within months, Elijah's expressive language began to soar. In the course of that transitional year at public school, he became a high-functioning yakker à la Asperger's syndrome. Visual images were his vehicle of communication, as he swiftly moved from naming colors to asking endless questions about the fine points of animation.

"Mom," he says to me as we sit on the bed together holding hands, watching the Disney production of *Pinocchio* one more time. "Is Pinocchio a *real* boy?"

"No, at this point in the story he's still a puppet. But at the end of the movie, he becomes a real boy."

"Mom?"

"Yes?"

"Do cartoons get hurt?"

"No . . . I mean, yes. Well, it depends on how you look at it."

"Am I two-dimensional?"

"No."

"Am I three-dimensional?"

"Yes."

"Are cartoons real?"

"No . . . actually, that depends too."

"Are cartoons dead?"

Elijah's questions are unremitting. He asks them hundreds of times a day, devoting himself to the problem of reality versus animation.

"Mom?"

"Yes?"

"Do cartoons get hurt?"

"That's a hard question, Elijah." I answer slowly, keeping my language as simple as possible. "Sometimes the characters in the stories get hurt—like when they fall off cliffs or get bonked on the head." Elijah laughs. "But then they always seem to feel better really fast, don't they?"

"Yes!"

"In *real life,* they're just pictures. They don't *feel* anything."

"Is Pinocchio a *real* boy?"

"Well . . . no . . . he's not. He's a cartoon character."

"Does Pinocchio get hurt?"

I'm thoroughly confused now as to how to answer Elijah. First I say Pinocchio is a puppet. Then I say he's a boy. Then I say he's a cartoon character. I say he's real. I say he's not real. I say he's just a moving image. Temple Grandin points out that autistic children don't necessarily make the presumed neurotypical connection that an image of an object is not the object itself. "They've got to learn that a line drawing is a picture." In other words, if you're going to teach an autistic child what a cup is, "you must show her the literal object first, then the image of the cup later."

During Elijah's headlong leap into animation, what began as his one-line colored marks on separate sheets of paper blossomed into elaborate drawings. By the end of his seventh year, sketching and talking cartoon talk were all that interested him. He came home from school, walked with me up the stairs to the apartment, kicked his shoes off just inside the door, and went directly to his bedroom, without a word, to all his special marker sets and sketch pads. As always, he wouldn't use just any kind of paper. At the art supply store, he was painfully selective about paper textures, sizes, and the degree of whiteness.

His first drawings were of hats, all of them taken strictly from cartoons he had seen before. For months on end, he compulsively sketched the floppy hats of the Seven Dwarfs from Disney's *Snow White,* all the while asking questions that seemed to involve the phenomena of motion and gravity.

"Mom?"

"Yes?"

"Is Sneezy's hat standing up?" He's watching *Snow White* on the VCR while I sit beside him, reading an academic essay on Else Lasker-Schüler's exiled life in Palestine after the Nazis came into power in Germany.

"Is Sneezy's hat standing up?"

I pass a glance at the television. "Yes, Sneezy's hat is standing up," I answer mechanically.

"Mom?"

"Hmm?"

"Is Grumpy's hat hanging down?"

I look up again. "Yes, Grumpy's hat is hanging down."

In Dr. Seuss's *Green Eggs and Ham,* the main character, Sam I Am, has a floppy hat that's reminiscent of the dwarfs' in *Snow*

White. Elijah drew hundreds of sketches of Sam's hat, often depicting its three-dimensionality by shadows or by the colors he chose. But the hat that Elijah liked to sketch most of all, and this he drew literally in the thousands, was a top hat that belonged to Jiminy Cricket.

"See that square shape?" I ask him, pointing to a sketch he's working on. Elijah doesn't answer, but I know that he's listening. We're sitting side by side on the wooden floor of the kitchen with dozens of sketches surrounding us. As usual, his hands are stained with marker ink. "That square you're drawing is a patch on Jiminy's *old* hat, the one that changes to a new hat when the fairy comes and touches him with her magic wand."

Elijah is still silent, but he likes it when I narrate for him what he knows more articulately in images than in words. Once he has finished the drawing, he stands up abruptly and walks to the other side of the room.

"Pinocchio, save yourself! Save yourself!" he calls out dramatically, then tosses his body onto the floor. Elijah is imitating Pinocchio's father, Geppetto. We are now moving into a deep media fixation (a topic Jim Sinclair did a presentation on at Autreat in 1999).

Elijah pulls himself up off the floor again and begins pacing around the apartment. He's got his "torn-up clothes" costume on, consisting of an array of ragged garments that look like the ones Geppetto wore during his days of crisis, when he was trapped inside the belly of the whale. Elijah designed this special costume himself, using the Disney animation as a strict visual source. He selected the colors for the "torn-up shirt" and the "torn-up vest" and showed me where to sew the patches on the knickers. The weathered knickers are necessarily ragged at the knees, and on the clogs he's wearing, we've glued gold buckles made of felt. Elijah sketches images of these torn-up articles of clothing again and again. They hover on the white page of the sketch pad, lined up in rows like fashion studies. He even wears a white wig that's shaped like Geppetto's hair.

"Pinocchio, save yourself! Save yourself!"

Elijah is reciting what Geppetto says when Pinocchio attempts to rescue his father from Monstro, the great whale who has smashed their tiny raft to bits. As Monstro is closing in on them for the final kill, Pinocchio sacrifices his own safety, grabs his helpless father, and manages to drag him ashore. Elijah spends day after day modeling on this scene in the animation. He sketches picture upon picture of hats and torn-up pants and shirts and shoe buckles. Sometimes he draws Pinocchio and Geppetto in their greatest moment of despair, seated side by side on a raft inside Monstro's belly, just before their big escape.

Many autistics have media fixations. They mimic the language of characters in movies and on TV. They replicate the gestures and memorize dialogue, just as Dustin Hoffman's character in the film *Rain Man* recited long stretches of the Abbott and Costello routine, "Who's on First Base." A media fixation can be motivated by a desire to understand the human social condition. Jim Sinclair speaks of his "television autobiography," of how he learned things that many neurotypicals take for granted through assiduous study of his favorite TV programs. The main revelation he gained from watching *Gilligan's Island,* for example, was realizing that people "can be recognized because they have the same appearance and the same name each time one sees them." Jim also practices reading facial expressions and can synchronically integrate a person's smile with the emotion of happiness, thanks to his media fixation on *It's Hercules: The Legendary Journeys.*

Elijah emulates the characters of *Pinocchio* on paper. He emulates them in clay. He emulates them in costume, gesture, and language. Sometimes he sketches with the stereo turned on, drawing to frisky accordion polkas. He likes the accordion music because in the Disney animation, Geppetto plays the concertina.

In moments such as these, Elijah is piecing the world together though his media fixations, through cartoons, through sound effects, and miming.

"Am I two-dimensional?"

"Am I three-dimensional?"

"Am I a real boy?"

"Do cartoons get hurt?"

My answers always seem insufficient, but Elijah is waiting for something that will untangle his complex of questions about reality, identity, and the moving image on the television screen. "You're three-dimensional, Elijah," I finally say, feeling a tug inside. There's something more to all of this, but I cannot translate it. "The limits of my language mean the limits of my world."

One day, as I was telling Sharron the excitement of Elijah's journey into visual art, she moaned a knowing moan over the telephone.

"The drawing is good," she pointed out. "Elijah needs that. But you gotta know that he's under a lot of stress if he's spending all that time doing it."

Her words were sobering.

Some researchers and autistics alike feel that the Austrian philosopher Ludwig Wittgenstein was a high-functioning autistic, probably with Asperger's syndrome. Wittgenstein was drawn to philosophy, his biographer writes, by a "compulsive tendency to be struck with . . . questions." Whenever I read Wittgenstein's philosophy of language, I see a mind glimmering with profound insight into the image and its relation to the spoken word. "When someone says the word 'cube' to me," he writes,

I know what it means. But can the whole use *of the word come before my mind, when I understand* it in this way? . . .

On the other hand isn't the meaning of the word also determined by this use? And can these ways of determining meaning conflict? Can what we grasp in a flash accord with a use, fit or fail to fit it? And how can what is present to us in an instant, what comes before our mind in an instant, fit a use? What really comes before our mind when we understand a word?—Isn't it something like a picture? Can't it be a picture?

Wittgenstein is compelled by how the utter specificity of a word in a given context is imagined in the mind. In his famous logical study, the *Tractatus logico-philosophicus,* he places images at the center of his theory of language. For him, a statement is a kind of picture. Wittgenstein scholar H. O. Mounce explains:

A man knows what a picture is about, say a painting of a wheatfield, not because the picture tells him, but because he can see from the picture what it is about. He can see this, as it were, in the picture even if what it pictures, the wheatfield, has never existed. Of course, what the picture is about can also be put into words. But Wittgenstein's point would be that when we say what the picture is about then what we are really doing is introducing another picture. The statement stands to the picture as, in another context, a picture might stand to a statement.

Wittgenstein was born in Vienna in 1889 and was raised as the youngest of eight children in one of the wealthiest families of the Austro-Hungarian Empire. His life span intersected with those of Leo Kanner, Hans Asperger, and Bruno Bettelheim, all of whom were fellow countrymen. Wittgenstein's childhood biography has familiar signs of the high-functioning autistic narrative. He didn't speak until he was four years old. Upon entering school, after being privately tutored at home for fourteen years, he was teased and bullied by classmates who ridiculed him, "chanting an alliterative jingle that made play of his unhappiness and of the distance between him and the rest of the school: '*Wittgenstein wandelt wehmutig widriger Winde wegen Wienwärts*' (Wittgenstein wends his woeful windy way towards Vienna)."

Marjorie Perloff concisely summarizes the tenor of what neurotypical culture might call Wittgenstein's "eccentric life":

> *The Wittgenstein paradoxes are indeed the stuff of legend. A fabulously rich man who gave away all his money so he wouldn't have to bother with it; a man, three of whose brothers committed suicide and who frequently contemplated suicide himself and yet told friends, on his deathbed, that he had had a wonderful life . . . an intellectual genius who, in his thirties, worked first as a gardener and then as an elementary school teacher in rural Austria . . . a man who had no interest in modernist art movements and lived in Spartan rented rooms furnished with assorted deck chairs, but who designed for his sister Margarete Stonborough a starkly beautiful ultramodernist house and attended to every detail of its construction from radiators to doorknobs. . . . [He is] the ultimate modernist outsider, the changeling who never stops reinventing himself, who never really "belongs."*

An autism researcher, M. Fitzgerald, writes that Wittgenstein had obvious "impairment in reciprocal social interaction." His relationships with others were fraught with difficulties, and his "method of small group teaching" as a professor of philosophy at Cambridge University "was distinctly strange. He basically spoke out his thoughts aloud, largely in a monologue." He was "given to being lost in thought and would dislike being interrupted." It wasn't that Wittgenstein didn't wish to interact with others, but his desire to do so was "always in relation to his special interest in philosophy." He was infamous for his emotional outbursts, which often tested the limits of his intense friendships with other intellectuals at Cambridge like Bertrand Russell. Wittgenstein once said that "normal human beings" were a "torment" for him and that "most human relationships" were "irksome," clearly remarking on the constant social run-ins he had with the expectations of neurotypical culture. "He was totally focussed," says Fitzgerald, "and showed a repetitive adherence to his interests. He felt that nothing was worth doing except producing great philosophical works which indeed he did. This research work was carried out often on his own in isolated places, for long periods, to the exclusion of other activities."

Compulsions and repetitions punctuated Wittgenstein's life. "He would return again and again to a passage of music or a poem" or "stay with a profound utterance and attempt to deepen his understanding of it." He was more a person of depth than of breadth, "never one for learning a multiplicity of things" simply "because it was expected of him." He preferred to spend his time "arranging and rearranging his philosophical works," copying them from one book to another. He listened to music the same way Elijah and I do, "over and over again," and he claimed to have heard Wagner's opera *Meistersinger* performed thirty times.

In the arena of nonverbal communication, Wittgenstein had the trademark stiff gaze and limited facial expression, and the people who encountered him had classic neurotypical responses to this. Wittgenstein came from "another world." He was a *Sonderling* (German for "eccentric") and "someone out of the normal run." When he talked shop with his philosophical colleagues, he often dominated their discussions, insisting rigidly on his own views or yakking in monologue late into the night

with little awareness that others might be tired or bored. Today, the main emphasis in the education of Asperger children is placed on learning social skills, such as how to take turns in conversation or how to broach a new topic gracefully.

Like many autistics, Wittgenstein had limited food interests, most likely due to sensory sensitivities. When he was living in Dublin, he ate precisely the same meal each day in Bewley's Café on Grafton Street, and at the end of his life, when he stayed with his family doctor, he requested the same things to eat every day. Elijah too has highly specific food interests, which seem to be dictated by his sensory experience. For a long time, the only things he ate were white or nearly colorless. White bread, white tofu, white rice, and chicken breasts. No two foods could be mixed together, or he would refuse his plate. Color, or the lack thereof, has always been important to him.

The autistic artist Jesse Park distinguished what she called "peacock blue" from "peacock green" long before she had much speech. Wittgenstein spent a lot of time thinking about color. He wrote a philosophical treatise devoted to it. "Let us imagine," he writes, "that someone were to paint something from nature and in its natural colours. Every bit of the surface of such a painting has a definite colour. What colour? How do I determine its name? Should we, e.g., use the name under which the pigment applied to it is sold? But mightn't such a pigment look completely different in its special surrounding than on the palette?" Wittgenstein points out that when we name a color, we have some concept of absolute purity, some ideal definition, when in fact, in "everyday life, we are virtually surrounded by impure colors." "I treat the colour concepts," he says "like the concepts of sensations."

"Val?" Elijah has begun to call me by my name, particularly when he wants me to pay close attention.

"Yes, Elijah?"

"What comes between Medium Blue and Dark Blue?"

"That's a hard question. What do you think?"

"What do you think?"

"No, what do *you* think?"

"What comes between Medium Green and Dark Green?"

"It's a good question. It's hard to answer, isn't it?"

"Yes."

"I love your questions, Skrumpshk. They make me think."

"Thank you, Val. Do cartoons get hurt?"

"Something that we know when someone asks us," says Wittgenstein, "but no longer know when we are supposed to give an account of it, is something that we need to *remind* ourselves of. (And it is obviously something of which for some reason it is difficult to remind oneself.)"

CHAPTER 10

∾

Life Under Glass

"Val?"

"Yes, Elijah?"

"Do you think Yosemite Sam is funny?"

"Yes, Elijah. I think he's funny."

"Do you think it's funny when his face turns black?"

"Yes, I think it's funny when his face turns black."

"Val?"

"Yes, Elijah?" I'm lying on the couch, watching Elijah, who is squatting on the floor, turning out confident sketches while he pelts me with his cartoon questions.

"Do you think Yosemite Sam is funny when he's wearing the blue pants and his face turns black? Do you think it's funny when the cannon explodes in his face?"

"Do you?" I ask, too tired to keep up with the banter. It's Sunday, late in the afternoon. We've been lazing around the apartment all day, never stepping outside even once for air. On the weekends, Elijah moves deep into his drawing, never pausing to do much else but eat. He lets the sketching play itself out because on school days, his time for drawing is limited. The only sound in the room is that of Elijah's marker moving agilely on the paper.

Sketches are strewn all around him on the floor, and soon the sun will set. Gold light swims through the window of my bedroom and beckons me to go in there and take a nap.

"Do you think it's funny when the cannon explodes?"

"Let's stop talking for a while, okay? I'm going to lie down in my room."

Elijah doesn't answer, but the marker continues making its fast strokes. He has completed at least twenty sketches in the past few hours, all of them the same image of Yosemite Sam, the ranting Looney Tunes character. Elijah has carefully filled in each drawing of Yosemite with a different color. There's Yosemite in red. Yosemite in blue. Purple Yosemite. Orange too.

Lying on my bed now, I muse about our recent time together at the college where I teach. Elijah had had a day off from school, so I brought him along to work where there were bureaucratic responsibilities to tend to. When lunchtime rolled around, I took Elijah to the faculty lounge, and we sat down at a big round table with some colleagues who were engaged in literary discussion. Finished with my dissertation now and my grandparents' money all spent, I was feeling particularly sensitive about my part-time status at an institution where I have taught intermittently for ten years, ever since I entered graduate school.

Though I have the Ph.D., there's no prayer in hell for a full-time promotion here. My political moment came and went years ago, when I was caring for Elijah's seizures, when any promise of an academic career had come to a grinding halt. I'm a stigmatized adjunct, and though I have no regrets about my responsibility to Elijah, we are nearly broke. As during the early years, we are living hand to mouth again.

This made the erudition among the tenured and the full-timers at the table all the more unnerving for me. I found their conversation utterly removed from everything I had become. Elijah, sitting beside me in a bubble of supreme focus, was rapidly working his way through the brand new sketchbook I had hoped would last a little longer. Within half an hour, he had filled nearly every page with views of Yosemite Sam, each drawing depicting the cartoon character from a different perspective. It was then that I realized, in my own bubble of nonparticipation at the table, that Elijah was drawing a storyboard for an animation. It began with Yosemite seen from behind—just the back of a large cowboy hat and a pair of squat, booted legs sticking out beneath it. Slowly, the view panned around his body moving from a profile, to a three-quarters view, and finally ending up above Yosemite from a bird's-eye view. This was followed by a series of direct frontal sketches from various distances, as if, page by page, a camera were zooming in on the cartoon character. Yosemite began as a speck of a figure, then gradually loomed into an extreme close-up, his wild eyes filling the entire page.

Elijah was particularly focused on his work that day at the college, and I sensed that he sensed my nervousness. Then someone sitting at the table began to talk directly to me about a volume of poetry by "so-and-so," a name I did not recognize.

"I haven't read that," was my distracted answer. Elijah's sketchbook was coming to the end. Soon he would necessarily want to leave.

"You haven't read 'so-and-so'?" My questioner was taken aback by my ignorance.

"No. I haven't," I heard myself reply with an edgy defiance. "I've been reading *other* books, *other* authors." With this I managed to alienate the guy and, it seemed, all the others at the table too.

So here I am, lolling on my bed at home on a quiet Sunday evening, wondering if I'll ever manage to find an academic position in a glutted university market and in an educational system that fell into its dull emulation of corporate culture during the decade of my graduate years. Rolling over on my side, I try to forget about it and open up a large catalogue from an Andy Warhol exhibition that I recently borrowed from a friend. I have begun to read Warhol's biography and to study his serial works of art, scanning them for autistic cues.

"Elijah, come here. Look at this."

"No, I'm busy now."

The next room is all silence and deep concentration. Elijah is taken up with "staying inside the lines," as he calls it whenever he uses color.

"It reminds me a lot of Yosemite Sam," I tempt him.

The silence in the living room grows louder. I can hear it about to pivot. Elijah puts his marker down on the floor. He's standing up. Intent footsteps are now approaching my room.

"Yes, Val, I will listen to you talk about Yosemite Sam," he says, stopping at the threshold.

"Look," I point at the catalogue beside me on the bed. "It's Campbell's soup cans, with the labels peeling off."

"Yes," Elijah answers disinterestedly.

"Just look at this." I turn the page of the catalogue. "Here are more Campbell's soup cans, lined up in pretty rows. These were done by the artist Andy Warhol. See, here's his picture. That's what Andy Warhol looked like." Elijah moves closer.

"Andy Warhol likes cartoons."

"Yes, he did."

"Is Andy Warhol scared?"

"I don't know," I reply looking at the photograph again. Andy's gaze is distracted, staring into seeming nothingness. "Do you think he's scared?"

"Yes." Elijah wants to walk away from this conversation and go back to the pressing work that's waiting for him in the living room. If what I have to say doesn't fit into his current stream of activity, he has little time for it.

"Wait! Don't go yet! There's something more I have to show

you. Just slow down, and really take a look at this. Andy Warhol, the artist of the Campbell's soup cans, made a lot of pictures of a person like Yosemite Sam. Her name was Marilyn. She was a famous movie actress. He made her many different times in many different colors." I open up the pages of the catalogue to Warhol's famous serigraphs. "There's Marilyn. See. She has blue lips and yellow hair here. And look, in this one she's all red. Here, she's green and pink. You and Andy Warhol have a lot in common."

"Yes! Andy Warhol is an animator!"

"Now wait. Don't go away." I get up from the bed, go out to the living room, pick up a stack of Elijah's drawings from the floor, then come back into the bedroom where I arrange them on my bed. Twelve images in pretty rows of four. Yosemite in green. Yosemite in blue. Purple Yosemite. Yellow, too. "Do you see what I mean now about Andy Warhol and Marilyn?"

"Yes." Elijah points at each of drawings on the bed. "Yosemite, here, is orange, and he was always that way. Yosemite, here, is blue, and he was always that way. Yosemite, here, is green, and he was always that way." When Elijah reaches the final drawing, he stumbles for a moment. He perceives a disruption, a duplicate color, a second Yosemite all in orange. He picks it up and gazes into it. "Val, throw this one away." He hands it to me and walks abruptly to the living room. "Throw it away, Val. I'm making a new one. This is a new Yosemite, in a new color, pink," he says from his squatting position on the wooden floor. When he's finished, Elijah returns to the bedroom and fits the pink image into its proper place. "Yosemite is pink here, and he was always that way."

Andy Warhol was probably not aware of Asperger's syndrome by name, but he was aware of what he called his "missing chemicals." Sometimes he called them "responsibility chemicals." He was missing these, he explained, and that's why he was such a "sissy," such a "mama's boy." It's why he didn't like being touched, why sex was "hard work," and why he was afraid of flying and heights. "I always bring every problem back to chemicals," he writes in his autobiography, "because I really think that everything starts and finishes with chemicals."

Warhol wore his "chemical problems" openly. In his media splash entry into pop art in the 1960s, Andy Warhol the person was as arresting and provoking as his art. His laconic speech, his cool attitude, and his bizarre looks were viscerally mistrusted by critics and journalists. Andy was getting a lot of attention, some of it unwittingly engaged not with his art but with his Asperger's syndrome.

"He was a liberator," said the New York gallery owner Ivan Karp, looking back on Warhol's early career. "The *idea* of painting the soup cans is what made him significant—his preoccupation with things as things." From 1961 to 1962, Andy painted thirty-two "portraits" of Campbell's soup cans, copying each and every flavor methodically from Chicken Gumbo, to Black Bean, to Split Pea, to Pepper Pot. What he didn't do in all the images was change the shape, the color, or the perspective. The result was arresting and provoking. Each soup can was a stark replica of the preceding one. At their first exhibition in Los Angeles in 1962, gallery visitors were dumbfounded and confused. They didn't know what to make of it.

Soon repetition and serial imagery became Warhol's trademarks. His high years as a pop artist had begun. With his assistant, he worked like the machine he'd always wanted to be, churning out multiple silk screens of all-American commercial products and famous personalities, of stars who dazzled him from a distance like Elvis Presley, Jackie Onassis, and Marilyn Monroe. Some critics found his art banal, lacking in feeling and painterly process. Others thought he was a revolutionary, a visual genius.

If the soup cans were cool and distant, the silk screens removed Andy one more degree from his so-called subject. Whether it was a Coke bottle or Jackie Onassis, he was duplicating them over and over again like a mimeograph machine. "My mind always drifts," he writes, "when I hear words like 'objective' and 'subjective,' I never know what people are talking about, I just don't have the brains." Andy moved in the realm of the literal, a common autistic trait. Abstractions, theories, and concepts are not as graspable as objects and images, which Andy rolled out in different colors. He lined them up in assorted rows and sizes. *210 Coca-Cola Bottles, 80 Two Dollar Bills, Sixteen Jackies, Twenty Jackies,* and 168 repetitions of the lips of Marilyn Monroe. Andy had always been captivated by repetition. Perhaps it was an autistic predilection for the serial and the literal.

Autism is a life of profound serial experience. It is a life of cataloguing repeated events and variations of events. Repeated images. Repeated language. Repeated movements and repeated gestures. Its expression is found, classically and clinically, in the lining up of things in rows, side by side by side, just as Elijah lines his water balloons up neatly in the muffin tins or his marker sets along the floor. In the visual arts, there is a classical propensity for repetition too. An artist does a study, or he does a sketch. Then he does another one, and another one, and another one, until the process is complete. The repetition is compelling, a mirror of internal drama and development. It is a place of border crossings, a place under glass, suspended somewhere between subject and object. It's a place, perhaps, of neurological transcendence.

Pepper Pot, Pepper Pot, Pepper Pot soup. Chicken Gumbo, and Tomato Rice. You can eat it every day, every day for lunch. Mom cooks it every day, yet every day is different. Andy's childhood was different too. He spent most of it as a loner. Shy, serious, withdrawn, and always drawing. He drew, and drew, and drew. He also spent most of his time in close vicinity of his mother, Julia. She knew just what Andy needed and just what he liked. She heated up the Campbell's soup every day for lunch. "I used to have the same lunch every day," Warhol says of himself, "for twenty years, I guess, the same thing over and over again." Like Elijah and Wittgenstein, Andy might have had sensory sensitivities to taste and texture.

Warhol was born in 1928, just as the Depression was getting under way. His parents were immigrants from a village in the Carpathian Mountains, somewhere along the border between Russia and Poland. His father was a laborer who died when Andy was still a boy. His mother was a housewife. They had little money, little education, nothing but their bits of broken English, their ramshackle house in the Soho ghetto of Pittsburgh, and their Byzantine Catholicism. The legend goes that the family couldn't afford better than Campbell's Soup, but Andy must have liked it too. In fact, he liked it enough to paint it perseveratively with precision, method, and design.

"Communication via objects was safe," writes Donna Williams in *Nobody Nowhere*. Williams also had a catalogue of special objects. The pay phone around the corner from her house, for example, not to mention the phone book inside it. Finding no love in her abusive home, she made many calls on that phone. She did it alphabetically, working her way through the book as methodically as Andy did when he carefully painted each and every flavor of soup. Williams would dial a number, then tell the voice that answered that his name was the first in the directory to start with the letter "B." This was the reason that she was calling. Dumbfounded, the listener either hung up or cursed at her angrily. Warhol's audience would respond similarly to his art. It was a stupid prank. It was a cause for rage.

This is the important crux of failed communication. It is the story of two ships passing in the night. One ship is sending out signals, via the object; it has an autistic sail. The other ship does not; it is navigating its neurotypical waters and doesn't require the objects to communicate. Warhol was also known for his fond admiration of the telephone (not to mention tape recorders and television sets). He said the telephone constructed his most intimate moments with other people, but he pooh-poohed what he called "personal love" and "personal sex."

The famous and beloved pay phone, hanging on the wall in his New York studio, the Factory, was the perfect medium for Andy's intimacy. On the phone, there wasn't too much social and sensory input to integrate. Personal contact was reduced to just a voice—to just a "B," as Andy would call the person on the other end of the line, referring to himself as an "A." The dialogue between A and B, conducted by way of phone or tape recorder or movie camera, was an important foundation in Andy's relationships. It was important for its mirroring effect and is best explained by the title of his memoir: *The Philosophy of Andy Warhol (From A to B and Back Again)*.

"The people I liked were their things," Donna Williams explains. For those who let her live this way, *through* the objects, without ridicule or harassment, Williams would begin to feel attachment. Andy associated the soup cans and other household objects, like Brillo boxes, directly with his mother Julia. After the exhibition of the 32 *Soup Cans,* he set out to duplicate her entire kitchen. It was a kitchen of things: cans, boxes, soaps, and special products. A kitchen full of American advertisements, repeated lunches, and reliable routines.

For Julia Warhola, there was a lot to keep track of when Andy was a little boy. He was often bullied by his brothers or by the tough kids at school, and he wasn't showing signs of the usual social graces. His brother Paul said he was full of mischief from ages three to six. He'd hear bad words from other kids and then repeat them in the most inappropriate social settings, so his family locked him out of the house. "It was really embarrassing," says Paul. "And the more you smacked him the more he said it, the worse he got." As Andy grew a little older and guests came around to the house to visit, he "kept his head down . . . and when he did look up it was furtively as if he was afraid of getting hit."

Andy was also known to make disappearances. He would often vanish in the middle of a softball game. A kid would hit the ball outfield where Andy was posted, but when the players looked out there for him to make the catch, he was long gone. Later, they'd find him at home on the porch drawing pictures. All the neighborhood told jokes and laughed about these "absent-minded" disappearances.

A nine-year-old autistic boy walked off into a Florida swamp once, then swam around alone there among the alligators. Two days later, he was discovered, safe and completely naked, by a fisherman in a boat. Elijah wanders off the sidewalk when cars are speeding by. He doesn't seem to know where or what the danger is. The "responsibility chemicals" that Warhol speaks of as the source of his "problems," the ones he says he was missing, might have something to do with autistic experience. It is a neurological phenomenon, a difference of mind. Thought is not absent, but somewhere else, linked to other things, stimming on some sensory object or perseverating.

"When people have a cool, calm atmosphere about them," Warhol writes, "they're usually spaced. They have those right kind of eyes, and they sit around and not bother anybody. Some people are like that naturally because of their chemicals, and other people are like that because of drugs." Maybe Warhol was writing about himself and about the distracted autistic gaze, the "lack of eye contact," which neurotypicals often perceive as rude aloofness, disassociation, or cool absence.

Why does Elijah leave the room when it is full of people? Why, when a friend stops over for a visit, does he stop talking and quietly take himself away to draw pictures in his room? Why did Warhol, at his first big opening in New York City at the Stable in 1962, plunge abruptly into nonverbal space? He stood "in a corner of the gallery and at the party afterwards with a blank expression on his face. . . . Many people were struck by his behavior."

The high-functioning autistics I have met at Autreat describe what neurotypicals perceive as withdrawal as a partial shutdown of the senses, as a busy cataloguing of events around them, or as a stimulating fascination with a nearby sensory experience. Sometimes there are just too many social cues to read and interpret all in the same moment. It's a question of executive function. A one-to-one relationship, often of intensity, is the preferred form of social interaction. One thing is certain: the apparent distancing is a necessary safety device, a way of navigating through neurotypical waters, even though it's wrongly read as shutting out, as a puzzling lack of social grace, or as just plain bad behavior. "I wasn't misbehaving," writes Donna Williams about her frequent "mysterious" disappearances from school. "If they'd have found me and told me where to go, I'd have followed."

"I wish you'd just tell me the words, and I can just repeat them because I can't . . . uh . . . uh . . . it's uh . . . I can't . . . uh . . . I'm so empty that I can't think of anything. . . . Why don't you just tell me the words, and they'll just come out of my mouth?" Andy Warhol said this to an interviewer on TV in 1966. He said it in a monotone voice that might have seemed aloof and arrogant. Was Warhol *misbehaving?* Many people thought so. In his interviews, he notoriously broke all the rules of social interaction as he exposed entrenched presumptions about standard communication.

In the interview, Andy, perched on a high stool with his hands carefully folded on one knee, is facing the camera directly. He is poised like a piece of china inside a glass vitrine. He looks "spaced," to use his own words, wearing dark sunglasses (Did he have visual sensitivities to light?), rarely making a gesture or a facial expression. In clinical terms, this is called "lack of affect." Behind Andy is a large double silk screen of Elvis Presley, standing in a wide gunfighter stance, his hand drawing out a pistol. Throughout the interview, Andy does not look once at the journalist who is smoking nervously and shifting in his seat. Instead, Warhol says he is "empty." He doesn't have the words he needs, situated there carefully between the silk screen and the camera. In this moment, he either cannot, or is refusing to, *pass* as neurotypical.

"Why don't you just tell me the words, and they'll just come out of my mouth?" Was Andy asking for an echolalic cue? Was he too stressed to summon forth the language himself? The interviewer is thrown off course, taking more wild puffs at his cigarette.

"No. Don't worry about it," he says. "Because we . . ."

"No. No. I think it would be so nice," Warhol interrupts him, a degree more confrontational. The interviewer is confused now.

"We'll loosen up after a while," he says and attempts to laugh it off.

"No, it's not that," Warhol corrects him. If you look closely enough at Andy's face, beneath the seeming coolness, a complex, pained frustration is growing there. "It's just that I can't . . . uh . . . I have a cold and I can't think of anything, and it would be so nice if you told me a sentence, and I just could repeat it."

"Okay, then," says the interviewer, "let me ask you some questions that you can answer."

"Oh, no," says Warhol, "but repeat the answers too."

Was this the manipulative creep who so perplexed the media, or was this the tenacious genius? Andy Warhol was shocking in his "behavior," but by this point in his life, at age thirty-eight, he was fed up with the expected discourse. He had honed his social awkwardness into a high form of mockery and cultural criticism. He was a high-functioning maverick, flamboyantly displaying his "missing chemicals" and his "missing responsibility" to mainstream neurological culture. If Warhol was an early underground pioneer of gay American life, as many view him today, the same might be said about him and autism.

What's the difference between subjective and objective? Uh . . . uh . . . uh . . . I don't know. "I'm sure I'm going to look in the mirror and see nothing," Warhol writes. "People are always calling me a mirror and if a mirror looks into a mirror, what is there to see?" One Asperger woman in Los Angeles calls autism "involuntary Buddhism," and a conversation with Elijah about Yosemite Sam is sometimes like a mantra, or a mirroring dialogue that gradually loses distinction between who is who and which one of us is talking.

"Val?"

"Yes, Elijah?"

"Do you think Yosemite Sam is funny?"

"Yes, Elijah. I think he's funny."

"Do you think it's funny when his face turns black?"

"Yes. I think it's funny when that happens."

"Val?"

"Yes, Elijah?"

"Do you think it's funny when his face turns black?"

"Yes, I think it's funny when his face turns black."

Conversation with Elijah has become a dialogue of complex, multiple reflections in the way that Warhol describes it in his memoir: "from A to B and back again." "I only know one language," Andy writes,

and sometimes in the middle of a sentence I feel like a foreigner trying to talk because I have word spasms where the parts of some words begin to sound peculiar to me and in the middle of saying the word I'll think, "Oh, this can't be right . . . this sounds very peculiar, I don't know if I should try to finish up this word or try to make it into something else, because if it comes out good it'll be right, but if it comes out bad it'll sound retarded."

Andy appears to have had delays in processing and generating speech, and he played with language recombinations. In moments of hesitation, he'd "graft" a piece of one word onto another. Sometimes, he said, it "made good journalism" and "looked good in print." Other times, it was "very embarrassing." Warhol's sensitivity about sounding "retarded" had a history to it. Long before he was a famous artist, he had internalized the negative stigma of the "retard." At the age of eight, he had a traumatic bout of Saint Vitus' dance, a disorder of the nervous system that causes involuntary jerking in the muscles. Being disabled in the 1930s was marginalizing and threatening, to say the least. Top professionals in the mental health field at the time were seriously debating the sterilization of "social enemies and mental incompetents," of people with familial feeblemindedness, schizophrenia (which at the time included autistics, for the two neurologies had not yet been distinctly defined), manic-depressive psychosis, epilepsy, and Saint Vitus' dance.

As his symptoms started coming on in school, Andy was teased and bullied by the other kids. "He became increasingly disoriented, was easily provoked to tears, and began to find the simplest tasks, like tying his shoes or writing his name, difficult to coordinate," his biographer writes. When the situation grew too extreme, Andy was removed entirely from school and stayed at home in bed for a month. Victor Bockris calls this "a golden time" for Andy because he "was able detach himself from the world." He drew a lot and pored over the comics, paper doll cut-outs, and coloring books his mother plied him with. In essence, this was Warhol's first studio. "I liked Walt Disney," Andy says about this month in bed. "I cut out Walt Disney dolls. It was *Snow White* that influenced me."

Though he eventually recovered from Saint Vitus' dance, Warhol's apparent learning differences didn't go away. As a boy and young adult, he struggled verbally, and his early childhood had been marked by strange language. Perhaps the strangeness was "talking in poetry." That's what Donna Williams calls the yak-yak-yakking of a person with Asperger's syndrome, the zealous speaking about a singular subject that to the uninitiated seems narrow-minded, obsessive, and bizarrely out of context.

"Do cartoons have blood?" Elijah asks, out of the blue, many times a day.

"Am I two-dimensional?"

"Am I three-dimensional?"

"Are cartoons dead?"

If Warhol had learning differences back then, they didn't have the names we're familiar with now. Was it dyslexia? Was it attention deficit disorder? Many teachers assumed there was a "language problem" at home because of his immigrant parents and the influence of their "hunkie accents," but there was more to it. A college teacher at Carnegie Tech says that Andy was "never very strong in his academics" and was incapable of forming his thoughts coherently in writing, but "that had nothing to do with intelligence." (In fact, Warhol didn't put pen to paper with his own writings that he published later in life, relying instead on others at the Factory to translate his thinking into words.) It was also "difficult for Andy to follow directions," the same teacher says, describing another key aspect of Asperger life. He "had already developed enough to be very self-directed."

Andy's way of relating seems to follow the Asperger model. Applying clinical language, one could say that his art, including his filmmaking, was "an all-absorbing, circumscribed interest" that "might change over time but usually dominates . . . in terms of both the time and energy spent in pursuit of the topic and the content of social interacting with others." This perfectly captures the structure of Andy's relations with his family, particularly Julia, and with his colleagues at the Factory. His sister-in-law reports that as a young teenager, Andy "never had much to say," but "when he did talk, it was always about his work."

Andy's *work* was his drawing and his media fixations. In high school, he drew "compulsively, constantly and amazingly," and he always carried a sketchbook everywhere he went. His artistic reputation, his biographer feels, gave him something to "hide behind" in school. This might be true from a neurotypical perspective, but maybe Andy had found a way to preserve himself and his energies from sensory overload and to cultivate enough semblance of normality to be accepted among the other kids. As the sensitive "class baby" with creative talent, he clung to his visual skills as the main source of his stability.

By the time he reached art school at Carnegie Tech, Warhol was producing "a lot of work, most of it at night," a college friend remembers. At home, no one in his family paid too much attention, except for Julia, who would bring meals up to his room. Andy holed up there for long hours, often never coming downstairs to be with the family. I think of Julia Warhola on my weekends at home with Elijah, who rarely wants to leave the house because he's got so much drawing to tend to, and like Andy, Elijah's sketching has become the center of our lives. We never go anywhere without art materials. As Andy and Julia both grew older, their relationship became a problematic mix of symbiosis and dysfunction that centered around Andy's unremitting work. It's possible that Julia herself, an eccentric recluse who rarely left the apartment, was somewhere along the autistic spectrum or of the broader autism phenotype.

Once, in a moment of visual revelation, Temple Grandin saw her isolated social life symbolically epitomized in an image of glass. She was a graduate student in her twenties, washing the bay window of the university cafeteria, which consisted of a series of glass sliding doors. Slipping in between two doors to clean them, Temple suddenly found herself trapped inside. "It was almost impossible to communicate through the glass," she writes. "Being autistic is like being trapped like this. The windows symbolized my feelings of disconnection from other people and helped me cope with the isolation." Donna Williams describes the separateness she felt at school—when her classmates laughed at her and called her "mad"—as like being "under glass," and Wendy Lawson, an Asperger woman, wrote a memoir titled *Life Behind Glass*.

Glass is the symbolic medium of division between autistic and nonautistic life. Glass is inscrutable and important. During his toddler years and the time of his seizures, Elijah was looking *into* the glass, not through it. He was focused on the fine layer of what lies in between, on the seemingly invisible places that neurotypicals overlook. It's another order of vision that in spite of a translucent medium causes profound separations. For high-functioning autistics, awareness of their own difference and separateness becomes painfully felt as one emerges from childhood into puberty and adolescence.

Andy Warhol once described unwittingly the social dilemma and ostracization of a person with Asperger's syndrome: "People who imagine me as the 60s media partygoer who traditionally arrived at parties with a minimum six-person 'retinue' may wonder how I dare to call myself a 'loner,' so let me explain how I really mean that and why it's true. At the times in my life when I was feeling the most gregarious and looking for bosom friendships, I couldn't find any takers." This is when, Andy explains, he became a "loner in his own mind."

Emptiness, emptiness, a place under glass. A place between mirrors perhaps. A place between a silk screen and a television camera. If constantly rebuffed attempts at communication with neurotypicals proves to be a pursuit in vain, not worthy of one's time and emotional well-being, there's always work. "Living is work," Warhol writes in his memoir. Time and again, I think of Sharron's telling groan on the phone that day when she said Elijah's drawing was terrific, but "if he's doing it a lot, you gotta know, he's under a lot of stress." Temple Grandin writes of work as her major source of satisfaction in a culture that has no place for her socially. Like Temple Grandin, Warhol eventually came to the conclusion that his work and his media fixations were the only antidote to his loner status, to a life under glass. By the time he reached his thirties, he had come into his own. He had *self-realized through the media.*

Since the emergence of television, feature films, and pop music in the second half of the twentieth century, something unprecedented has happened for autistics. Contemporary life for many has become a systematic self-construction through media fixations. Elijah has Yosemite Sam, Geppetto, and Jiminy Cricket, and Andy Warhol had *Snow White* and Shirley Temple. From the moment Andy first saw Shirley on the movie screen, she became his idol and his "role model." In fact, he "would imitate her standard gestures" well into his adult life, "folding his hands in prayer and placing them next to his cheek, or twisting them together and holding them out to the right just below his waist."

Growing up as he did in the dawn of the mass media era, Andy might be counted among the first generation of autistics to ride this liberating wave. He says he would listen to pop songs over and over and over again, until he understood their meaning. Relentlessly, he monitored film, television, music, advertisement, comics, and newspaper images beginning in his early childhood. His brother John says that when he was seven, Andy "wanted a movie projector. We didn't have the money to buy the screen but you could show the pictures right on the wall. It was just black and white. He'd watch Mickey Mouse or Little Orphan Annie and he got ideas and then he would draw a lot." As he grew older, Andy's media fixations became a reaction to mainstream neurotypical culture. "When I got my first TV," he writes, "I stopped caring so much about having close relationships with other people. I'd been hurt a lot to the degree you can only be hurt if you care a lot. So I guess I did care a lot, in the days before anyone ever heard of 'pop art' or 'underground movies' or 'superstars.'"

In the late 1950s, just before his artistic emergence, Andy "started an affair" with his television. He would "play around" in his bedroom, he says, "with as many as four at a time. But I didn't get married until 1964 when I got my first tape recorder. My wife. My tape recorder and I have been married for ten years now. When I say 'we,' I mean my tape recorder and me. A lot of people don't understand that."

Warhol's "wife" made it possible to be alone in a room with someone who wasn't a "B." "B"s were familiar. "B"s were colleagues or freaks from the Factory. But if he met someone new or someone who was sending out sexual innuendo in his direction, Warhol's "wife" made him feel safe and lessened his anxiety. The tape became a solution to some of his social dilemmas. Whether it was a sound tape or a film tape, these recordings were a safety device, a buffer, and a way of relating to others. They were a means of border crossing, of getting through the glass. "The acquisition of my tape recorder really finished whatever emotional life I might have had," Warhol writes,

> but I was glad to see it go. Nothing was ever a problem again, because a problem just meant a good tape, and when a problem transforms itself into a good tape it's not a problem any more. An interesting problem was an interesting tape. Everybody knew that and performed for the tape.

You couldn't tell which problems were real and which problems were exaggerated for the tape. Better yet, the people telling you the problems couldn't decide any more if they were really having the problems or if they were just performing.

Warhol's films gave him the notorious reputation of being a voyeur. As a visual thinker who was probably nonverbal or speech delayed in stressful situations, it's only natural that he would be a watcher. His films and his sexuality went hand in hand. Sex, too, was a "problem" for Andy. Perhaps he had heightened sensory sensitivities, and there was the ever-present necessity of relating through things, through objects, and through the media. The tape recorder and the movie camera made sex possible. In his memoir, Warhol records a dialogue with a friend who asks him about his fear of being touched.

"You do hate it when people touch you," the friend says. "I remember when I first met you, I bumped into you and you jumped about six feet. Why is that? Afraid of germs?"

"No. Afraid of getting attacked."

"Did you get this way after you were shot?"

"I was always like this. I always try to have a corner of my eye open. I always look behind me, above me."

High-functioning autistics who experience tactile sensitivity often describe the feeling of being touched as similar to sunburn. Still others stress the importance of peripheral vision. Warhol seems to have had these sensitivities and coping mechanisms. His jumping at the unexpected touch of another person and his peripheral scanning for danger might have had, as Temple Grandin points out in her book, comparative links to animal behavior. Grandin writes about her "antipredator system" that gets activated deep within her brain whenever she comes into contact with threatening stimuli. These "old animal instincts for safety and grooming" are probably triggered more readily in autistics than in neurotypicals. Andy, often perceived as a coward, was always on the lookout for attack.

Though renowned for his visual virtuosity, few people know that Warhol had keen olfactory sensitivity too. In his memoir, he writes about "perfume space" and about his "smell museum," a beloved assortment of various scents that he collected. Guerlain's *Sous le Vent*, Lucien Le Long's *Opening Night*, Ciro's *Surrender*, Lenthèric's *À Bientôt*. The list goes on and on. It's a catalogue of scents Warhol could identify the moment he walked into a room, or whenever he got a stray whiff from someone passing by him on the street. "I'm embarrassed to admit it," Temple Grandin writes in her memoir, "but when I was a young child, I liked to sniff people like a dog. The scents of different people were interesting." Warhol also lists many other olfactory situations in his memoir.

> *When I'm walking around New York, I'm always aware of the smells around me: the rubber mats in office buildings; upholstered seats in movie theaters; pizza; Orange Julius; espresso-garlic-oregano; burgers; dry cotton tee-shirts; neighborhood grocery stores; chic grocery stores; the hot dogs and sauerkraut carts; hardware store smell; stationery store smell; souvlaki; the leather and rugs at Dunhill; Mark Cross, Gucci; the Moroccan-tanned leather on the street-racks; new magazines, back-issue magazines; typewriter stores; Chinese import stores (the mildew from the freighter).*

If autistics were beginning to reach new levels of personal freedom at the dawn of the TV era, their liberation, unlike other liberations of the 1960s and 1970s, was largely silent. This was all the more so because of the state of medicine and psychiatry at the time, but true to form, Warhol was planting the seeds for a neurological revolution. A great autistic opening and emergence in our culture are observable in his life's work. For years, scholars and critics have discussed the "puzzle," the "enigma," the "eccentricity" of Andy Warhol the person. For years, there seems to have been an unspoken consensus that he was pulling the wool over our eyes, remaining aloof and unrevealing behind those dark sunglasses. But the "enigma" of Andy is much larger than a single eccentric life. It's more than one individual could ever be held accountable for, with or without his "responsibility chemicals."

Victor Bockris writes that in the early 1960s, "repetition was in the air." Man Ray "had written about it in his recent autobiography. John Cage thought that it was a basic concept of twentieth-century art." Was autism in the air? Was a neurological revelation on the rise? Was it the advent of mass media that brought the many high-functioning voices of autism forward today? What made it possible finally to look at Hans Asperger's studies, nearly buried for more than fifty years? Did these high-functioning people, through film, TV, and the pop song, finally have the liberty and the means that are necessary to emerge as a socially accessible group of human beings? I think, yes. And Andy Warhol, the jack-of-all-marginal-trades, was an unwitting pioneer of autistic emergence who passed, back and forth, back and forth, between the mirrors, between the glass.

CHAPTER 11

⌒

Playground Comedian

I am going to try a comedy like that.
I am going to like a comedy like that.
Like that is like that it is like that I am going to like that.
I am going to like it like that.

—Gertrude Stein, from "A Comedy Like That"

"Listen, I'm in a slight predicament," Oliver Hardy says to his best pal, Stan Laurel, in the film *Helpmates*. Stan has just walked in the door, and they're standing together in Oliver's living room. Oliver is agitated: "My wife's coming home today at noon, unexpectedly, and *look* at this house!" There's a long pause. Old comedy has its silences and generous close-ups. Oliver's face is grimacing. After a drunken night of cards with the boys, he needs to convince Stan of helping him clean up the place, and quickly! Cigarettes are smoldering in overfilled ashtrays. Empty bottles of alcohol are crammed onto every surface. Chairs are overturned. Furniture is broken. The curtains are down, and the wife's due back in just a few hours! There's no time to lose!

Stan, the sensitive harlequin, scans the living room, making a concerted effort. His empty, honest, open face perceives the crusty dishes with half-eaten food and the spilled cocktail glasses that are dripping onto the floor, yet he seems to miss the point entirely. "What's the matter with it?" he asks, gazing vacantly.

"What's the matter with it!?" Oliver's pulse is rising. "You never *met* my wife, did you?"

Stan pauses to think, "Yes . . . I never did." He's bemused with his own answer.

"Whaddya mean '*Yes,* I never did'?!" Oliver is aggravated to no end. He snatches a photo of his wife off a nearby commode and shoves it in Stan's direction. "*That's* my wife!" He points at a foreboding image of a tough biddy.

Stan studies the photograph conscientiously. He wants to say the right thing. "Isn't she sweet?"

"Charming!" Oliver yells, fed up now with his vain attempts at elucidating the dire situation he's in. Stanny remains good-natured. Angry wife or no angry wife, he's happy to help clean up. His humor lies in the social cues he naively overlooks and in the words he interprets far out of left field. Oliver Hardy's humor, on the other hand, is in his outbursts, which are frequent and improper. This comic duo fascinates Elijah with their missed cues and sophisticated social transgressions. He guffaws and har-hars and asks a million questions about them, always beginning with the words, "Is it funny when . . . ?" as if he were cataloguing every possible instance of humor that exists.

"Is it funny when Stan looks at the picture of Oliver's wife?" Elijah asks.

"Yes, it is."

"Why?"

Comedy is a swift art. Before I can answer Elijah, I have to put the video we're watching on pause, then I move into lengthy descriptions about the plot, the facial expressions, and the meaning of a gesture.

"Oliver's wife is *mean-looking,*" I reply, dramatizing my words while the two comedians stand frozen on our TV screen waiting for me to finish. "Did you get a look at her face?!"

"Yes!" Elijah happily squeals.

"Did you see that *frown?* It was shaped like a horseshoe!"

"YES!" Elijah throws his head back and howls with laughter.

"Well, when that grumpy wife of Oliver's comes home, she's going to be *REALLY* mad because he and his cronies trashed the house last night. JUST LOOK AT THAT MESS!"

Elijah can't stop laughing now. He likes it when I exaggerate the understatement. "That's hilarious!" he yells, using his newly learned synonym for the word "funny." He's always prodding me for more terms he can use in his new investigations into comedy. There's "humorous." There's "witty." There are "side-splitting" and "droll," and, in special circumstances, there's "absurd." Elijah chatters away about the different genres of humor: slapstick, romantic and stand-up comedy, satire, and sarcasm. He collects joke books and memorizes their contents.

"Why did the cow jump over the moon?" He's been telling this one all week.

"I don't know. Why?" I ask, setting him up for the punch line, as if we were a team performing our own material.

"Because the farmer has cold hands."

These days Elijah is less likely to leave the room when friends come over for a visit. Sometimes he even takes center stage, spooning the jokes out with a delivery that is just atypical enough in prosody and pragmatics to keep his listeners rapt and off balance.

This is at home, where everybody knows Elijah and where, as he says, he's "used to people." At school, it's a different story. Elijah is nine. He's in the fourth grade and comes home each afternoon distraught and full of complaints about being teased by the other boys in his class. When he isn't distracted by his comedy, he's easily agitated, withdrawn, and sad. I visit the school, thinking I might get to the bottom of it. The first thing I see there is Elijah's stereotypy, a mild flapping of his hands, something he no longer does at home. It's just enough unusual movement to make another kid feel uneasy and keep a distance.

This year, for the first time in his school career, Elijah has been pegged as an oddball. He wants to interact with the other kids. He approaches them and tells a joke, for that's the way he's taught himself to communicate successfully. But in school, with his peers, it just doesn't fly. After observing him in his morning lesson in the classroom, I stay on for lunch and walk down the hall with him to the raucous din of the cafeteria.

"Wow! It's loud in here," I say as we walk through the doors. "Does the noise in here bother you?"

"Nope!" Elijah answers proudly, as he sits down at a long table and unpacks his ritual bag lunch of tuna fish. In the past year or so, his sensitivity to sound has decreased dramatically. It's now limited mainly to low rumbling noises, like thunder or the sound of a large truck trundling down the road. Other boys are sitting at the table with us, some of them from Elijah's "special ed" class, some of them from the "regular ed" fourth grade. The boys invite Elijah to a game of kickball after lunch.

"No thanks," he says disinterestedly, chewing his sandwich.

"Why don't you play with them?" I ask, encouraging him to take up the offer. Reluctantly, he accepts, asking me to stay for recess and watch him play.

After lunch, on the way outside to the blacktop, Elijah reveals to me that the boys who asked him to play kickball were "lying" because I happened to be sitting there at the lunch table today. There's no time to talk about what he means exactly because the kickball game is already getting started. Elijah trots out onto the blacktop to join in. Within a matter of minutes, I've grocked the situation. I see that the boys who arranged the game are a clique of boisterous fellows, full of mischievous energy and raw interest in teasing. Some of them have emotional issues, the ones in Elijah's special ed class. They inch their way up the hierarchical pyramids of stickers that hang on the classroom wall, indicating the level of their self-control each day. Behavioral modification.

These boys need structure, and like Elijah they are black sheep. They have a status at school they are becoming all too painfully conscious of. Unfortunately, Elijah is the only autistic in his class, a common occurrence. His needs are sometimes very different compared to his majority peers, and in his subdued passivity and good-naturedness, I suspect that his needs are often overlooked.

The rowdy boys, banding together with other rowdy boys from regular ed, have selectively set themselves up to play against a group of underdogs, including Elijah. They boss their opponents around, telling them to take the outfield.

"You're out there with them, Elijah," one of the boys directs him. "Your team pitches. We kick."

"Okay." Elijah runs outfield in a half-directionless manner, joining his motley teammates who have taken up their places at various points. Their pitcher is a very short boy who can't manage to get the ball rolling too fast along the gravelly blacktop. This makes it easy for the teasing team to kick the ball to far-flung places. The ball flies right past lanky Elijah several times, who is spaced out and smiling distractedly like Stan Laurel. Gregory is outfield too. Gregory is the "fat boy," as the clique taunts him. He also has a conspicuous speech delay. After the short boy has pitched a few rounds and the bully team has scored too many points running around the bases, Gregory tries to make it clear that he wants to take a turn at pitching. But the tough kids won't let him. They yell and laugh, "No! No! Off the field!" Gregory stands his ground, plants himself center field, and holds up the game. His sense of dignity and fairness is intact, as he screeches at his taunters, outraged, unable to talk. But it only eggs them on even more. He screeches again, an octave higher, which puts the playground aides on alert. They rush over and remove Gregory from the game, telling him he needs to calm himself down. Nothing is said to the rambunctious gang. Disgusted, Gregory storms away from the placating aides and walks over to the grass where I'm standing. He mills about, cursing in words that I can't fully make out.

"You're right to feel angry," I tell him. "You're a good kid." He curses some more. I nod my head in agreement.

There's only one girl playing kickball today. That's Jenny. She's on Elijah's underdog team, and she's the only girl in his class too. This is a typical gender paradigm in special education, where boys with disabilities and behavioral problems tend to outnumber girls by a wide margin. Jenny gets picked on all the time. She's "dumb." She's "gross." I also happen to know that Jenny has been abused at home and is no longer living with her parents. Elijah's desk is right beside hers in the classroom. One evening, when I went to a parent open house at the school, I saw that both Elijah and Jenny had failed to complete a science project correctly. All the other kids in the class had successfully constructed dioramas of ecosystems that proudly crowned the tops of their desks, sculptural depictions of the habitats of iguanas, tarantulas, and bats. On Elijah's desk, however, pushed into a far corner, were three very small clay figures so obscure in form that I couldn't make them out. On Jenny's desk was the word "DREAMER," spelled out with colorful buttons that she had glued to a piece of cardboard.

Jenny, the dreamer, happened to be the best pitcher in the kickball game. She relieved the short boy and started firing out balls to her opponents with good aim and confidence. All the while, Elijah continued smiling, balls flying right past him. Then a whistle blew. Recess was over.

"Come say good-bye to me!" I called out to him.

"Okay, Val!" He ran across the playground all gangly and happy to see that I was still there.

I kissed him. "Have a good day."

"Okay." Off he went, clumsily, like a puppy, and disappeared into the school.

That night, when Elijah was getting ready for bed, he told me that he didn't like playing kickball and that he usually says "no thanks" when those boys ask him to play.

"I understand why now. I didn't at first," I tell him. "They were very unfair to Gregory, and I heard them say cruel things to Jenny."

I was beginning to absorb more fully the paucity of tools that the teachers, the aides, and the children themselves had to work with when it came to bridging gaps. At age nine, Elijah had not yet had the experience of a good close friend, but if he was going to have one, I was going to respect his choices and not push him into forging relationships just to ease my own concerns about his autistic isolation. "When I make contact with someone," Jim Sinclair writes, "it's special—and not just because a lot of time and effort have gone into producing a response that's a pale imitation of normal social responses. Pale imitations of normalcy aren't worth any of my time and effort at all."

This is a common theme I hear among autistic adults who feel the constant pressures of having to pretend to be normal. As an activist, Jim is invested in preserving authenticity in autistic communication, which is sometimes threatened by neurotypical preoccupation with the "deficits." "When I make a connection," Jim says,

> *it's special because I don't have to do it, but I choose to do it. It's special because I don't generalize very well from one person to another, so everything I do is intensely focused on just that one person. It's special because, having no idea of what's normal and little talent for imitation, I have created something entirely new for that person and that occasion. It's special because I don't know how to take people for granted, so when I'm relating to someone, that person is the most important thing in my world for the duration of*

the contact. . . . I have exactly as many relationships as I want. I relate only as myself, only in ways that are authentic to me. I value people only as themselves, not for their roles or status, and not because I need someone to fill empty spaces in my life. Are these the severe deficits in communicating and relating that I keep reading about?

Actually, there are some pretty serious deficits, but not in my ability to care. There are deficits in my ability to recognize people who aren't able to care, people who aren't authentic, who don't value me as myself, or who aren't connected at their own cores. It's hard for me to tell when someone is lying. It took me a very long time, and a lot of painful experience, just to learn what lying is. And in the social area, as with everything else, I have trouble keeping track of everything that's happening at one time. I have to learn things other people never think about. I have to use cognitive strategies to make up for some basic instincts that I don't have.

"Are girls smarter than boys?" Elijah asks, lying in his bed one night not long after my visit to the school. Our bedtime conversations are very different from the busy comedy patter of daytime, which tends to be more routine and repetitive. At night, we have involved discussions about emotions and social phenomena.

"No," I answer his question. "Girls are smart, and boys are smart too."

"Girls . . . aren't stupid . . . right?"

"You mean because they're girls?"

"Yes."

"Some people think that way about girls, but it's not true."

"The boys in my class think Jenny is stupid."

"Jenny isn't stupid."

"I know."

"Do you like her?"

"Yes."

"Then she's your friend. It's okay to have friends who are girls. *Anyone* who treats you decently can be your friend."

The school year continued, and so did the teasing. Jenny was the only person in Elijah's class whom he wanted to relate to, but whenever we sent notes home to her aunt inviting Jenny over to our house to play, we never received a reply. I was told by Elijah's teacher that the family was very protective and that Jenny didn't go out much.

I was making little progress in my conversations with Elijah's teacher, who, when asked about the teasing and bullying, explained to me that fourth graders in general were just awful to one another. I wanted to find out more about the school culture he was living in. It was obviously taking its toll. Elijah was becoming more depressed and shut down. He began hitting himself on the head again, something he hadn't done since he was a toddler, and he talked about "killing himself" and "jumping off a cliff." I volunteered to be a parent aide in the after-school chess program, which Elijah had expressed interest in. One afternoon a week, I waited in the cafeteria for my charges to be released from their classrooms at the end of the school day. The eight kids participating in the chess class, with the exception of Elijah, were all from regular ed. They swarmed about the cafeteria amid the chaos of parents picking their children up from school and other groups assembling for their after-school subjects. Once all the kids in my group had made it to the cafeteria, I led them down the hall to the library, where the chess instructor was ready for us.

On the second day of the class, while waiting for my group to gather itself, I saw that Elijah's stereotypy was most pronounced in the loud cafeteria. I observed him from afar as he flapped about, excited that it was the end of the school day and that I was there for the chess class. Then a boy named Trevor walked into the cafeteria. He was one of the chess players. Elijah recognized him instantly and made his way across the cafeteria in Trevor's direction. He wanted to make contact, so he stood at some remove facing Trevor and waved his arms up and down and undulated his body, looking like Steve Martin when he does his "wild and crazy guy" routine. Trevor was flabbergasted and afraid. He didn't know what to do. When Elijah began to approach him, he stood there paralyzed.

"Why did the chicken cross the road?" I clearly heard Elijah say through the loud echoes of children's voices bouncing off the cinderblock walls of the cafeteria.

Trevor, deeply confused by Elijah's opening, called out, "Get away from me!"

The rejection sent Elijah flapping back to a distant point where he remained, still looking at Trevor, unsure of what to do and unable to walk away. He laughed nervously and began undulating again. Then a second boy from the chess class walked in and joined Trevor, who was visibly relieved to have another person there beside him. Trevor began whispering things into the other boy's ear, and now both of them were staring at Elijah, sometimes pointing at him. Elijah flapped harder. The phenomenon of otherness unfolded before my eyes. My throat grew swollen with emotion. I walked over to the three boys and, suppressing my tears, told them it was time to go down to the library.

On the way to the library, Elijah walked with me, holding my hand and watching all the other children running wildly ahead of us as they screamed and joked with one another.

"Val, does Trevor think I'm crazy?"

Stung to the core by his question and by what I had just witnessed in the cafeteria, I imagined that Elijah's long days at school often contained such incidents.

"We'll talk about it later, after chess class, okay?" I muttered.

"Okay."

When we entered the library, Elijah immediately ran to the table where Trevor and the other boy were sitting and took a place right beside Trevor.

"Why did the chicken cross the road?"

"Get away from me!" Trevor yelled again. "Don't sit next to me!"

Without a second thought, I walked directly to the boys' table, ignoring the chess teacher, who had just begun a talk on the ins and outs of castling. I squatted down, making my gaze the same level as Elijah's and Trevor's.

"Listen, guys," I said firmly. They both looked startled by my sudden appearance on the scene. "We need to clear something up here. Trevor, Elijah has a disability that isn't easy to see. That's why you're feeling uncomfortable. Elijah, you're feeling uncomfortable because Trevor keeps telling you to go away." Elijah nodded his head. I turned to Trevor again. "Elijah likes you. He wants to get to know you, but he's nervous, and when he talks to you, he might say things that seem odd." Trevor looked surprised and relieved. "Elijah," I said, "Trevor is uneasy with how you're approaching him. You need to slow down a little and say something like 'Hi, Trevor, I'm Elijah. I'm in your chess class.'" Elijah nodded his head again. "Okay, that's all, guys. Just take it slowly." I walked away trembling.

"Hi, Trevor. I'm Elijah. I'm in your chess class," I heard Elijah say behind me. I spun around on my heels.

"Hi." Trevor answered nervously.

"Can I sit here?" Elijah asked.

"Yes."

"Why did the baby cross the road?"

"I don't know. Why?"

"It was stapled to the chicken."

Trevor laughed out loud. At last, some comic relief! Elijah was thoroughly satisfied with himself. I apologized to the teacher, who nodded and returned to his lecture, pointing to a felt chess-board that was hanging on the wall. The board had movable Velcro chess pieces that he maneuvered while talking fast strategy to the kids. Then he set all the children up with their own boards to play against one another. Trevor began to loosen up. He even helped Elijah with some moves, and from time to time I heard them both laughing. When class ended and it was time to go, I took Trevor aside.

"Thanks, Trevor. You're a great kid."

He was silent, nodded good-bye, and walked out the door of the library.

Back home that evening, while Elijah was in the bathtub, he asked, "Val, does Trevor think I'm crazy?"

"We didn't get a chance to talk about that, did we?"

"No. Does Trevor think I'm crazy?"

"No, you're not crazy."

"Is Trevor my friend?"

"He might become your friend. Give it some time."

"Am I crazy?"

"Why do you ask that? Did someone tell you that you're crazy?"

"No. Why did I say the wrong answer in chess class?"

"You mean when you raised your hand and the teacher called on you?"

"Yes."

"You forgot that you were making a move for white, and you tried to play for black. It was a mistake. Every kid in that class makes mistakes."

"Really?" Elijah said incredulously.

"Yeah. Trevor made a mistake once, too. And so did Jennifer. Forgetting things doesn't mean you're crazy, and making mistakes doesn't mean you're crazy. It means you're learning."

"Really?"

"Yeah."

⌒

Late that same night while we were fast asleep, a violent thunder-storm boomed though Woodstock, and Elijah screamed aloud in the dark. I ran into his bedroom to find his thin body sitting bolt upright in bed.

"I'm going to puke!" he cried. "It's too loud!"

I took him by the hand and led him down the hall to the bath-room. Wild lightning illuminated our way. Once in the bathroom, Elijah leaned over the toilet and threw up. I wiped his mouth off with a washcloth and put my arms around him. "It's okay. Let's go back to your room."

In the bedroom, I turned a small lamp on. I held Elijah in my arms in his bed, as the lightning became more infrequent and the thunder moved into the distance.

"Why am I so sensitive to thunder?" he asked.

"It has to do with your senses. Do you know what those are?"

"No."

"Well, your eyes see things. Your tongue tastes things. Your nose smells things, and your ears hear things."

"Oh, right."

"You're very sensitive to certain sounds."

"Am I crazy?"

"No. You're not crazy. You're autistic."

"Is it hard in school because I'm autistic?"

"Sometimes. Let me tell you something."

"Okay, Val."

"It's about a man named Albert Einstein. He was an important scientist who helped people understand many new things about space and the universe. He was able to do this because he could think in pictures. It had to do with his senses and how his brain worked. Albert Einstein happened to be autistic, just like you, and he used to have hard times in school when he was a kid."

"He did?"

"Yes."

"And there are others. Our friend Sharron, for example."

"Sharron?!"

"Yes. Other kids at school used to call her 'Simple Sherry.'"

"That makes me sad."

"Me too."

"Oh, boo-hoo." Elijah performs his expression of sadness, looking forlorn like Stan Laurel when he tweaks the top of his head and makes a melancholy face.

"The kids at school don't know you're autistic, and they don't know how to react when you do something they're not used to, like Trevor did today. But it doesn't mean you're doing anything wrong. It doesn't mean you're crazy. You're being yourself. That's the biggest thing a person can do in a life, and you're doing a fine job."

"Thanks, Val." Elijah sighed and moved close into my body. "Is Jenny autistic?"

"I don't think so, but she's kind like you. She's *compassionate*. Do you know what that means?"

"No."

"It means she has a lot of understanding for other people, no matter what they're like or what they do. She treats you decently. We'll find out if Trevor treats you decently, too. It takes time to figure that out. It took our friend Jim Sinclair a long time to figure it out."

"It did?"

"Yeah. Jim didn't know when people were lying or being unkind. You're sensitive. That's why it's hard sometimes, but sensitivity is also a strength. And there are other things you're good at, like drawing pictures and spelling."

"Yeah, and I'm a good comedian."

"Yes, you are."

Elijah pats me gently on the back. The movement is slightly mechanical and sweet. "Thanks, Val."

"You bet. I'm lucky to have you as my son."

Another mild round of thunder peals in the far distance. Elijah stiffens in my arms. "Oh no! It's coming back!"

"No. It's not coming back. It's moving farther away."

"Is it going to get loud again?"

"No. Soon it will be all gone."

He sighs. "I love you, Val."

"I love you, Elijah." We lie there in silence for a while. "Can you hear the rain on the window? It's very soft."

"Yes. It's relaxing." He sighs again. "Val?"

"Hmmm?"

"Are we like this?" Elijah holds his hand close to my face, so that I can see the gesture he's making. His fingers are crossed into an X. Immediately, I recognize the allusion. It's to a Laurel and Hardy routine in the film *March of the Wooden Soldiers*. Oliver uses the same gesture to describe to Stan the special nature of his relationship to their cranky boss. "Why he and I are like this," Oliver says, crossing his fingers emphatically when Stan challenges him, doubting very much that the boss is going to give them a raise when Oliver asks for it. Later in the film, it turns out that the boss and Oliver aren't as close as the finger gesture implies. In fact, Stan concludes, they're more "like this." He holds his two hands out far apart in the air. Since that night of the thunderstorm, Elijah began using the two gestures to differentiate between people he felt "used to" and those he didn't care to get used to.

"I keep reading that autistic people lack empathy and are unable to take others' perspectives," Jim Sinclair writes, but empathy "is a nebulous term that is often used to mean projection of one's own feeling onto others." He elaborates further:

It is therefore much easier to "empathize" with (i.e. to understand the feelings of) someone whose ways of experiencing the world are similar to one's own than to someone whose perceptions are very different. . . . While [neurotypicals] vary in how much they examine their own assumptions about my experience and take care to communicate their own perspectives in terms I can understand, I have never interacted with [a neurotypical] who was as careful about these things as I am. The extent to which communication occurs in the course of my interactions seems to depend on how effectively I am able to identify discrepancies in understanding and to "translate" both my own and the other person's terms to make sure we're both focussing on the same thing at the same time.

Jim asks an important question that I have yet to see raised in professional literature or in special educational settings. "If I know that I do not understand people and I devote all this energy and effort to figuring them out, do I have more or less empathy than people who do not understand me, but who do not even notice that they don't understand me?"

"Elijah?"

"Yes, Val."

"Do you usually play with other kids on the playground, or do you play alone?"

"Alone."

"What do you do?"

"Oh, comedy . . . or I make up adventures, and I save people."

What is it about the playground comedian? The wacky loner? The solitary oddball? Around this time of Elijah's budding self-awareness of his autistic differences, the film *Man on the Moon* came out, the story of the comedian Andy Kaufman. I remembered Kaufman from his infamous days on *Saturday Night Live* when he was doing Elvis impersonations long before they became a national pastime. By this point in my career as Elijah's mother, I knew a media fixation when I saw one. Was Andy Kaufman a high-functioning autistic? I had to ask myself this, for what little I knew of him was resonant.

Kaufman's mother says that as a very small child, Andy always stared out the window, for very long periods of time. Perhaps he was stimming. He also listened, over and over again, to a set of small children's records, each of them a different bright color. He "would watch the colors spin" on the record player, Kaufman's biographer writes, and "see how the needle went from one edge to the other edge to make the sound come out," "totally content" whenever the record player was on. A few years later, his "programming" began—TV show routines Andy put together and acted out every single day. Eventually, Andy "would break the afternoon down into eight half-hour shows. He would sing and dance, play heroes and apes, judges and defendants, villains and monsters, damsels and dogs." Kaufman himself says that he didn't remember much about the shows, except that one "was like an old-time silent comedy":

> *In those days they showed a lot of silent movies instead of cartoons [on TV]. I didn't understand what was going on in these movies—all I knew was that these people were walking around faster than usual, with music playing . . . when I was re-creating them for myself, there wasn't any plot. It was just me for a half hour walking around fast and doing all kinds of faces and falling down and stuff like that. . . . My parents would say, "Why don't you go out and play?" and I would say, "I can't! I'm putting on my shows."*

Andy's parents often remarked that he had a "sad face" when he wasn't animated by his performances and swung back and forth between these dispositions. "Such energy, enthusiasm! A delight! Then later the withdrawal, the shell, the lonesome eyes," writes his biographer. Andy's first psychological assessment took place when he was in preschool, prompted as it was by the "sad face" and odd behavior his teacher had grown concerned about. There would be more psychological testing throughout his school years and into college. All the while his programs were developing into sophisticated, professional routines. With time, Andy became a paid performer at children's parties, produced his own children's television shows, and appeared as the wacky, unsettling comedian of *Taxi* and *Saturday Night Live*.

"I guess I always had a tendency towards [entertainment] ever since I was a little *little* boy," Kaufman says in an interview.

I used to stay in my room all day long every day while all the other kids were out playing ball . . . and imagine that there was a camera in the wall. . . . I was putting on a television show and . . . it was going out to somewhere in the country or in the world and it was being seen by people. I had about four hours of programming every day. . . . When I got too old to stay at home and I had to go to school, I would continue my programming on the playground. I would go into a corner of the woods [and] put on . . . my television shows, alone. And everyone would just see me in the corner of the woods. It would look like a crazy person talking to [himself]. But one day a little kid was chasing a ball from the ball game and he passed by me and he heard me putting on my show and he stopped and started watching it and he was so fascinated by it. . . . So the other kids started coming around and every day I got more and more kids watching me until I had a big audience. . . . I had this

large following of kids . . . and they stopped playing ball on
the playground. They came into my corner of the woods.

Kaufman's father, Stanley, was known for his angry outbursts
and yelling fits, a shadow trait that often turns up in the parents
of autistic children. He was concerned about his son's future
because Andy "didn't work hard at all" in school. He was disinterested in his studies and distracted all the time, thinking about
his programs. "He was a very, very smart kid," Stanley says, "but
he never wanted anyone to know it." He got mediocre grades
without studying and showed little interest in sports. "It never
occurred to him," his biographer writes, "to adapt or to change
or to be better or to dedicate himself to any popular endeavor
that disinterested him. His nonconformity was not meant as a
statement, although it would be taken as such. If it was rebellion, it was causeless rebellion."

Who is to distinguish the trees from the forest? Who are the pioneers along the borders of social paradigms? I invited Jim Sinclair and Scoot, a boy Jim mentored in the public school in
Syracuse, to come to Woodstock for a visit. Elijah and Scoot
had met earlier that summer on our now yearly journey to
Autreat. Scoot had attention deficit hyperactivity disorder and
was exuberance personified. He had bright red hair and big red
freckles. He was loud, innocently obnoxious, and constantly
way ahead of himself, always running full steam and getting
into touchy incidents like a puppy who doesn't know any better.
Scoot inspired Elijah, who tends to be subdued and less verbal.
They complemented one another that summer at Autreat, running all over the 4-H camp and frolicking in the swimming pool.
Scoot taught Elijah how to make fart noises at loud decibels by
blowing against the palms of his hands. It was a genuine friend-

ship, and Elijah anticipated his buddy's arrival to Woodstock with great excitement.

"Mom, I'm more excited about Scoot and Jim coming than I am about classic comedy." That was saying a lot.

Jim and Scoot traveled by train, along with Jim's service dog, Isosceles, an astute German shepherd–Labrador mix whom Jim had trained. Jim is *the* pioneer who expanded the use of service dogs, or "social signal dogs," into autism spectrum disabilities, beyond their conventional association with assisting the blind. Social signal dogs can help autistic people, who "often seem to be unaware of their environment or uncomprehending of dangers." High-functioning people, Jim says, "may lose track of where they are even in familiar surroundings, or may become confused and disoriented in unfamiliar places." In situations such as these, a social signal dog can be trained to lead the person home or to other destinations. Whenever I see Jim with Isosceles, Jim is bright and alert. The communication between them is subtle and poignant to witness.

Elijah and I are waiting on the platform as Jim's train pulls into the station. Elijah, his hands clapped to his ears, watches the big wheels come to a halt on the tracks. A conductor comes out, opening the door and letting down the noisy metal stairs for the passengers to disembark. Isosceles is first to emerge, followed by Scoot.

"Scoot!" I hear Jim's voice call out sternly from the interior of the train, but the affectionate redhead has already given wild hugs to Elijah and me and is now making a mad dash down the platform.

"C'mon, Jim! An elevator!"

"Scoot! Wait 'til I get off the train!"

Scoot turns around smiling broadly. "Sorry, Jim," he calls out, running back to us. Elijah is amused by the whole scene and laughs joyfully. I help the conductor lift Jim's wheelchair and

bags off the train. Then Jim's figure descends down the two large steps to the platform, balancing itself on crutches. When I first met Jim at Autreat five years ago, he wasn't using a wheelchair yet, but a motor disability that's not associated with his autism has continued to worsen.

"Does she have everything?" the conductor asks me, referring to Jim.

"Yes." I answer, wincing internally at the conductor's faux pas, not because he didn't get Jim's gender right (how could he?), but because he asked me, the nondisabled person, a question he should have asked Jim directly.

Scoot, hearing the conductor feminize Jim, protectively calls out, "He's a boy, not a girl!" But the conductor doesn't seem to hear all this. It's a comedy of errors, and Jim hasn't even gotten off the train yet. Isosceles is sitting alertly on the platform, watching Jim's every motion as he comes down the steps. I open up the folding wheelchair. It's purple, Jim's favorite color. Then I hang Jim's bags on it, most of them purple too, and pick up Scoot's duffel. Jim sits down in the wheelchair, exhausted. His blue eyes look into mine for a moment with emotion, as he hands me the crutches.

"Everyone on that train now knows who Scoot is," he says with a dry wit I have come to love about Jim. "Isosceles, come." He attaches a leash to Isosceles' purple harness.

"Jim! Jim! An elevator! C'mon!" Scoot takes off running again. Elijah, who generally feels no compunction to join in on such rash movements, follows right on Scoot's heels. Then Isosceles begins to pull Jim down the platform in his wheelchair, swiftly catching up with the boys, who run beside them all the way to the elevator at the end of the platform.

We load up the car and pile in. It's a tight fit. Isosceles, sitting in the back seat between the two boys, lets out a loud yelp just as we're pulling out of the parking lot.

"Scoot!" Jim says firmly, as if he were training a young pup. "Leave Isosceles alone."

"Sorry, Jim," Scoot apologizes genuinely, though he will soon forget and pull the dog's tail once more, and Jim, who is utterly devoted to his charge, will remind him again.

Back home, Elijah and Scoot go sledding with a friend of mine while Jim and I stay inside and talk on the couch. Jim is my contemporary in age. He grew up in the sixties and seventies when autism was said to be an emotional disorder.

"I was in treatment with one or another mental health professional starting with kindergarten," he tells me. At that time Jim was put on the drug Mellaril. "They were trying it on everybody," but in Jim's case, there was no indication for it. "I wasn't self-destructive. I wasn't hyperactive. I wasn't violent."

"What is Mellaril?" I ask.

"It's an antipsychotic. It's a major tranquilizer. It's used for people who are very out of control and destructive. The effect it had on me was basically to move me from being withdrawn to being catatonic." The point was not that Jim personally felt Mellaril was an appropriate drug to use on people, especially on those who cannot or do not give informed consent (an unsettling chapter in disability history), but that it was being prescribed for behaviors Jim did not have. At that time, people were also buying into the idea that autistic people were psychologically trapped inside their shells. This was when many clichés about autism were established.

"I always heard this phrase: 'Come out of your shell,' and that there was this normal little kid in there waiting to come out," Jim tells me. "But the more that I became able to communicate, the more apparent it became that what was inside was a lot more peculiar than anyone had suspected when I couldn't communicate."

Jim didn't speak until he was twelve years old. "The shorthand way that I put it is that up until I was twelve years old, there was talk about putting me into an institution because I couldn't talk, or I didn't talk, and then after I started talking, they wanted to put me in an institution because of the things that I said when I did talk."

Jim and Scoot stayed the weekend, and Elijah's spirits soared. He stopped hitting himself and saying self-deprecating things, like "I'm stupid" or "I'm worthless." Jim has a theory that many autistic people can preserve identity in the unremitting neurotypical environment by spending time with each other. Plus, it can be a lot of fun. I saw this clearly in Elijah's turn of mood.

That night at dinner, while the boys ate pizza with me at the dinner table, Jim sat in the corner of the room where he was able to eat in our midst and still be able to swallow. Jim has trouble with some aspects of motor planning when he has to integrate socializing and eating at the same time. Munching their pizza, the two boys joked and pranked and gave each other big smiles. Occasionally, Jim said something to us from his quiet corner. We were talking about autism and how few and far between autistic people can sometimes be in the neurotypical environment.

"It's a strange world out there, Jim!" Elijah suddenly called out to him.

"You don't have to tell me that, Elijah."

In the film *The Music Box*, Stan Laurel and Oliver Hardy play two deliverymen who have a piano to bring to an exquisite home that's perched at the top of a steep San Francisco hill. A long outdoor staircase leads up to the top. The boys attempt the hill several times, heaving and pushing the crated piano up and up, but time and again it goes catapulting back down to the bottom. On one attempt up the stairs, the two deliverymen encounter a fine gentleman who is on his way down. The gentleman is wearing an expensive top hat and a fine suit, carrying a pair of fancy white gloves in his hand. Upon seeing the two good-for-nothings standing in the way, the fine gentleman stops in his tracks. He twists his handlebar mustache impatiently, then frantically waves his white gloves at them. The boys are too tired. They just don't see him, resting, as they are, against the large wooden crate, staring into nothingness.

"Well!" the gentleman explodes. "When are you two numbskulls going to take this thing out of the way?!" He has a thick German accent.

Oliver, who seems to have met his match, retorts, "What's it to you?"

"I should like to pass," says the man, incredulous that Oliver does not see the obvious.

"Why don't you walk around!" Ollie replies, equally agitated. He makes an emphatic gesture waving his hand slowly around the big crate.

"What?! Walk around?! Me?! Professor von Schwarzenhofel, M.D., A.D., D.D.S., F.L.D., F.F.F. and F. should walk around?!!!!!" This is the 1930s, when a professor with a thick German accent is synonymous with Freudian psychoanalysis, but our two deliverymen could care less about his academic status. "Get that thing out of my way!!!!" the professor screams hysterically, moving into a tantrum long before even Oliver can work one up. In heated excitement, the professor knocks his top hat off his own head, causing it to fall down, down, down the long stairs, to where it lands in the street far below. A few seconds go by. Then a truck runs over the hat.

"I'll have you arrested for this!!! I'll have you put in jail!!!" the professor bellows, belligerently pushing his way past Stan and Oliver and storming down the hill.

Elijah always laughs his head off at this segment of the film and wants to rewind it again and again. We all need a little irreverence to stay happy. Take Muskie's Web site, for example. Muskie is an ANI member and an autism activist who designed a Web page that parodies neurotypical culture and its othering

attitudes toward autistics. The Web page is a spoof on a disorder called "neurotypical syndrome": "Neurotypical syndrome is
a neurobiological disorder characterized by preoccupation with
social concerns, delusions of superiority and obsession with
conformity. Neurotypical individuals often assume that their
experience of the world is either the only one, or the only correct one. . . . Tragically, as many as 9,625 out of every 10,000
individuals may be neurotypical." It's all in jest, and it's refresh-
ing to see the tables turned, to see Elijah move entirely out of his
depression and have renewed energy to deal with the teasing
and constant misfirings in communication at school. Who is
crossing borders?

By the time Andy Kaufman was a young man,

> *he was known to all perimeters of the Kaufman family as
> the most unusual/colorful specimen ever to emerge from
> their gene pool. At every family Passover seder, for instance,
> Andy would famously disappear from the dinner table, run
> around to the front door, reappear clad in linens and wear-
> ing a long false beard, then wordlessly reenter to take the
> ceremonial seat saved for the Hebrew prophet Elijah, so as
> to sip Elijah's unsipped wine and entertain the relatives.*

Elijah's cup is full. He has his special interests. He has his
comedy and his ups and his downs. He has his autistic mentors
and his friends.

"Val, can I be a comedian and be autistic too?" he asks me one
evening shortly after Jim's and Scoot's visit.

A friend of ours who is sitting with us, a computer specialist,
has a ready answer for him: "Can I be a network engineer and
have blonde hair?"

"Yes," Elijah says.

"Can Val be a writer and have brown eyes?"

"Yes."

"Well, you can be a comedian and be autistic."

Elijah smiles mischievously at the thought of this.

"What is it, Elijah? What are you thinking about?" I ask him.

"Why did the chicken cross the road?"

CHAPTER 12

Cracking Code

"It feels like home here," Elijah says, sleepily viewing all the objects that line the narrow windowsills of Sharron's boat. It's six in the morning. The sky coming in is a mix of blue and pale orange from the floodlights that illuminate the marina where *Sojourner* is docked. I've been awake for hours, lying beside Elijah, gazing out at the otherworldly sky.

"This is Sharron's home sweet home," I say as he stretches his long limbs in the small cubby bed we shared last night.

"Hey, you guys. You're awake," Sharron calls from inside the dark bow of the boat where she slept, having given up her bed for us. "I'm glad you like it here, Elijah."

"Yeah." He stretches again. "It's . . . cozy . . . Sharron," he yawns.

"It's cozy all right. You bed hog!" I tease him, shoving his sprawling arms and legs back over to his side of the bed.

Elijah chuckles, proud of himself, then puts his arms around my neck and squeezes.

"Hey, Elijah!" Sharron speaks out from the darkness again. "Guess what?"

"What?"

"We're going to Disneyland!"

"When?!"

"Today!"

"Cool!"

In the past few months, Elijah has begun to use small collo-quialisms and insert them purposefully into his slow-paced speech. "Is Hal coming with us?"

"Yeah. Hal's coming too," Sharron replies.

"All right!"

Hal, whom Elijah and I know from our yearly trips to Autreat, is a mild-mannered fellow with Asperger's syndrome and a good pal of Sharron.

"Hey, guys," I interrupt their banter, "I need to pee. Do you have to go too, Elijah?"

"Nope."

"Okay, then, I guess I'm on my own."

"Yep."

"Take the key with you," Sharron says, emerging in her night-gown. "It's hanging near the telephone."

While Sharron busies herself with milk and cereal for Elijah, I get up from the narrow bed and join her in the limited floor space of the boat, throwing on yesterday's clothes. They are soft from the long flight across the country and the sweaty drive from the airport in Hal's Jeep.

"You know, I could use a cup of coffee," I say. "Is there a place around here that's open this early in the morning?"

"There's a diner where all the fishermen go. It's out on the pier."

"Okay. See you guys in a little while."

Heartened by the promise of caffeine, I step outside the small door of the boat onto the stern and into the open air. The orange light of the marina lamps has now fully dissolved into the blue sky. The whole scene here reminds me of the bohemian days when

Sharron and I first met in Woodstock. Cramped quarters, little sleep, late nights, and good satiric humor. There's a small grill on the back deck of the boat where Sharron sometimes cooks up a meal. Her scooter and mountain bike are neatly tucked beside it. Potted flowers are blossoming, and there is a place to hang up wet laundry. I step over the side of the boat, place a firm foot on the dock, then swing the rest of my body over to the other side.

Sojourner has given Sharron the reliable shelter she needed when we first met. She sold some of her paintings to purchase the boat, whose two old engines no longer work. But she floats, and with a slip rent at the marina of $300 a month, Sharron can manage to keep a place of her own, using the monthly social security checks that she qualified for not long after her diagnosis. Sharron once told me that without those checks, she'd be living under a bridge. The marina is no middle-class romantic idyll, no trendy port for the rich and the beautiful. It is tough and gritty, particularly at night, but it's a place where Sharron's hermit nature can thrive. I love Sharron for this, for her dogged self-reliance and her unpretentious wisdom.

The morning air coming off the ocean moves into my lungs. It's soothing to be on water, to walk with this slight spring under-foot down a long dock and amble past a row of fishing boats. I read all their names, taking my time, then begin to drift in and out of some lines from "Journey Out," a poem by Ingeborg Bachmann about being at sea:

> *The first wave of night hits the shore,*
> *the second already reaches you.*
> *But if you stare sharply yonder,*
> *you can still see the tree*
> *which defiantly lifts an arm*
> *—the wind has already knocked one off*
> *—and you think how much longer,*

how much longer
will the twisted timber withstand the weather?
Of land there's nothing more to be seen.
With your hand you should have dug into the sandbank
or tied yourself to the cliff with a strand of hair.

For Bachmann, looking back on a receding shore is an act of memory, of taking stock of hardships so well endured they have softened into beauties one never wished to leave behind. It's good to be near Sharron's unearthing mind again where my past and present with her and Elijah have become a tumble of beauties.

I continue walking the straight and narrow path of the dock. When I reach the end, I push open a heavy metal gate that clangs firmly shut behind me. The sound of the gate is familiar, as if I've opened it and let it fall closed again many times before. The bathroom, which only residents of the marina have keys to, is a few steps farther away. Later, I think as I unlock the door, I'll come back here to take a shower and wash away the sweat and salt from yesterday. After picking Elijah and me up from the airport, Hal and Sharron had taken us directly to the beach where the sea opened itself up so large to Elijah that he ran, overjoyed, right into the big waves and gleefully allowed them to toss him anywhere they pleased.

Bachmann continues in her poem,

Then something happens with the ropes,
you are called and you are happy
that you are needed. Best of all
is the work on ships
that sail far away,
the knotting of ropes, the bailing of water,
the caulking of leaks, the guarding of freight.
Best to be tired and at evening

to collapse. Best in the morning
to awaken clear to the first light,
to rise up beneath the immovable sky,
to ignore the impassable water,
and to lift the ship over the waves
towards the forever recurring shore of the sun.

It has been well over seven years since Elijah had his first seizure and since the revelation of autism was upon us. Though I would not have had the mind back then, today I can acknowledge this: best of all has been the hard work, the tiredness, the journey out with Elijah.

Beyond the bathroom, large asphalt parking lots extend all the way to the distant pier. I walk through one lot after another, training my eyes on the wide ocean, keeping the fast food conglomerates—the builders of the vacant, sterile lots that interrupt the continuity of our lives—pushed into my blind periphery. This place between Sharron's marina and the pier is a no-man's-land, a built-up trap of Denny's and Wendy's and Red Lobster. Sharron's neighborhood, on the other hand, has character and currency. Immediately opposite her dock is a worn-down pedestrian zone, a strip of older establishments, greasy spoons, and dingy bars that predate the modern asphalt that encroaches from all sides.

"It's safe here," she assured me late last night while Elijah slept, though I wasn't to go out alone to the bathroom in the dark. "No one would ever guess that people live here," she added. "They think it's all fishing boats."

Sharron is living in her unassuming paradise. Her neighborhood is a microcosm of working-class people who run the cafés, along with a few alcoholic regulars who haunt the bars at night. She knows everybody, and they greet her when she's out and about. Yesterday evening, after our swim in the ocean, we ate fish and chips at one of the cafés with trusty *Sojourner* in full view from our table. The night air was balmy. We sat outdoors in sturdy wooden chairs at a checkered vinyl tablecloth. Sharron talked with the waitress, while Hal and I drank a pitcher of beer that tasted weak but made me dizzy nonetheless.

"I like California!" Elijah exclaimed. He was having a grand time. Sharron had unloaded her scooter off the boat and pushed it along the dock all the way to the café. After our meal, Elijah rode up and down the strip, zooming past our table from time to time, grinning broadly and pumping hard with his foot on the pavement. Each time he passed by, Sharron positively beamed with pride for her grandson.

"Maybe you and your boyfriend will get back together again," she encouraged me as we followed Elijah's motions. I had been bemoaning my separation, one month ago, from a man I thought would be a companion. Ever since Ben and I split up, I had had my share of attempts at new relationships, always unable to sustain them longer than a year. Inevitably, tension would build up. I had too many responsibilities living with an autistic child and pursuing my professional ambitions. There was little time left for a partner, and I suppose I never really expected to cultivate something of longevity during those hard years when Elijah and I slogged through the long days of unrelenting crises. But hadn't things changed? For here before me is Elijah, gliding up and down the marina on his own two feet, pausing now and then to call out independent opinions: "I like California!" "I like the beach!" "I like the big waves. Let's go back to the rough ocean!" He speeds off again, and Hal gets up from the table to join him.

"You know," I tell Sharron, "Ben and I are becoming friends again."

"Maybe you two will get back together," she responds, not surprised in the least. Sharron always manages to say things that hang in the air, things that few have the pluck to speak aloud.

"It's uncanny," I reply.

"What is?"

"On the day that my boyfriend and I split up, so did Ben and his girlfriend. I went to Ben's house to pick Elijah up. It was Mother's Day. I took Ben aside, intending to tell him about my breakup, but before I could even say a word, he was telling me about his own separation. I guess it sounds sorta like a soap opera."

"Yeah," Sharron repeats, "maybe you two will get back together again. Maybe he's changed."

"Maybe we've all changed."

Elijah speeds by again. Hal follows casually behind him. I'm now lost in thoughts of Mother's Day and how Ben and I revealed our mutual losses to one another as if we were confessing something else. What else? Instinctually, I had put my arms around him and had sought some kind of union in that embrace. Ben was my comrade. We were weary veterans who understood the thick and the thin of each other's lives and the life of our son.

What will happen? Is there a code in the ever-shifting sea of events that wants to be cracked open? All I know is right now I'm content, right now, right here on the pier where I'm watching the sea. Inside the diner, fishermen are laughing and eating their hearty breakfasts. I pay the waitress at the counter a dollar for coffee. She pours it into a Styrofoam cup. I add some cream and walk out onto the pier to lean against the railing and watch the sea arch visibly beyond the horizon down to distant points of the earth. This is a place to recollect and collect myself. "What will happen," asks Ingeborg Bachmann, "if we survive the test of the beauty?"

Refreshed by solitude and back at the boat again, I find Sharron and Elijah preoccupied with their respective projects. Sharron is reading e-mail from a philosophical friend in San Francisco who recently completed treatise titled "A Topological Theory of Autism."

"Greg is one of the Autastics," Sharron tells me.

"Who are they?"

"They're one of the biggest groups of Asperger people in the country. There are about a hundred members, and they meet once a month in San Francisco. LA has its own version called Agua. I'm a member of that. California is happening, man! The Autastics and Agua aren't going away!"

Elijah, lounging on the bed, is playing a handheld electronic game, a gift from Sharron that prompts him to make words from jumbled sets of letters and spell them correctly. Every so often Sharron leans over him to check his answers.

"Good spelling! Good spelling!" Then she turns to me. "Wanna see my new painting? It's for the Autism Society of Los Angeles' annual Christmas card. They asked me to do it."

"Sure!"

"It's a religious motif," she adds with a tinge of mischief in her voice. She takes out a photograph of the painting and hands it to me. "It's the baby Jesus and Mary and Joseph."

The implications of the painting are quietly radical. Only the initiated among Sharron's audience would know about the recent debates in the disability community on Jesus' neurobiological status. Was he a high-functioning autistic? Was he manic-depressive? Sharron has made the holy family in her painting a family of color. Jesus is a curly-haired baby with brown skin. Radiant, colorful light shines forth from his head, while his admiring parents have slightly concerned expressions on their faces. They know their child is unusual. They are awed and afraid.

"Another beautiful painting, Sharron. I like your religious art."

"Thanks."

This year, Sharron participated as a guest speaker at a big autism conference in LA. She sat on a panel and spoke about her life experience, after which she was awarded a special certificate printed in fancy gold lettering.

"Everything was fine, but when they gave me that certificate, I thought, 'Oh-oh, I'm not *normal*.' I didn't know I was still that prejudiced about autism."

As she talks about the phenomenon of internalized normalism, Elijah moans from where he's sitting on the bed. He's frustrated because he can't get the spelling of a word right. His temper is getting up.

"You'll get it," Sharron assures him, then turns to me again. "I like Elijah's long hair."

"So do I. He wants it that way."

"Do people think he's a girl sometimes?"

"All the time. But he says he doesn't care."

"That's good."

Elijah is immersed. The frown has left his face now, and perky sounds are emitting from the little box in his hands.

"You should get him a Gameboy for his tenth birthday," Sharron advises me. "Elijah would like that." She peeks over his shoulder. "Good spelling!"

"Thanks, Sharron," he replies, fixed on the small screen.

We all lay around the boat a little longer, waiting for Hal to arrive.

"I have plans for a new painting," Sharron announces.

"Oh yeah?"

"It's going to be a big circus, a big autism conference. Crowds of people are attending, and there are different acts going on. The circus people doing the tricks are performing for the mainstream people who are watching them. That's what it's like at an autism conference. The Asperger people always seem like they're having more fun than the neurotypicals who organized it!" Sharron cackles at this realization, then continues with her description. "High up above all the conference participants. I'm gonna have Temple Grandin, holding a small parasol, walking the tightrope. A bear holding another parasol will be following behind her. And little Puzzle Head is in the painting, too."

"Who is that?"

"You know, the logo for the Autism Society of America."

"Oh! That thing!" Little Puzzle Head, as Sharron calls him, is an object of derisive criticism among autistic activists. The logo is an image of a child whose head is composed of puzzle pieces. In some of the newsletters I've received in the mail over the years from various ASA chapters, a piece is often missing from the puzzle head. The person, the logo implies, is incomplete and mysterious.

"In my painting, Little Puzzle Head is wearing a top hat! He'll look kinda like Elijah." Sharron laughs. "I wanna sell it as a poster at the big, national ASA convention next year. Do you think they'll get mad at me?"

Although the ASA is an important organization that was established in the 1970s by parents who were fed up with psychoanalytic dogma, people like Sharron, Jim Sinclair, and Muskie have moved things a step further along in the process. They are autism's direct voices, and because of this, from time to time, they must challenge even the ASA and its values regarding disability.

"One day," I tell Sharron, "I'd love to see the ASA commission an autistic person—you know, a visual thinker—to design the logo. Who knows, maybe it'll be you."

Elijah is now cracking code with ease on his new game, finding hidden words in the jumbled letters. Then Hal arrives and sticks his head in through the door of the boat.

"Hey, Elijah!"

"Hi, Hal." Elijah looks up from his game. "Is it time to go to Disneyland?"

"That's right."

"Yahoooooo!" Elijah tosses the plastic box aside, gets up from the bed, and joins Hal out on the stern.

"Don't you need your shoes?" I hear Hal ask just outside the door.

"Oh, right . . . Duh!" Elijah answers, jesting about his own forgetfulness.

The peak of the Matterhorn shines with meaning in the distance. We have walked through the grandiose gates of Disneyland and into nostalgia. The Matterhorn, with its white peak and its strange synthetic surface that glistens in the hot Anaheim sun, has suddenly conjured up my father. Dr. T loved amusement parks, especially with his six progeny tailing him like goslings from one ride to the next.

"Let's go on The Pirates of the Caribbean again!" I remember him calling out to me and my brothers and sisters on a visit to Disneyland more than twenty-five years ago, when I was about Elijah's age. My father walked with a quick stride at amusement parks. "Look! Hurry up! There's no line!" he yelled, happily gesticulating a hundred yards ahead of us. I remember quite a lot about The Pirates of the Caribbean. I remember stimming on the electric fireflies that gently pulsed above the calm dark waters just before our galleon ship plunged down into the underworld caves of the pirates.

"Grandpa Mel loved this ride," I tell Elijah just as our boat is entering the secret grottos and the lyrics of the pirates' theme song surround us in perfect stereo. *Yo-ho, yo-ho, the pirate's life's for me!* Elijah is enamoured. I saw him stimming on the fireflies as we passed by them a moment ago, and now he's dragging his hand through the water beside the boat, absorbing all the awesome goings-on around him. The mechanized mannequins who talk and drink and gamble and brawl once hypnotized my father with their bizarre humor and theatrical scenarios.

"Grandpa Mel is here. I saw him!" Elijah reveals to me later, after we've disembarked from the ride. Elijah is always playing tricks on me when I get wistful about my dear old dad.

"Yes!" I play along with Elijah. "Grandpa Mel is here in *spirit*." We're just getting into a long line for The Haunted Mansion. "I'll bet he's inside that haunted house! Ha, ha, ha, ha, ha, ha!" I laugh ghoulishly and point at the big mansion.

"Did Grandpa Mel like Raiders of the Lost Ark?" Elijah wants to know.

"That ride wasn't here when I came to Disneyland with him."

"It wasn't?! When did you come here?"

"That was way back in the summer of '73," I answer, making my voice into a shaky old woman's. "I was about your age back then, sonny." I pat him on the head with a trembling, elderly hand, and he chortles.

"Hey, Elijah. Do you wanna go on Raiders of the Lost Ark again?" Sharron asks with a twinkle in her expression. "That's my favorite ride. That's why I'm wearing my Indiana Jones hat today."

"It is?"

"Yeah."

"Let's go!" Elijah abandons the line we're standing in and takes off running in a random direction, until Hal, who has a map of the entire park incised perfectly in his mind's eye, sets things straight.

"This way, Elijah."

"Oh! Duh!"

They hold hands and begin walking in the right direction, just a pace ahead of me and Sharron.

"The last time I was in Disneyland," Sharron remembers rather loudly, "all the lines for the rides were short, so we perseverated on Raiders of the Lost Ark. We went over and over and over again. It was like going to heaven."

"It was?!" Elijah is amazed.

"Yeah, and the more you go on Raiders of the Lost Ark, the more you become desensitized to the sound. Do you know what that means?"

"No."

"If you go on Raiders of the Lost Ark enough times, you don't have to cover up your ears anymore."

"Really?!" Elijah is incredulous. All day long, he's been holding his hands close to his ears, blocking out the loud noises of the rides.

We reach the entrance to Raiders of the Lost Ark and find no visible line spilling out from its main gate. "Yahhooooo!" We glide inside, freely moving through the cool, cavelike passageways that are typically packed with slow queues of bored people. We are swift and liberated, and the air-conditioning feels good. Eventually, we'll reach the huge subterranean chambers of this fantastic ancient mine, and the big Jeeps will take us on a perilous journey of death-defying adventure. The lanterns on the stone walls flicker and grasp at Elijah's attention. Low rumbling sounds come and go, as if the heavy rock above us were threatening to collapse. Elijah stops a moment, dead in his tracks.

"Wait!" he yells, stimming on one of the lanterns, his hands tightly sealing his ears. "Wait!" he says again. Then, cautiously, still gazing fixedly into the flickering light, he removes his hands. There's more rumbling, the mine grows dim, the lanterns nearly snuff themselves out, then miraculously they brighten again.

"Look, Val! I don't need to cover my ears!"

"I see that! Terrific!"

Elijah pries his eyes away from the lantern, smiles happily at the three of us, and darts ahead, leading the way back and forth, back and forth through a zigzagging path that is unpeopled. Thunder booms. The volume is growing more intense. It rises sharply as we reach the colossal chamber where the giant Jeeps are pulling in for passengers to board. Elijah claps his hands to his sensitive ears, turns around, and looks at us with a pained expression on his face.

"It's okay. One step at a time," I assure him, hearing the concern in my own voice.

He smiles at Sharron and Hal who have moved in behind me.

"Sharron!" he yells through the din.

"What?!"

"Are you ready?!" He sounds as if he's announcing the beginning of a horse race.

"Yeah!" Sharron joins his enthusiasm.

"I wanna ride with you!"

"Okay!"

They board the front seat of a Jeep that has just pulled in. An usher tells them to put on their seat belts, then directs Hal and me to sit behind them. After clicking my belt into place, I see that Elijah is struggling with his own, nearly in a panic. He has freed a hand from his right ear while attempting to block the noise out by squeezing the ear into his shoulder. The Jeep is revving its engine, preparing for departure. The sound is huge. The ride could take off before Elijah's safely buckled in! But then his hand quickly moves back over the exposed ear. He's managed to click the belt into place. I tap him on the shoulder. He turns around with an adventuresome grin on his face, and I give him the thumbs-up sign. He yells something in reply.

"What?! I can't hear you!"

"I . . . LIKE . . . CALIFORNIA!" his voice makes its way through the cacophony all the way to me. "THIS . . . IS . . . MY . . . FAVORITE . . . RIDE!" Then, removing a hand from one ear, just for a flash of a moment, Elijah gives me a swift thumbs-up, and our wild Jeep takes off!

Sharron's advice to give Elijah a Gameboy for his tenth birthday was typically on target. In no time, he was applying the logical structures of the game to nearly every aspect of his waking life. When Elijah wasn't actually holding the small green box in his hands and deftly manipulating the moving images on the screen with the small control buttons, he was sketching situations inspired by games like Ray Man and Dragon Dance. The house filled up with drawings again, all of them depicting some point of action on a particular level of a game as it appears on the Gameboy screen. He'd ask me to take a marker in my hand and trace a path, just as the movement would happen on the screen, through the dangerous landscapes he had originated on paper.

It was a summer of Gameboy levels and passwords and special lists. In a five-subject spiral notebook, Elijah filled page after page with titles for Gameboy games he intended to design someday. When asked about any title on the list, he seamlessly launched into the details of how the future game would be structured. He improvised fantastic names for all the levels one would rise to and what a player would achieve by maneuvering the hero through sundry perilous obstacles.

His longest list of titles nearly topped a thousand entries. Often they involved him as the protagonist-hero of the game. There were Elijah in the Earth, Elijah's Prisoned World, and Elijah Is Up to Mischief (versions I and II). There was a comedian series that included the Charlie Chaplin Game Pack and the Adventures of Jim Carrey. There were Evil Ape and its companion, Evil Monkey. Crack the Code. Be Bossy! Pinocchio Saves the Day. Feast on It! Underground Meany. Blood Meany. Speak French. Knuckle Sandwich.

Sometimes the titles read like telegraphic diary entries of a day in the life of Elijah. After spending an afternoon with a Buddhist friend, for instance, he entered Chanting Boy onto his long list. One night I rented the film *Rain Man* and watched it with

Elijah, to find the following morning that he had added Rain Boy as a new entry on the list. Most of Elijah's conversations, especially during the day, were infused with Gameboy lingo. "I'll bet you're wondering what it's like in level two of Spellbound Forrest" was a common opener to his conversations with me or anyone else who happened to be around.

Summer flew by. Elijah's long lists were proof of the passage of time. One late August night, Ben and I stumbled into one another at a concert in town.

"Hi. Where's Elijah?" I ask, for it's Ben's night to have Elijah at his place.

"He's sleeping over at my parents'."

"Are you here alone?"

"Yeah."

"Me too."

Ben and I sat beside each other at the concert, then decided afterward to go out for a drink somewhere. Considering our options on a late night in tiny Woodstock, standing out on Tinker Street beneath the sky, we heard music wafting over from a nearby restaurant.

"Let's go in there," I suggested. "They have a bar upstairs."

We walked across the street and went inside. The place was full of young men and women in their twenties listening to techno. A strobe light was on, and Ben, as if he were in an old silent movie, brought two brandy snifters of Grand Marnier from the bar, sitting down at the small table I had found for us. We sipped our liqueur and watched an eccentric young woman with a bandanna on her head take up a microphone and sing, artfully placing her voice among the shifting synthesized rhythms and the spliced-in lyrics from familiar old tunes. The room filled up with dancers. They moved their arms about in the vibrating light.

"Do you want to dance?" Ben asked.

"Sure."

We got up and moved onto the floor, experimenting with our bodies in the music that was so far from our experience. Ben and I were the oldest people there. We didn't speak at all to one another. It was too loud for that, but I watched everything. I glimpsed Ben's face in the strobe light, taking in his familiar worry lines, noting the new gray in his hair just above his ears. Seeing me watching him, Ben's lips moved into a generous smile. We held a friendly gaze until, overwhelmed by emotion, I averted my eyes and returned to dancing. Our bodies didn't touch that night, but we danced in an intimate space of memory among these young people and their scene.

Before Elijah was born, Ben and I had traveled around the world together. We lived in Tokyo for a year as a kind of daring honeymoon after our marriage, then moved on through the rest of Asia and into parts of Europe. Being here in this bar scene reminded me of all the other foreign situations we had walked into together, sometimes willingly, sometimes not: strip bars in Pataia, Kabuki and sumo wrestling in Tokyo, abandoned temples in Pagan, and emergency rooms of hospitals. The strobe lights put me into a trance. I felt both close and far away from Ben. After a few songs, we sat down on a couch and watched the dancers some more. Then Ben said he was tired and we agreed that it was time to go home. We got up, walked out into the summer air on the street, embraced one another, said "Good-bye" and "It was fun" and "It was sweet," then walked back to our separate cars and drove them to our separate homes, mutually wondering what had just happened.

"I love your eyes! They are gold like diamonds!" Elijah says to me the following night as I'm putting him to bed. He's speaking like a gypsy with a mysterious accent. "I love your nose! It is silver like Russian coins!" This summer Elijah has been seeing a reading tutor once a week. Recently she taught him how to make similes, and now it's become a language game during his bedtime routine. He concocts wacky constructions and laughs at himself. "I love your chin! It's like . . . it's like . . . it's like a pizza!"

"My chin is like a pizza?! How attractive!"

"Yeah!" he screeches, satisfied with his Dada experiments. Then the room falls silent for a moment. At last, Elijah is getting sleepy, I think, until he says, "I'll bet you're wondering what it's like on level three of Rocky Peaks."

"Yes . . . I'm wondering," I reply for the umpteenth time.

He launches into a long-winded description, telling me his strategies for tomorrow's Gameboy session. He knows he's allotted only forty-five minutes each day, and in that time, he has premeditations about what he will accomplish.

"Do you think I'll get to level four of Rocky Peaks tomorrow?"

"I don't know, but if you do a little every day, eventually you reach your goals."

"Yes!" he sighs, happily imagining himself ascending higher and higher up the levels.

What will happen? What will come of this?

"Val, I had a dream last night," he says, abandoning the Gameboy thinking.

"What was it about?" I'm lying beside him, feeling sleep about to overcome me.

"I was a detective, and I was saving all my friends on the playground."

"You're a good guy, Elijah."

"I know. You were in the dream too, Val."

"I was? What was I doing?"

"You were cracking code." As he says this, Elijah wriggles in the blankets, as if a bolt of joyfulness has moved through his body so profoundly he cannot contain it. "You were cracking code, my mom," he repeats and sweetly pats me on the shoulder. Then he turns his back toward me and snuggles his long body into mine. I put my arms around him.

"Time to sleep now."

The room is all silence for a long time. Elijah, I think, has surely drifted off to sleep, until I perceive him softly whispering something to himself.

"The wheels on the bus go round and round, round and round, round and round . . ."

"I haven't heard that song since you were a toddler! Did you know that was your favorite when you were three years old?"

"Nope." He continues singing. "The wipers on the bus go swish swish swish, swish swish swish, swish swish swish . . ."

What will happen if we survive the test of beauty?

"Guess what, Val?" Elijah abruptly stops his singing. "I can tell the future!"

"You can?"

"Yep."

"What's going to happen?"

"In two years . . ."

"Yeah?"

"I'll be twelve years old."

Web Sites by and for Autistic People and for Autistic Advocacy

http://www.loree.org

> *Sharron Loree's Web site, where you can view Loree's art and learn more about her.*

http://www.autistics.org

> *Resources by and for persons on the autistic spectrum, one of the most politically forward-looking sites on autism. From this site you can also send greeting cards that celebrate neurodiversity and autism.*

http://www.ani.autistics.org

> *Web site of Autism Network International, an autistic-run self-help and advocacy organization for autistic people that sponsors the annual Autreat featured in Chapter 8 of this book.*

http://www.amug.org/~a203/index.html

> *Asperger/Autism On-the-Same-Page, an autistic-run resource site (with great visuals!).*

Notes

CHAPTER 2: THE GIFT OF LOSS

18 *"The limits of my language"*: Ludwig Wittgenstein, trans. C. K. Ogden, *Tractatus logico-philosophicus* (New York: Routledge, 1988), no. 5.6.

18 *"The world is all"*: Ibid., no. 1.

19 *When using Phenobarbital:* http://www.onhealth.com (search: "phenobarbital").

19 *Symptoms of a Phenobarbital overdose:* Ibid.

20 *Less serious side effects:* Ibid.

20 *Phenobarbital is habit forming:* Ibid.

24 *"No new world without a new language"*: Ingeborg Bachmann, trans. Michael Bullock, *The Thirtieth Year* (New York: Holmes and Meier, 1996), 50.

26 *"Are you waiting for somebody?"*: Franz Kafka, trans. Willa and Edwin Muir, *The Castle* (New York: Random House, 1974), 20.

29 *"Whereof one cannot speak"*: Wittgenstein, *Tractatus logico-philosophicus*, no. 7.

CHAPTER 4: THE COINCIDENCE OF SHARRON LOREE

45 *"Kafka is perhaps not meaningless"*: Franz Kempf, *Everyone's Darling:*

Kafka and the Critics of His Short Fiction (Columbia, S.C.: Camden House, 1994), 69.

52 *"I can't shut out background"*: Temple Grandin, *Dr. Temple Grandin Speaks on "Visual Thinking of a Person with Autism,"* video, Future Horizons, 1999. The material quoted from this video is being used here as a means of reconstructing the content of an unreleased video that was shot of Temple Grandin in 1993 but that no longer exists. The content of both videos is similar.

53 *"All my thinking"*: Ibid.

53 *"This thing that people call thought"*: Ibid.

57 *"If you looked into nothingness"*: Donna Williams, *Nobody Nowhere* (New York: Avon, 1992), 3.

CHAPTER 5: NIETZSCHE IN THE BATHTUB

59 *"New paths do I tread"*: Friedrich Nietzsche, trans. Thomas Common, *Thus Spake Zarathustra* (New York: Prometheus Books, 1993), 106–107.

59 *"blessed isles"*: Friedrich Nietzsche, trans. Walter Kaufmann, *Thus Spoke Zarathustra: A Book for None and All* (New York: Penguin, 1966), 85.

59 *"New speech comes to me"*: Nietzsche, *Thus Spake Zarathustra*, 106–107.

59 *"lack," "deficiency," "impairment"*: American Psychiatric Association, *Diagnostic and Statistical Manual of Mental Disorders*, 4th ed. (Washington, D.C.: American Psychiatric Association, 1994), 70–71, 77.

60 *"Every cretin is an idiot"*: Wilhelm Griesinger quoted in Leo Kanner, "Historical Review of Mental Retardation: 1800–1965," *American Journal of Mental Deficiency* 72 (September 1967): 167.

60 *publishing in 1935 the first book*: Leo Kanner, *Child Psychiatry* (Springfield, Ill.: Charles C. Thomas, 1948).

60 *he published, in 1943, his first case studies*: Leo Kanner, "Autistic Disturbance of Affective Contact," *Nervous Child* 2 (1943): 217–50.

61 *"they were buffeted"*: Edward Shorter, *A History of Psychiatry: From the Era of the Asylum to the Age of Prozac* (New York: Wiley, 1997), 303.

61   *They criticized the inclusion:* Ibid., 305.

61   *In the midst of this sea change:* Lorna Wing, "Asperger's Syndrome: A Clinical Account," *Psychological Medicine* 11 (1981): 115–29.

61   *Coincidentally, Asperger called the condition:* Ami Klin, Fred R. Volkmar, and Sara S. Sparrow, eds., *Asperger Syndrome* (New York: Guilford, 2000), 32.

61   *"a lack of or inadequate":* Ibid., 33.

62   *Wing coined the phrase:* Ibid.

63   *The euthanasia killings:* Henry Friedlander, *The Origins of Nazi Genocide: From Euthanasia to the Final Solution* (Chapel Hill: University of North Carolina Press, 1995), 22.

63   *Let us try to recall:* Leo Kanner quoted in Victor D. Sanua, "Leo Kanner (1894–1981): The Man and the Scientist," *Child Psychiatry and Human Development* 21 (Fall 1990): 9.

64   *"History," writes Shorter:* Shorter, *A History of Psychiatry,* 166.

65   *such as* The Empty Fortress: Bruno Bettelheim, *The Empty Fortress: Infantile Austism and the Birth of the Self* (New York: Free Press, 1967), and *The Uses of Enchantment: The Meaning and Importance of Fairy Tales* (New York: Knopf, 1977).

66   *In fact, it was Kanner:* Kanner quoted in Sanua, "Leo Kanner," 15–16.

66   In Defense of Mothers: Kanner quoted in Sanua, 8.

67   *one "can never be sure":* Uta Frith, ed., *Autism and Asperger Syndrome* (Cambridge: Cambridge University Press, 1991), 68–69.

67   *Asperger said their language:* Ibid., 70.

67   *Asperger called his patients "little professors":* Lawrence Osborne, "The Little Professor Syndrome," *The New York Times Magazine,* June 18, 2000, 56.

67   *In fact, researcher Uta Frith writes:* Uta Frith, ed. *Autism and Asperger Syndrome* (Cambridge: Cambridge University Press, 1991), 9.

68   *His daughter, Maria Asperger Felder:* Christopher Gillberg, "'Aspergermänniskan'—en kylig särling utsatt för stora psykiska påfrestningar," *Läkartidningen* 87 (1990): 2973. (Translated for the author by Katarina Ricken.)

68   *During his first year in school:* Ibid.

68   *Asperger himself once said:* Frith, *Austism and Asperger Syndrome*, 32.

68   *Asperger's paper was apparently delayed:* Ibid., 86n.

69   *the "power in [present-day] psychiatry":* Shorter, *A History of Psychiatry*, 170.

69   *"Illness categories have ballooned":* Ibid., 319.

70   *Some autism researchers warn:* Klin, Volkmar, and Sparrow, *Asperger Syndrome*, 15.

70   *"Do you really believe":* Friedrich Nietzsche, trans. Walter Kaufman, *The Gay Science* (New York: Random House, 1974), 240.

71   "Where are your greatest dangers?": Ibid., 220.

75   *"Our personal and profoundest suffering":* Ibid., 269.

75   *"But whenever people* notice": Ibid.

75   *"They wish to help":* Ibid.

CHAPTER 6: MY FATHER WAS A YAKKER

83   *I know I must whisper softly:* Valerie Tekavec (Paradiž), *Peacocks and Beans* (Detroit: Ridgeway Press, 1996).

85   *In recent autism research:* Ami Klin, Fred R. Volkmar, and Sara S. Sparrow, eds., *Asperger Syndrome* (New York: Guilford, 2000), 86.

86   *It's also said that to varying degrees:* Ibid., 84.

86   *Some autism researchers:* Geoffrey Cowley, "Understanding Autism: Why More Kids and Families Are Facing the Challenge of 'Mindblindness,'" *Time* magazine, July 31, 2000, 46–54.

86   *"First-order . . . involves prediction":* Klin, Volkmar, and Sparrow, *Asperger Syndrome*, 84.

86   *In her book* Mindreading: Sanjida O'Connell, *Mindreading: An Investigation into How We Learn to Love and Lie* (London: Heinemann, 1997), 18.

86   *They do not have "the ability":* Ibid., 5.

87   *[i]n concept, BAP is:* Klin, Volkmar, and Sparrow, *Asperger Syndrome*, 161.

88   *"Who is the person with a hidden form":* John J. Ratey and Catherine

Johnson, *Shadow Syndromes* (New York: Pantheon, 1997), 219.

91   *Asperger specialist Tony Attwood writes:* Tony Attwood, *Asperger's Syndrome: A Guide for Parents and Professionals* (Philadelphia: Jessica Kingsley Publishers, 1998), 142.

CHAPTER 7: ECHOLALIA FUN FUN FUN

102   *If you make a deep study of words:* Gertrude Stein, ed. Richard Kostelanetz, with an introduction by Kenneth Rexroth, *The Yale Gertrude Stein* (New Haven, Conn.: Yale University Press, 1980), xv.

102   *Temple Grandin says:* Temple Grandin, *Dr. Temple Grandin Speaks on "Visual Thinking of a Person with Autism,"* video, Future Horizons, 1999.

102   *Gertrude Stein, describing the development:* Stein, *The Yale Gertrude Stein*, xvi.

103   *Who was born January first:* Ibid., 72.

103   *"Echolalia is a good sign":* Grandin, *Dr. Temple Grandin Speaks.*

104   *March the eighteenth:* Stein, *The Yale Gertrude Stein*, 79.

107   *July because July because because:* Ibid., 87.

109   *November first. First and ferries:* Ibid., 94–95.

109   *Who was born January first:* Ibid., 72.

CHAPTER 8: BALLOON DAYS

121   *As a small child, Einstein was:* Ilana Katz, "Was Einstein Autistic? The Einstein/Autism Meld" (lecture at the National Autism Convention, Autism Society of America, 1994).

121   *"He was well past two":* Dennis Overbye, *Einstein in Love: A Scientific Romance* (New York: Viking, 2000), 5.

121   *Ilana Katz, an Einstein scholar:* Katz, "Was Einstein Autistic?"

121   *When he reached school age:* Overbye, *Einstein in Love*, 8.

122   *On the one hand, Overbye writes:* Ibid., 7.

122   *His Greek professor:* Ibid.

122   *During his summer vacation:* Ibid.

122   *His peers reported:* Katz, "Was Einstein Autistic?"

123   *"There were the strange occasions":* Overbye, *Einstein in Love,* 83.

124   *"For example," writes Steven Pinker:* Steven Pinker, "E = mc²: His Brain Measured Up," *New York Times,* June 24, 1999, A31.

124   *Temple Grandin compares:* Temple Grandin, *Thinking in Pictures and Other Reports from My Life with Autism* (New York: Doubleday, 1995), 183.

Chapter 9: Cartoons Don't Get Hurt

132   *I've got no strings to hold me down:* Walt Disney Productions (producer), *Pinocchio,* 1940.

140   *"Expecting that we learn to 'act normal' socially":* Jim Sinclair, personal communication, December 31, 1996.

140   *Instead of teaching:* Ibid.

141   *He likes the sound of "galumph":* Louis Untermeyer, ed., "Jabberwocky," in *The Golden Treasury of Poetry* (New York: Golden Press, 1959), 208.

143   *"They've got to learn that a line drawing":* Temple Grandin, *Dr. Temple Grandin Speaks on "Visual Thinking of a Person with Autism,"* video, Future Horizons, 1999.

146   *Jim Sinclair speaks of his "television":* "Stories About Stories: Learning and Building Through Popular Media" (lecture at Autreat, Autism Network International, 1999).

147   *"The limits of my language mean":* Ludwig Wittgenstein, trans. C. K. Ogden, *Tractatus logico-philosophicus* (New York: Routledge, 1988), no. 5.6.

147   *Wittgenstein was drawn to philosophy:* Ray Monk, *Ludwig Wittgenstein: The Duty of Genius* (New York: Penguin, 1990), 3.

147   *"When someone says the word 'cube'":* Ludwig Wittgenstein, trans. G.E.M. Anscombe, *Philosophical Investigations* (Englewood Cliffs, N.J.: Prentice Hall, 1958), 54e.

148   *Wittgenstein scholar H. O. Mounce:* H. O. Mounce, *Wittgenstein's Tractatus* (Chicago: University of Chicago Press, 1981), 3.

148   *Upon entering school:* M. Fitzgerald, "Did Ludwig Wittgenstein Have Asperger's Syndrome?" *European Child and Adolescent Psychiatry* 9 (2000): 62.

149   *The Wittgenstein paradoxes are indeed:* Marjorie Perloff, *Wittgenstein's Ladder: Poetic Language and the Strangeness of the Ordinary* (Chicago: University of Chicago Press, 1996), 7–8.

149   *An autism researcher, M. Fitzgerald, writes:* Fitzgerald, "Did Ludwig Wittgenstein Have Asperger's Syndrome?" 62.

150   *"He was totally focussed":* Ibid.

150   *Compulsions and repetitions punctuated:* Ibid., 63.

150   *In the arena of nonverbal communication:* Ibid., 62.

151   *The autistic artist Jesse Park:* Valerie Tekavec (Paradiž), "Art from the Realm of Uncanny Acuity," *Woodstock (N.Y.) Times,* May 12, 1994, 15.

151   *"Let us imagine," he writes:* Ludwig Wittgenstein, trans. Linda M. McAlister and Margarete Schättle, ed. G.E.M. Anscombe, *Remarks on Color* (Berkeley: University of California Press, 1977), 26e.

151   *Wittgenstein points out that when we name:* Ibid.

151   *"I treat the colour concepts":* Ibid.

152   *"Something that we know when someone asks us":* Wittgenstein, *Philosophical Investigations,* 42e.

CHAPTER 10: LIFE UNDER GLASS

157   *Andy Warhol was probably not aware:* Warhol was probably not aware of Asperger's syndrome because he died in 1987, seven years before it was included in the *DSM-IV.* Although autism researchers, led by Lorna Wing in 1981, were becoming ever more engaged in articulating the nature of the high-functioning end of the autism spectrum, this knowledge had not yet reached the general population. It wasn't until the 1990s, and Uta Frith's translation of Asperger's original study of 1944 into English, that public awareness began to grow. This coincided with the phenomenal increase in the number of diagnoses.

158   *It's why he didn't like being touched:* Andy Warhol, *The Philosophy of Andy Warhol (From A to B and Back Again)* (San Diego: Harcourt, Brace, 1975), 97–98, 111.

158 *"I always bring every problem":* Ibid., 181.

158 *"He was a liberator":* Kim Evans (director and producer), *Andy Warhol: Portrait of an Artist,* film, RM Productions (London), 1987.

159 *"My mind always drifts":* Warhol, *Philosophy,* 184.

160 *"I used to have the same lunch":* Kynaston McShine, ed., *Andy Warhol Retrospective* (New York: Museum of Modern Art, 1989), 460.

160 *"Communication via objects was safe":* Donna Williams, *Nobody Nowhere: The Extraordinary Autobiography of an Autistic* (New York: Avon, 1992), 6.

161 *"The people I liked were their things":* Ibid.

162 *"It was really embarrassing":* Victor Bockris, *Warhol* (New York: Da Capo, 1997), 24.

162 *As Andy grew a little older:* Ibid., 30.

162 *"When people have a cool, calm atmosphere":* Warhol, *Philosophy,* 158.

163 He stood *"in a corner of the gallery":* Bockris, *Warhol,* 156.

163 *"I wasn't misbehaving":* Williams, *Nobody Nowhere,* 67.

163 *"I wish you'd just tell me the words":* Evans, *Andy Warhol.*

165 *"I'm sure I'm going to look in the mirror":* Warhol, *Philosophy,* 7.

165 *"I only know one language":* Ibid., 147.

166 *In moments of hesitation, he'd "graft":* Ibid., 147–48.

166 *"He became increasingly disoriented":* Bockris, *Warhol,* 38.

166 *Victor Bockris calls this "a golden time":* Ibid.

166 *"I liked Walt Disney":* Ibid., 39.

167 *Perhaps the strangeness:* Williams, *Nobody Nowhere,* 53.

167 *Many teachers assumed:* Bockris, *Warhol,* 60.

167 *A college teacher at Carnegie Tech says:* Ibid.

167 *It was also "difficult for Andy":* Ibid.

167 *Applying clinical language:* Ami Klin, Fred R. Volkmar, and Sara S. Sparrow, eds., *Asperger Syndrome* (New York: Guilford, 2000), 37.

168 *His sister-in-law reports:* Bockris, *Warhol,* 53.

168 *Andy's work was his drawing:* Ibid., 52.

168 *His artistic reputation:* Ibid., 53.

168 *By the time he reached art school:* Ibid., 61.

169 *"It was almost impossible":* Temple Grandin, *Thinking in Pictures and Other Reports from My Life with Autism* (New York: Doubleday, 1995), 36–37.

169 *Donna Williams describes:* Williams, *Nobody Nowhere,* 66.

169 *Wendy Lawson, an Asperger woman:* Wendy Lawson, *Life Behind Glass* (London: Jessica Kingsley Publishers, 2000).

169 *"People who imagine me":* Warhol, *Philosophy,* 23.

169 *This is when, Andy explains:* Ibid.

170 *"Living is work":* Ibid., subtitle under "Work" on the Contents page.

170 *Temple Grandin writes of work:* Grandin, *Thinking in Pictures,* 139.

170 *From the moment Andy first saw Shirley:* Bockris, *Warhol,* 41.

170 *In fact, he "would imitate her":* Ibid.

170 *His brother John says:* Ibid., 36.

171 *"When I got my first TV":* Warhol, *Philosophy,* 26.

171 *In the late 1950s:* Ibid.

171 *"The acquisition of my tape recorder":* Ibid.

172 *"You do hate it when":* Ibid., 181.

172 *Grandin writes about her "antipredator system":* Grandin, *Thinking in Pictures,* 144.

173 *In his memoir, he writes about "perfume space":* Warhol, *Philosophy,* 150–52.

173 *"I'm embarrassed to admit it":* Grandin, *Thinking in Pictures,* 166.

173 *When I'm walking around New York:* Warhol, *Philosophy,* 152–53.

174 *Victor Bockris writes:* Bockris, *Warhol,* 150–51.

CHAPTER 11: PLAYGROUND COMEDIAN

175 *I am going to try a comedy like that:* Gertrude Stein, ed. Richard Kostelanetz, *The Yale Gertrude Stein* (New Haven, Conn.: Yale University Press, 1980), 98.

175   *"Listen, I'm in a slight predicament":* Hal Roach (producer) and James
       Parrot (director), *Helpmates,* film, Metro-Goldwyn-Mayer, 1932.

181   *"When I make contact with someone":* Jim Sinclair, "Bridging the Gaps:
       An Inside-Out View of Autism (or Do You Know What I Know?)," in
       Eric Schopler and Gary B. Mesibov, eds., *High-Functioning Individuals
       with Autism* (New York: Plenum Press, 1992). My source is posted on
       Sinclair's Web site: http://www. members.xoom.com/_XMCM/ Jim Sin-
       clair/bridging.htm, page 9.

181   *"When I make a connection," Jim says:* Ibid. My source is posted on Sin-
       clair's Web site: http://www.members.xoom.com/_XMCM/ Jim Sin-
       clair/bridging.htm, pages 9–10.

189   *"Why he and I are like this":* Charles R. Rogers and Gus Means (direc-
       tors), *March of the Wooden Soldiers,* film, Metro-Goldwyn-Mayer,
       1934. Based on Victor Herbert's *Babes in Toyland.*

189   *"I keep reading that autistic people":* Jim Sinclair, "Thoughts about
       Empathy," *The Maap* (spring 1989). My source is from Sinclair's Web site:
       http://www.members.xoom.com/_XMCM/ Jim Sinclair/empathy.htm,
       page 1.

190   *"If I know that I do not understand people":* Ibid. My source is from
       Sinclair's Web site: http://www.members.xoom.com/_XMCM/ Jim Sin-
       clair/empathy.htm, page 2.

191   *Kaufman's mother says that:* Bill Zehme, *Lost in the Funhouse: The Life
       and Mind of Andy Kaufman* (New York: Random House, 1999), 14.

191   *He "would watch the colors":* Ibid., 11.

191   *Eventually, Andy "would break the afternoon down":* Ibid., 18.

191   *Kaufman himself says:* "Andy Kaufman Soundstage Show," WTTW,
       Chicago, 1983.

192   *Andy's parents often remarked:* Zehme, *Lost in the Funhouse,* 70.

192   *"Such energy, enthusiasm!":* Ibid.

192   *"I guess I always had a tendency":* "Andy Kaufman Soundstage Show."

193   *He was concerned about his son's future:* Zehme, *Lost in the Funhouse,* 26.

193   *"He was a very, very smart kid":* Ibid.

193   *"It never occurred to him":* Ibid., 49.

194 *Social signal dogs can help:* Jim Sinclair, "What Do SsigDogs Do?" http://www.members.xoom.com/_XMCM/Jim Sinclair/ dogtasks.htm, page 2.

194 *High-functioning people:* Ibid.

198 *"Well!" the gentleman explodes:* Hal Roach (producer) and James Parrot (director), *The Music Box,* film, Metro-Goldwyn-Mayer, 1932.

199 *"neurotypical syndrome":* http://www.isnt.autistics.org.

199 *By the time Andy Kaufman:* Zehme, *Lost in the Funhouse,* 105.

CHAPTER 12: CRACKING CODE

203 *The first wave of night:* Ingeborg Bachmann, trans. Peter Filkins, *Songs in Flight: The Collected Poems of Ingeborg Bachmann* (New York: Marsilio Publishers, 1994), 7.

204 *Then something happens with the ropes:* Ibid.

207 *"What will happen," asks Ingeborg:* Ibid., 15.

207 *Sharron is reading e-mail:* Greg Yates, "A Topological Theory of Autism," http://www.aascend.org, 2000.

211 *Yo-ho, yo-ho, the pirate's life's for me!* Disneyland, Pirates of the Caribbean.

219 *What will happen if we survive:* Bachmann, *Flight,* 15.

Acknowledgments

I wish to express my deep gratitude to all our autistic friends, especially the members of Autism Network International, who welcomed me and Elijah into their community and generously shared their lives with us. I give special thanks to Sharron Loree, whose friendship, wit, and artistic sensibility completely redirected the path that Elijah and I were on and led us into realms of untold richness. I thank Jim Sinclair for his graceful intelligence, his visionary mind, and his love for my son. Dan Asher pushed me hard to ask important ethical questions as I was beginning this book, and Hal Messinger is our traveling buddy and Disneyland companion whom I thank for the fun times. I am also grateful to Professor Temple Grandin for her helpful conversations on the telephone while I was researching *Elijah's Cup*, and to Donna Williams, whose memoir, *Nobody Nowhere*, has been a guiding light for me.

My heartfelt appreciation and thanks go to Jamey Wolff, co-director of the Children's Annex of Kingston, and all the gifted staff in that marvelous school who have touched Elijah's life. Researchers in the field of autism who offered their kind support were Uta Frith, Ph.D., a researcher in the MRC Cognitive Development Unit of London; Steve Safran, professor of special education at the Ohio University College of Education; and Ami Klin, Ph.D., at the Yale Child Study Center in the Yale University School of Medicine. In the area of disability studies, I thank Professor Mark Jeffreys of the University of Alabama at Birmingham for slogging through early drafts of chapters and offering his generous comments.

The kind staff in the library of the New York Academy of Medicine were especially helpful when I conducted research on Hans Asperger and Leo Kanner there, and I express my special thanks to Dr. Maria Asperger Felder for generously offering me biographical information about her father and about Sister Viktorine Zak. Paul Trehin, honorary general secretary of the World Autism Organization, kindly provided me with early historical information about autism, and my Swedish translator, Katarina Ricken, helped me uncover important biographical information about Hans Asperger.

Residencies at Hedgebrook and at the Millay Colony for the Arts, where I received a generous grant from the Concordia Foundation, gave me time and solitude to work on *Elijah's Cup* without the distractions of daily life. In Woodstock, New York, I am grateful to the community of friends who supported me in the writing of the chapter on Andy Warhol, and I am deeply grateful to my sister, Margot O'Dell, for always believing in my work and for her support while I was in the very vulnerable, early stages of developing this book.

The brilliant, multitalented women in my writers' group, who are my mainstay and lifeline as a writer, saw this effort through from its conception to its completion with steadfast support and a professional camaraderie that is rare: Judy Upjohn, Jeanne DeMers, Gail Bradney, Prudence See, and Lisa Phillips. I give especially warm thanks to Colette Dowling, my first writing buddy and publishing mentor, who showed me the ropes in countless ways during our spirited, and sometimes raucous, late-night discussions in the Chinese restaurant. I am grateful to Dennis Overbye, whose research on his book about Albert Einstein was an inspiration to me.

I thank my agent, Elizabeth Kaplan, who took me on when *Elijah's Cup* was still in its infancy and believed in the project from the get-go. I am deeply grateful to my editor at The Free Press, Philip Rappaport, who from day one made me feel right at home. Philip's editorial insight, sensitive courtesy, and impeccable and genuine attention to my project pushed me to do my best.

Finally, there are family and friends whom I thank: Avis and Greg Gebert, and their three wonderful sons, Andrew, Nathan, and Carter. My German family, the Schneiders, are with me in every literary endeavor I undertake. I feel profound gratitude toward Emma Missouri for always being there, for always loving us, for always pushing the envelope on new adventure. I thank my mother Corrine, a child psychologist and a woman of depth and warmth who understood Elijah from the day he was born. I thank my grandmother Monica, to whom I feel deeply united, for we both share the experience of raising a child with a disability. I thank all my dead ones—my father, Mel; my grandmother Jennie; my grandfather Max. My loss of them during the moment of Elijah's diagnosis opened up a view of autism I had no clue awaited me. I thank my ex-husband, and I am joyous about our newfound friendship! I thank his parents, Grace and Jerry, who are family through and through. Daniel, Elijah's great-uncle, shared breakfasts with me that gave me deep respect for schizophrenia and its historical resonance with autism. Fannie, Elijah's great-grandmother, is my inspiration, my role model, my true friend and counselor. Finally, I am grateful to my closest friends and art pals, the whole rascally bunch: Bart Friedman, Anna Grace, David Chambard, Martina Dörr, Erika Laurion, Georges Jacquemart, Andrew Gebert, George Crane, Wendy Klein, Bob

Berky, Bet Williams, John Hodian, and Cecilia Hae-Jin Lee.

I am deeply grateful to my literary influences, all of them dead, but their writing and their thinking are alive and kicking inside me: Else Lasker-Schüler, Ingeborg Bachmann, Franz Kafka, Friedrich Nietzsche, and Ludwig Wittgenstein.

Finally, I say, THANK YOU, ELIJAH, my precious bird of a feather, my wacky soulmate.

Index

Abbott and Costello, 146
absent-mindedness, 78, 85, 162
affect, lack of, 164
Agua, 208
American Psychiatric Association, 56
anticonvulsants, 11, 17–20, 25,
    27–31, 33, 85, 91
    "designer," 21
    weaning off, 120, 131
    see also specific drugs
antidepressants, 101
antipsychotic drugs, 196
Apgar scores, 6
Asher, Dan, 136
Asperger, Hans, 61–62, 67–69, 87,
    90, 148, 174, 227*n*
Asperger's syndrome, 55–56, 61–62,
    74, 87, 89, 106, 165, 202, 209
    diagnosis of, 69–70
    Einstein and, 121
    inclusion in *DSM-IV* of, 59–60,
        227*n*
    language in, 67, 85, 103–4, 142,
        167

organizations of people with, 208
parental shadow traits and, 91
theory of mind and, 86
Warhol and, 157, 158, 167, 169,
    227*n*
Wittgenstein and, 147, 151
attention deficit disorder, 69, 167, 193
Atwood, Tony, 91
aural-visual jumbling, 54–55
Autastics, 208
Autism Network International
    (ANI), 131, 139, 198
Autism Society of American (ASA),
    137, 210
Autism Society of Los Angeles, 208
autistic personality disorder, 61
autistic spectrum, 56, 62
Autreat, 131–42, 145, 163, 193, 195,
    202

Bach, Johann Sebastien, 106
Bachmann, Ingeborg, 24, 203–5, 207
barbiturates, 20
    see also phenobarbital

behavioral modification, 178
benzodiazepines, 21
Bettelheim, Bruno, 65–67, 69, 90, 148
Bible, the, 11
birth, complicated, 5, 6, 8, 23
blacklisting, McCarthy-era, 64
blind, 194
blood tests, 13, 30–31
Bockris, Victor, 166, 174
Bogart, Humphrey, 38
Braille, Louis, 137
broader autism phenotype (BAP), 87, 89, 90, 168
Buddhism, 102, 215

Cage, John, 174
Cambridge University, 149–50
Carnegie Tech, 167, 168
Castle, The (Kafka), 26–27
Chaplin, Charlie, 27–28, 44
Chicago, University of, 65
Children's Annex (Kingston school), 48, 51, 91, 92, 104, 117
   daybook from, 111, 113, 119
   special education program at, 71
   toilet training at, 111
chloral hydrate, 13, 25, 27
clonic movements, 24
colloquialisms, 202
colors, naming, 113, 134–35, 142, 151
communication
   autistic, 181–82, 190, 196–97, 199
   nonverbal, 150
   via objects, 160–61
   rebuffed attempts at, 170
   with social signal dogs, 194
   standard, presumptions about, 163–64

visual, 142
   see also language
computerized tomography (CT) scans, 4

danger, scanning for, 172–73
deaf community, 137
depression, 90, 95, 100, 101, 110, 119, 120, 183
developmental examination, 41
developmental milestones, 8
Diagnostic and Statistical Manual of Mental Disorders (American Psychiatric Association), 60–61, 69
   Fourth Edition of *(DSM-IV)*, 56, 59–60, 62, 227n
disability movement, 137
disappearances, 162, 163
Disney, Walt, 166–67
Disneyland, 202, 210–14
drawing, 144–47, 153–55, 162, 163, 168, 170–71, 215
dyslexia, 69, 167

echolalia, 40–41, 91, 101–4, 107, 121, 125, 164
Einstein, Albert, 120–25, 132, 187
electroencephalogram (EEG), 10, 14–16, 24, 25
empathy, 189–90
Empty Fortress, The (Bettelheim), 65
epilepsy, 81, 108, 123, 166
   biology of, 16
   diagnosis of, 10
   idiopathic generalized, 24
   see also seizures
eugenics, 62–63

euthanasia, Nazi program of, 63, 68
executive function, 85, 89, 163
eye contact, 140
  lack of, 86–87, 162

facial expressions
  limited, 150, 164
  reading, 146
Family of Woodstock, 31, 37
fascism, 62–65
feeblemindedness, familial, 166
feeding difficulties, 7
Felbatol, 13, 85, 91
Felder, Maria Asperger, 68
feminism, 61
Fitzgerald, M., 149–50
Folstein, Susan, 87
Freudian theory, 61, 64–67, 69
Friedlander, Henry, 63
Frith, Uta, 67, 227n

Gameboy, 209, 215–16, 218
gays, 61, 165
  Nazi extermination of, 63
Gay Science (Nietzsche), 31, 70, 75
gaze, autistic, 67, 86, 150, 162
genetics, 69, 84–88, 90, 96
Gilligan's Island (television program), 146
glass, symbolic meaning of, 169
Gould, Glenn, 105, 106
grand mal seizures, 6, 11, 24
Grandin, Temple, 56, 70, 104, 125, 143–4, 210
  "antipredator system" of, 172–73
  childhood experiences of, 102, 103
  video of lecture by, 51–55, 222n

visual thinking of, 124, 168–69
  work as source of satisfaction for, 170
Green Eggs and Ham (Seuss), 144–45
Griesinger, Wilhelm, 60
Grillparzer (poet), 68
gypsies, Nazi extermination of, 63

Halcion, 21
Hardy, Oliver, 175–76, 189, 197–98
head banging, 7, 23, 46, 51, 183
hearing, sense of, 52
  see also sound, sensitivity to
Helpmates (film), 175–76
Hoffman, Dustin, 87, 146
Holocaust, 63
homosexuality, psychiatric view of, 61
Hudson River school painters, 49
humor, autistic, 142, 176–77

idiopathic generalized epilepsy, 24
In Defense of Mothers (Kanner), 66
Indians, 49
informed consent, 196
intellectuals, Nazi extermination of, 63
internalized normalism, 209
Internet, 131, 198
invisibility, autistic, 118, 125
It's Hercules: The Legendary Journeys (television program), 146
IV needles, 7

Jews, Nazi persecution of, 63
  refugees from, 64, 65

Johns Hopkins University, 64
Johnson, Catherine, 88

Kafka, Franz, 26–27, 31, 45, 50, 74
Kanner, Leo, 60–69, 89, 148
Kanner's syndrome, 60–61, 85
Karp, Ivan, 158
Katz, Ilana, 121
Kaufman, Andy, 191–93, 199
Kaufman, Stanley, 193
Keller, Helen, 137

language, 44–45, 68
  in Asperger's syndrome, 67, 85,
    103, 142, 167
  colloquial, 202
  delayed, 2, 17, 40, 57, 121
  echolalic, *see* echolalia
  games with, 218
  reappearance of, 27–29
  spontaneous, 117
  visual, 135
  Warhol on, 165–66
  Wittgenstein's philosophy of,
    147–48
Lasker-Schüler, Else, 119, 125, 144
Laurel, Stan, 175–76, 179, 188, 189,
  197–98
Lawson, Wendy, 169
learning disabilities, 125, 167
Life Behind Glass (Lawson), 169
list-making, 215–16
Loree, Sharron, 31–41, 45–58, 60,
  84–85, 117, 125, 132, 147, 170
  Asperger's syndrome diagnosis
    of, 55–56, 62, 70, 74, 203
  childhood experiences of, 54–55,
    57, 65, 188, 215

departure from Woodstock of, 75,
  82
Jim Sinclair and, 84, 131, 136,
  137
portrait of Elijah by, 130–31
visit in California with, 201–14
Luitpold gymnasium (Munich), 122

magnetic resonance imaging (MRI),
  10–14, 25, 27, 34, 40–42
manic-depressive psychosis, 166
Man on the Moon (film), 190–91
March of the Wooden Soldiers
  (film), 189
Martin, Steve, 184
Mayo Clinic, 20
McCarthy era, 64
media fixations, 145–47, 168,
  170–71, 191–92
Mellaril, 196
meltdown states, 140
"mental deficiencies,"
  differentiation among, 60
mental retardation, 20, 24, 62, 140,
  166
mind, theory of, 86–87
Mindreading (O'Connell), 86
mirroring, 161
Missouri, Emma, 98–101, 105, 106,
  108, 111, 120
Monroe, Marilyn, 157–59
More Advanced Autistic People
  (MAAP), 137
motor disabilities, 138, 194, 197
Mounce, H. O., 148
MRI, *see* magnetic resonance imaging
Music Box, The (film), 197–98

Nazism, 62–65, 68, 144
neurobiological perspective, 62, 67, 69
neurologists, pediatric, 8–11, 24–25, 29, 40, 120
    interpretation of tests results by, 15
New York, University of, at Syracuse, 131
New Yorker, The, 51
Nietzsche, Friedrich, 31, 59, 70–72, 75
Nobody Nowhere (Williams), 51, 160
nonverbal communication, 150
normalism, internalized, 209

object impermanence, 102
obsessive-compulsive disorder, 69–70
O'Connell, Sanjida, 86
olfactory sensitivity, 173
Onassis, Jacqueline Kennedy, 158, 159
Orthogenic School for Disturbed Children, 65–66
Ostranders, 2–3
othering, ideology of, 70
otherness, phenomenon of, 184
Overbye, Dennis, 120–23, 125

Park, Jesse, 151
Passover, 12
pentobarbital, 13
peripheral vision, 172
Perloff, Marjorie, 149
perseveration, 89, 116, 122, 123, 139, 160, 162, 212
petit mal seizures, 6, 11

pharmaceutical companies, 69
phenobarbital, 11, 13, 17–21, 25, 27, 41
    side effects of, 19, 20
    symptoms of overdose of, 19
phenotype, autistic, *see* broader autism phenotype (BAP)
Philosophy of Andy Warhol (From A to B and Back Again), The (Warhol), 161, 165–66
Pinker, Steven, 124
Pinocchio (film), 132–33, 139, 142, 145–46
pity, Nietzsche on, 71–72
pop art, 158
preoccupations, serial, 122
Presley, Elvis, 158, 164, 191
psychoanalysis, 61, 64–67, 69
psychodynamic perspective, 62, 67, 69
psychopharmacology, 69
    Asperger's syndrome and, 70
    see also specific drugs

Rain Man (film), 87, 146, 215
Ratey, John, 88
Ray, Man, 174
"refrigerator mother," 65, 66, 90
relativity, theory of, 124
repetitions, pervasive, 91, 92, 113, 141, 142
    in Warhol's paintings, 158, 159, 174
Rexroth, Kenneth, 102
Russell, Bertrand, 150

Sachs, Oliver, 51
Saint Vitus' dance, 166–67

Santangelo, Susan, 87
Saturday Night Live (television program), 191, 192
savantism, 87–88
scatter, 121–2
Schiklgruber (neurologist), 63, 64
schizophrenia, 61, 166
Schumann, Robert, 105–6, 135
Scoot (Elijah's friend), 193–97, 199
seizures, 1–16, 23, 30, 34, 36, 48, 57, 81–83, 99, 107, 108, 154, 169
    diagnostic tests for, 4–5, 11–15, 24, 25, 27
    examination by specialist for cause of, 24–25
    helping person through, 9–10
    language and, 40, 15, 27–29, 44–45
    medications to prevent, 11, 17–20, 25, 27–31, 33, 85, 91, 120, 131
    onset of, 1–4, 95, 205
self-advocacy, 137
self defeating syndrome, 61
sensory sensitivities, 52–55, 138–39, 150, 160, 164
    sexuality and, 172
serial images, 158
service dogs, 194
Seuss, Dr., 144–45
sexism, 61
shadow traits, 87, 88, 91, 142, 193
shame, Nietzsche on, 72
Shorter, Edward, 61, 64–65, 69
shyness, 89
side effects, drug, 13, 19, 20, 25
similes, 218
Sinclair, Jim, 84, 131, 188, 210

on authenticity in autistic communication, 181–82
at Autreat, 136–40
on empathy, 189–90
on media fixations, 145, 146
visit to Woodstock of, 193–97, 199
sleeping pills, 21
smell, sense of, 52
Snow White (film), 144–45, 167, 170
social signal dogs, 194
social skills training, 125, 140, 150
sound, sensitivity to, 42, 52–53, 178, 187, 194, 213–14
special education, 71, 125, 142, 178–80, 190
speech, *see* language
speech therapy, 125
spontaneous speech, 117
Stable Gallery (New York), 163
status epilepticus, 11, 19, 25
Stein, Gertrude, 102–4, 106, 174
stereotypies, 140, 177, 183
sterilization of disabled, 62, 68, 166
stiff gaze, *see* gaze, autistic
stimming, 104, 114, 123, 162, 191, 211, 213
Stonborough, Margarete, 149
Swiss Federal Polytechnical School, 122–4

tactile sensitivities, *see* touch, sensitivity to
tantrums, 99
taste, sense of, 52, 160
Taxi (television program), 192
Tegretol, 13, 25, 27, 29–31, 33
Temple, Shirley, 170

toilet training, 111, 119
tonic movements, 24
touch, sensitivity to, 90, 124, 172
Tractatus logico-philosophicus
    (Wittgenstein), 148
tranquilizers, 20–21, 196
Turk, Bill, 38, 47

urine tests, 13
Uses of Enchantment, The (Bettle-
    heim), 65–66

Valium, injections of, 21, 25, 28, 33, 36
Vienna, University Pediatric Clinic
    of, 68
visual sensitivities, 164
visual thinking, 53–54, 124–25, 172,
    210
    communication and, 142

Wagner, Richard, 150
whooping cough, 20
Warhol, Andy, 156–74, 227n
Warhol, John, 170–71
Warhol, Julia, 160, 161, 168
Warhol, Paul, 161–62
Williams, Donna, 51, 57, 70, 125,
    160, 161, 163, 167, 169
Wing, Lorna, 61–62, 69, 227n
Wittgenstein, Ludwig, 18, 29,
    147–52, 160
Wollstonecraft, Mary, 125
Woodstock Elementary School,
    72–73, 142, 177–80, 183,
    199
Woolf, Virginia, 125
World War II, 64, 67–69

Zak, Viktorine, 68